Betty & Veronica®
Vixens®

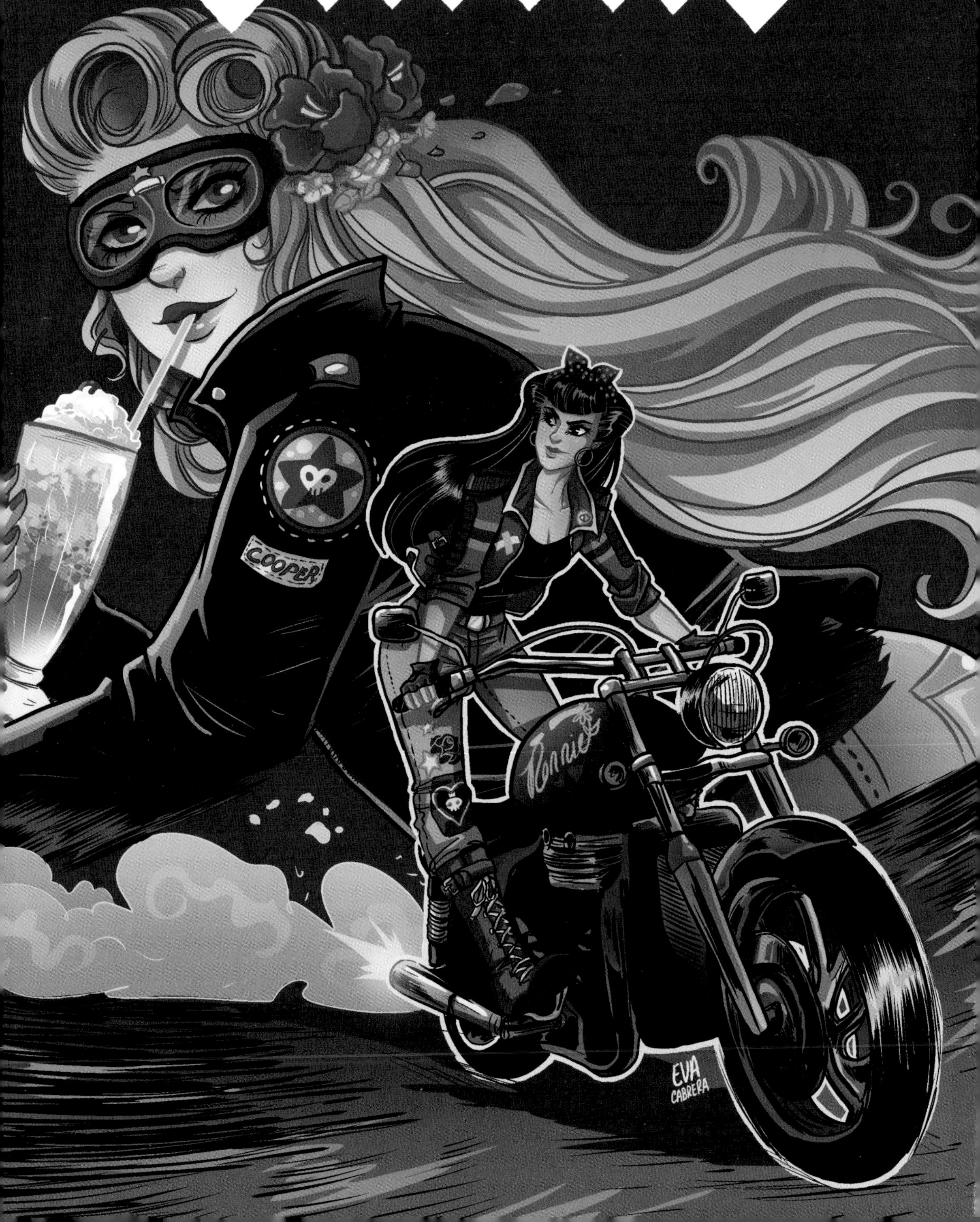
COOPER
Ronnie
EVA CABRERA

Betty & Veronica Vixens

JAMIE LEE ROTANTE

EVA CABRERA

ELAINA UNGER

RACHEL DEERING

ALEX SEGURA
VINCENT LOVALLO

FIONA STAPLES

STEPHEN OSWALD

KARI MCLACHLAN

VICTOR GORELICK

JON GOLDWATER

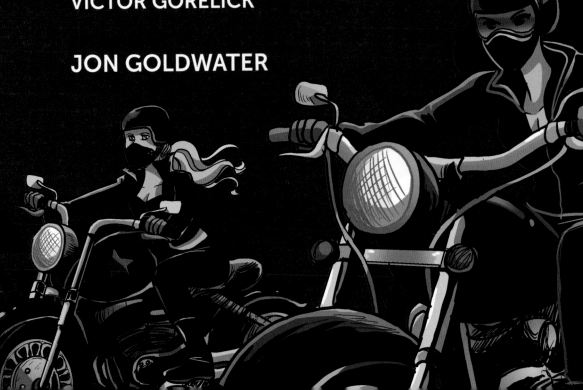

What if Betty and Veronica started their own girl gang?

The premise of *Betty & Veronica: Vixens* is simple enough: the iconic duo lead an all-female motorcycle gang. There's leather, brass knuckles and an appropriate amount of ass-kicking. It's what you'd get if you made the two BFFs the stars of a Russ Meyer film akin to *Faster Pussycat, Kill, Kill!*

We wanted to take everyone's preconceived notions about Betty and Veronica and completely turn them on their ear. It only made sense to let the ladies of Archie Comics take center stage—what if the girls were cheerleaders by day and a gang by night? There's already an established motorcycle gang featured in the classic *Little Archie* stories and the *Riverdale* TV series—the Southside Serpents—so the groundwork was already laid out for us.

But it's not just about motorcycles. It's not just about a subversion of classic characters. Hell, it's not even just about Betty and Veronica—there's a larger story that spins out of it, one that extends past the comic page itself. It's about women who have waited their turn for decades finally getting the chance to take charge. It's about Betty, Veronica and a host of the other ladies of Archie Comics who have only ever been explored as passing characters. And it's about these female characters coming together to rise above. It's women helping women.

I couldn't be more honored to get the chance to write two characters that were so influential to me growing up. I'm grateful that Archie CEO/Co-Publisher Jon Goldwater has allowed these characters to grow and change in so many different ways over the past few years, as we see in the Archie Horror and *Riverdale* series. And I couldn't have done it at all without the support of Mike Pellerito, Victor Gorelick and Alex Segura and the editorial team of Vincent Lovallo and Stephen Oswald.

I'm also incredibly honored to be working with a team of vastly creative, hard-working women. Eva Cabrera gives a new twist to the classic style in a way that captures the essence of the book so well. Elaina Unger's color palette so perfectly fits the mood of each and every scene she colors. Rachel Deering is a powerhouse when it comes to lettering, making my words look so much prettier on the actual page. And the logo and design of the very book you hold in your hands is thanks to our immensely talented lead designer Kari McLachlan.

I'd argue that there is never a bad time to publish a comic that lets its female characters lead the way, but now more than ever it's necessary. It's not doing it to fit a niche or to appeal to a demographic; it's doing it because it's right. Women are working hard both behind the scenes and within every comics panel—and that's not going to change any time soon.

Writer, BETTY & VERONICA: VIXENS

Chapter One

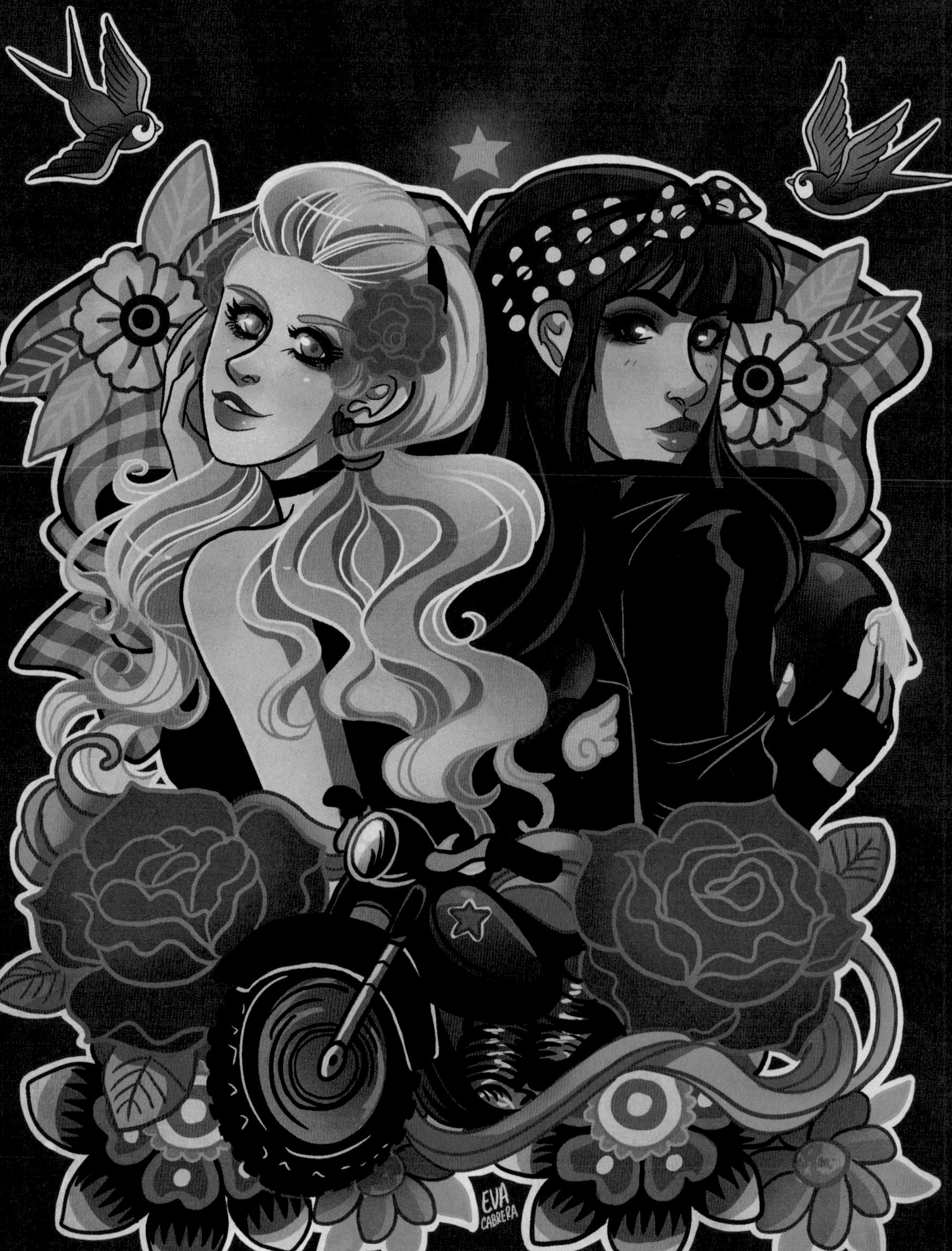
EVA
CABRERA

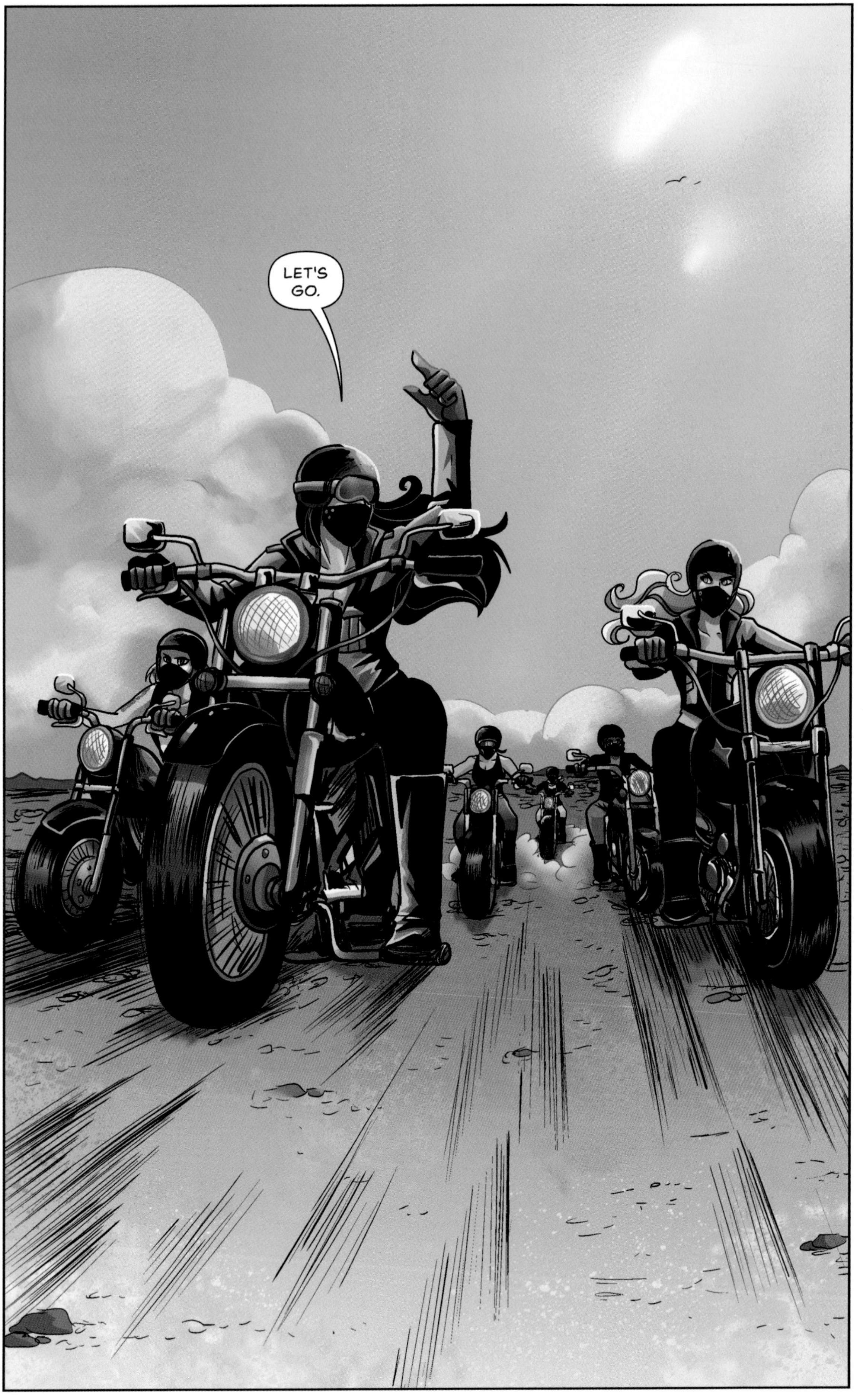
LET'S GO.

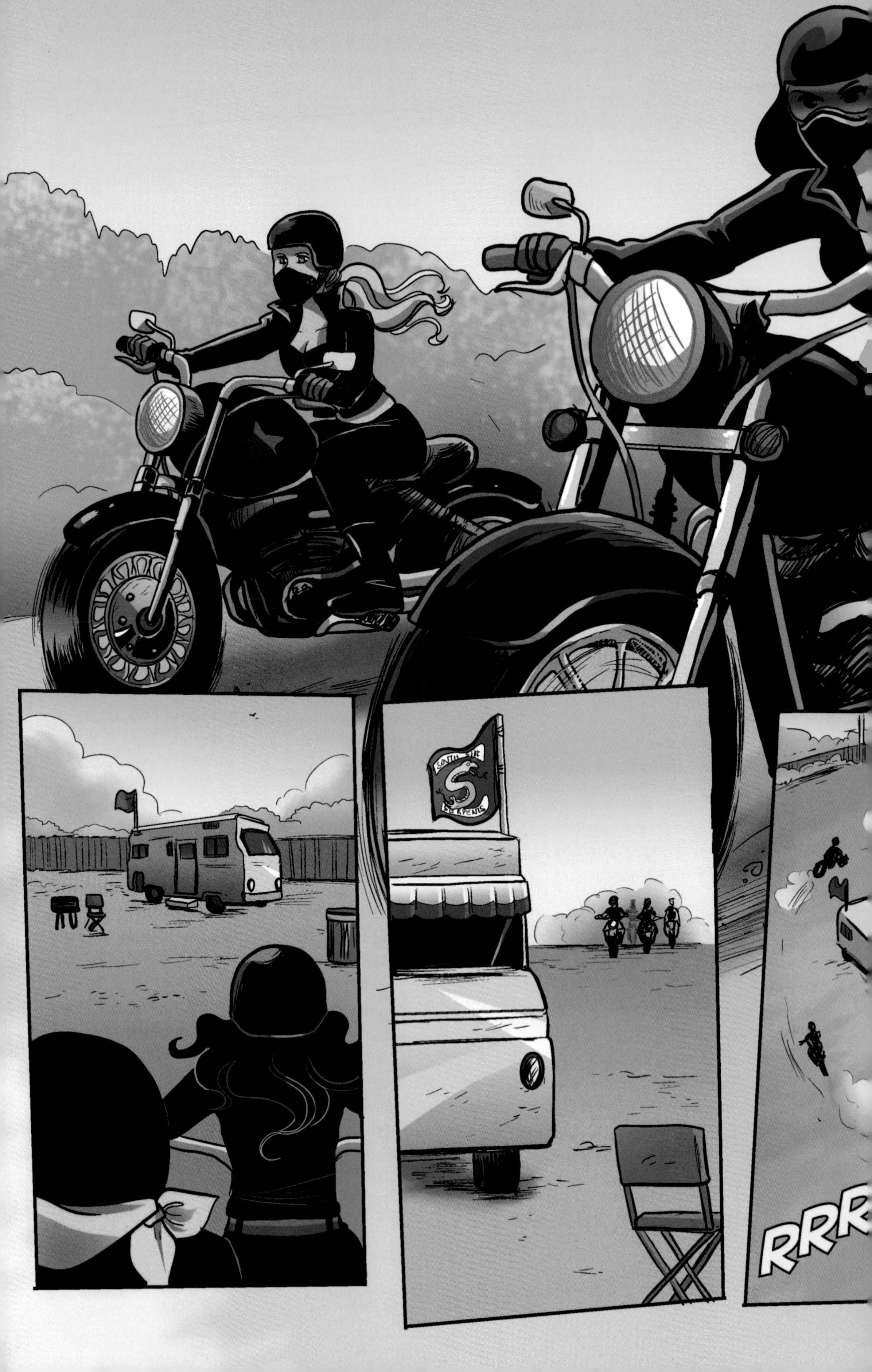
SOUTH SIDE
SERPENTS
RRR

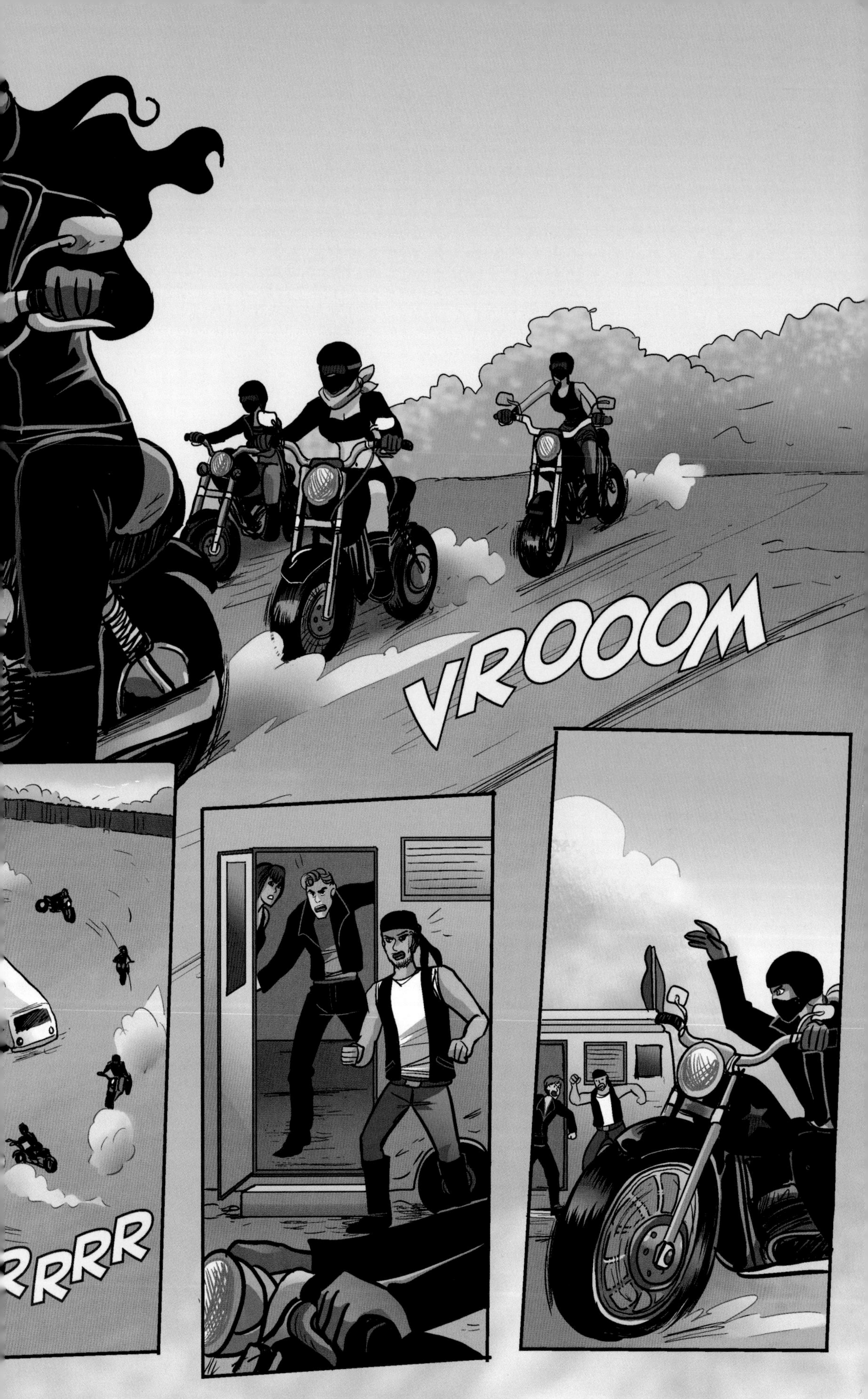
VROOOM
RRRR

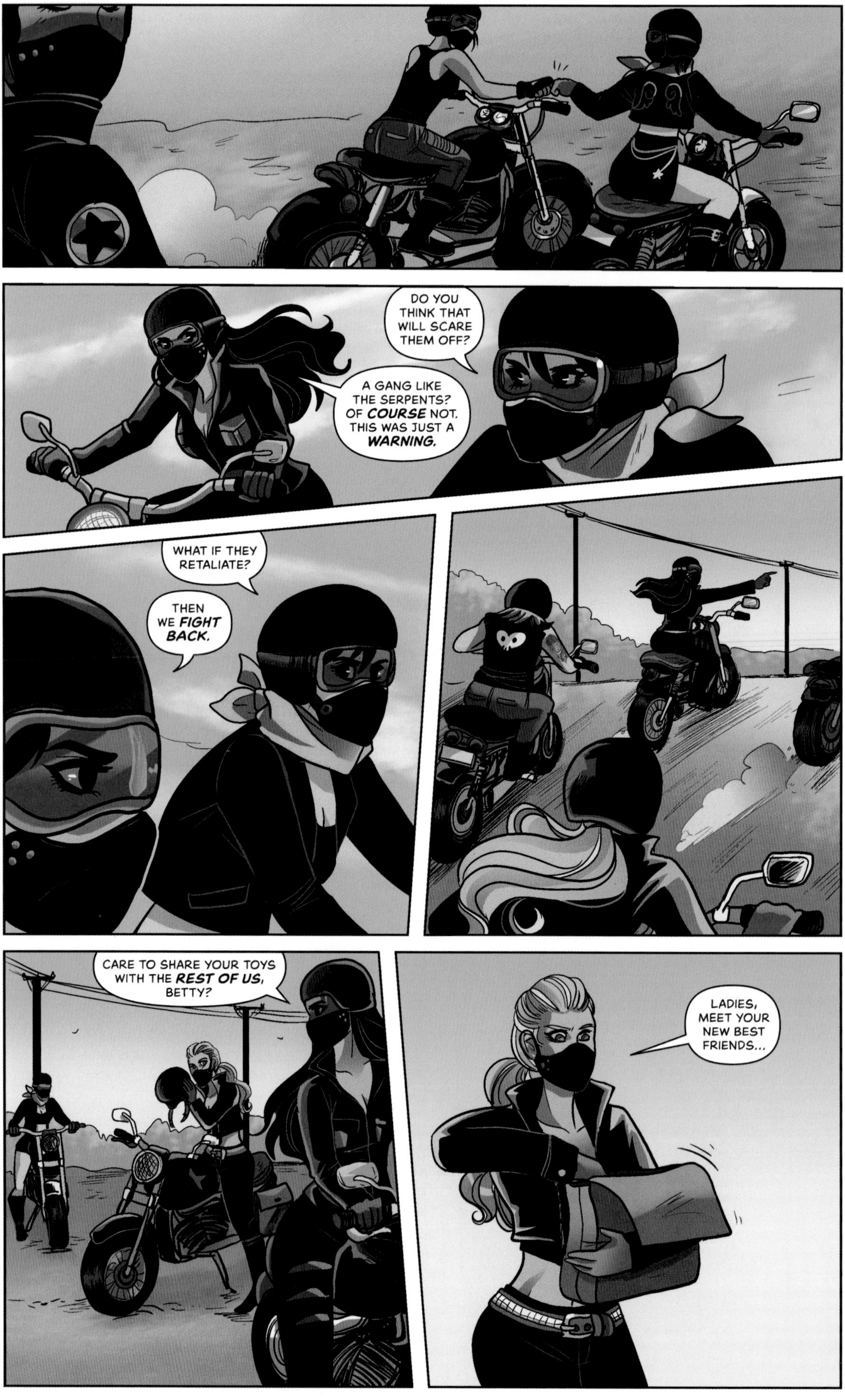
DO YOU THINK THAT WILL SCARE THEM OFF?
A GANG LIKE THE SERPENTS? OF COURSE NOT. THIS WAS JUST A WARNING.
WHAT IF THEY RETALIATE?
THEN WE FIGHT BACK.
CARE TO SHARE YOUR TOYS WITH THE REST OF US, BETTY?
LADIES, MEET YOUR NEW BEST FRIENDS...

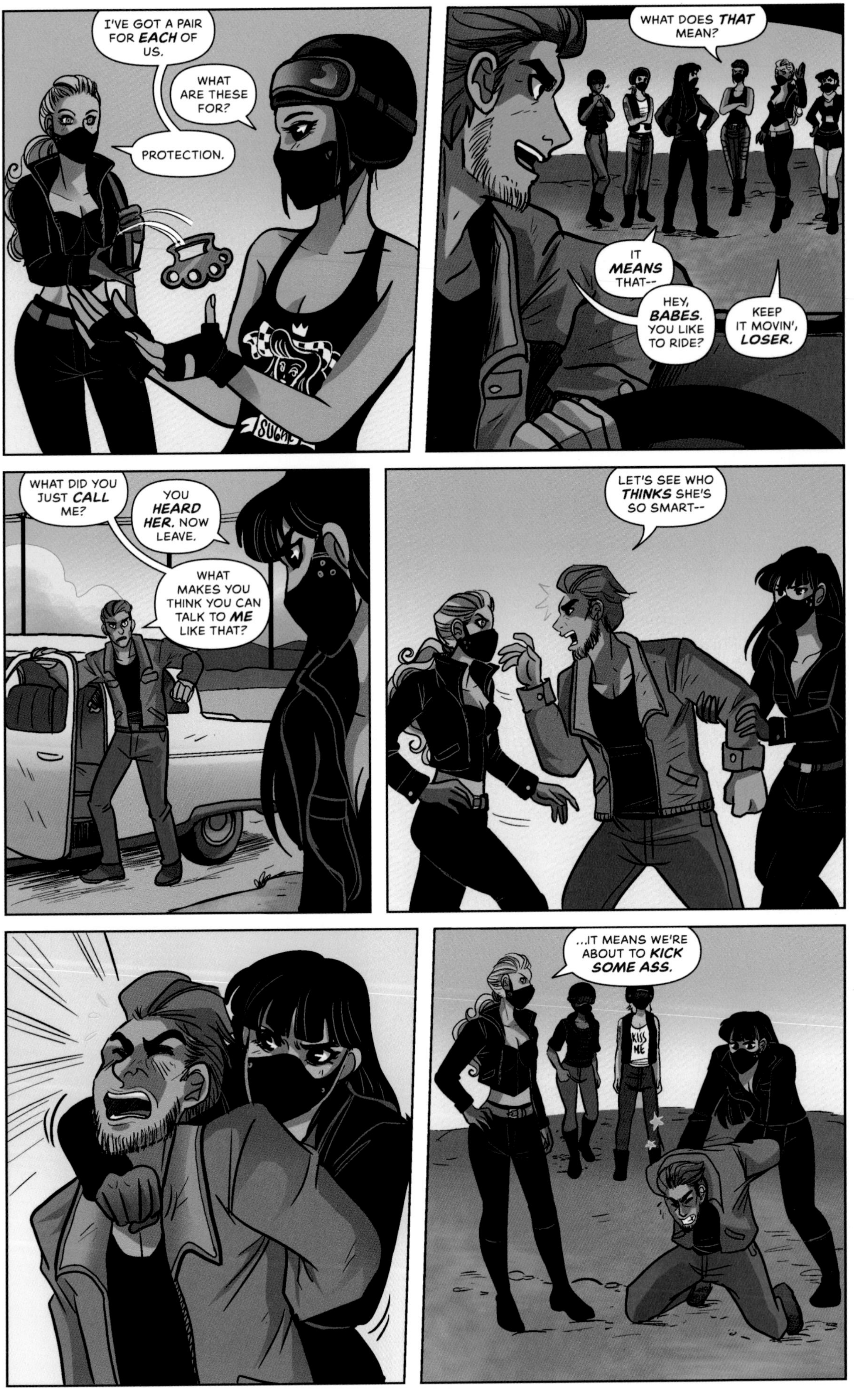

I'VE GOT A PAIR FOR EACH OF US.
WHAT ARE THESE FOR?
PROTECTION.
WHAT DOES THAT MEAN?
IT MEANS THAT--
HEY, BABES. YOU LIKE TO RIDE?
KEEP IT MOVIN', LOSER.
WHAT DID YOU JUST CALL ME?
YOU HEARD HER. NOW LEAVE.
WHAT MAKES YOU THINK YOU CAN TALK TO ME LIKE THAT?
LET'S SEE WHO THINKS SHE'S SO SMART--
...IT MEANS WE'RE ABOUT TO KICK SOME ASS.

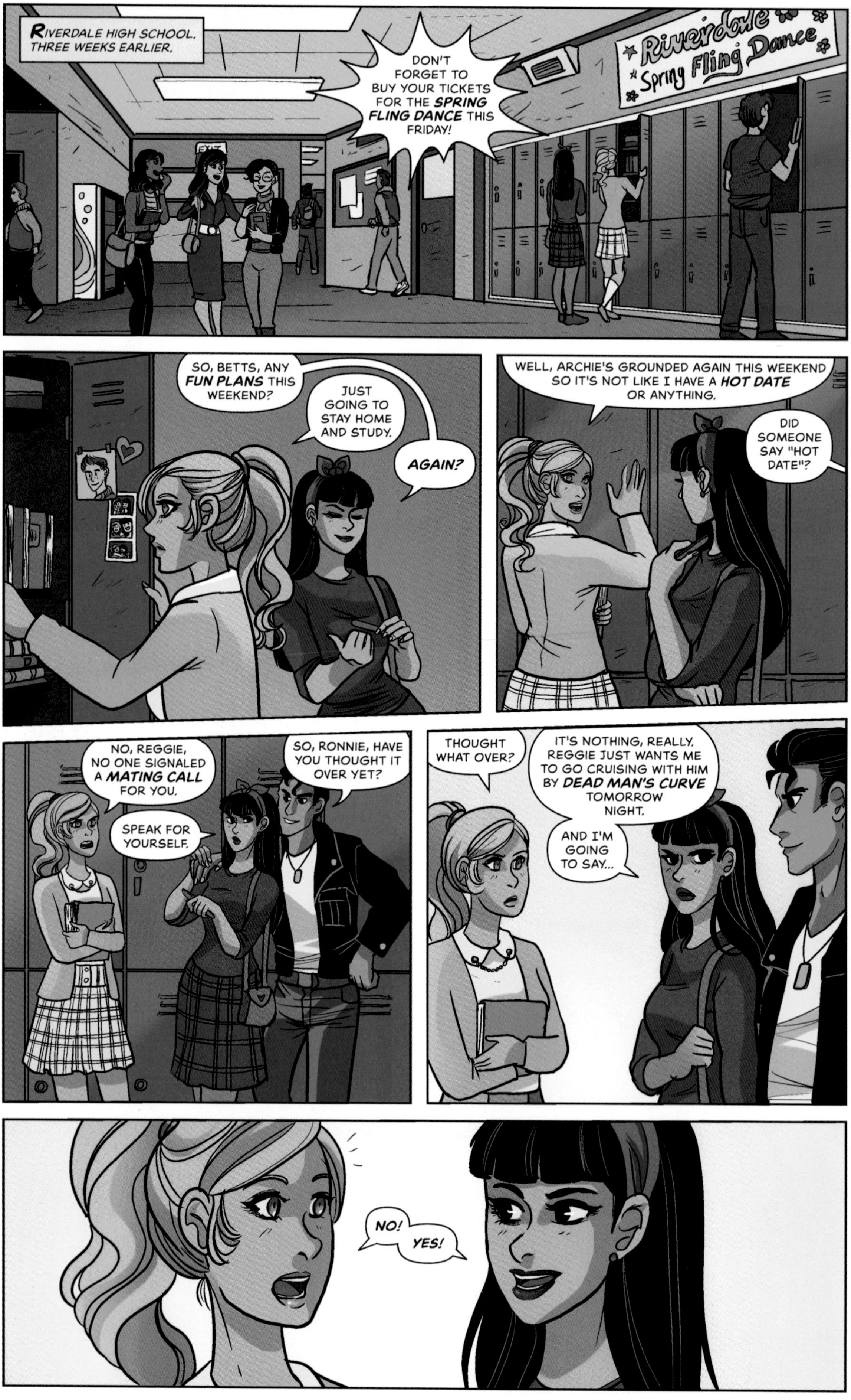
RIVERDALE HIGH SCHOOL. THREE WEEKS EARLIER.
DON'T FORGET TO BUY YOUR TICKETS FOR THE SPRING FLING DANCE THIS FRIDAY!
Riverdale Spring Fling Dance
SO, BETTS, ANY FUN PLANS THIS WEEKEND?
JUST GOING TO STAY HOME AND STUDY.
AGAIN?
WELL, ARCHIE'S GROUNDED AGAIN THIS WEEKEND SO IT'S NOT LIKE I HAVE A HOT DATE OR ANYTHING.
DID SOMEONE SAY "HOT DATE"?
NO, REGGIE, NO ONE SIGNALED A MATING CALL FOR YOU.
SPEAK FOR YOURSELF.
SO, RONNIE, HAVE YOU THOUGHT IT OVER YET?
THOUGHT WHAT OVER?
IT'S NOTHING, REALLY. REGGIE JUST WANTS ME TO GO CRUISING WITH HIM BY DEAD MAN'S CURVE TOMORROW NIGHT.
AND I'M GOING TO SAY...
NO!
YES!

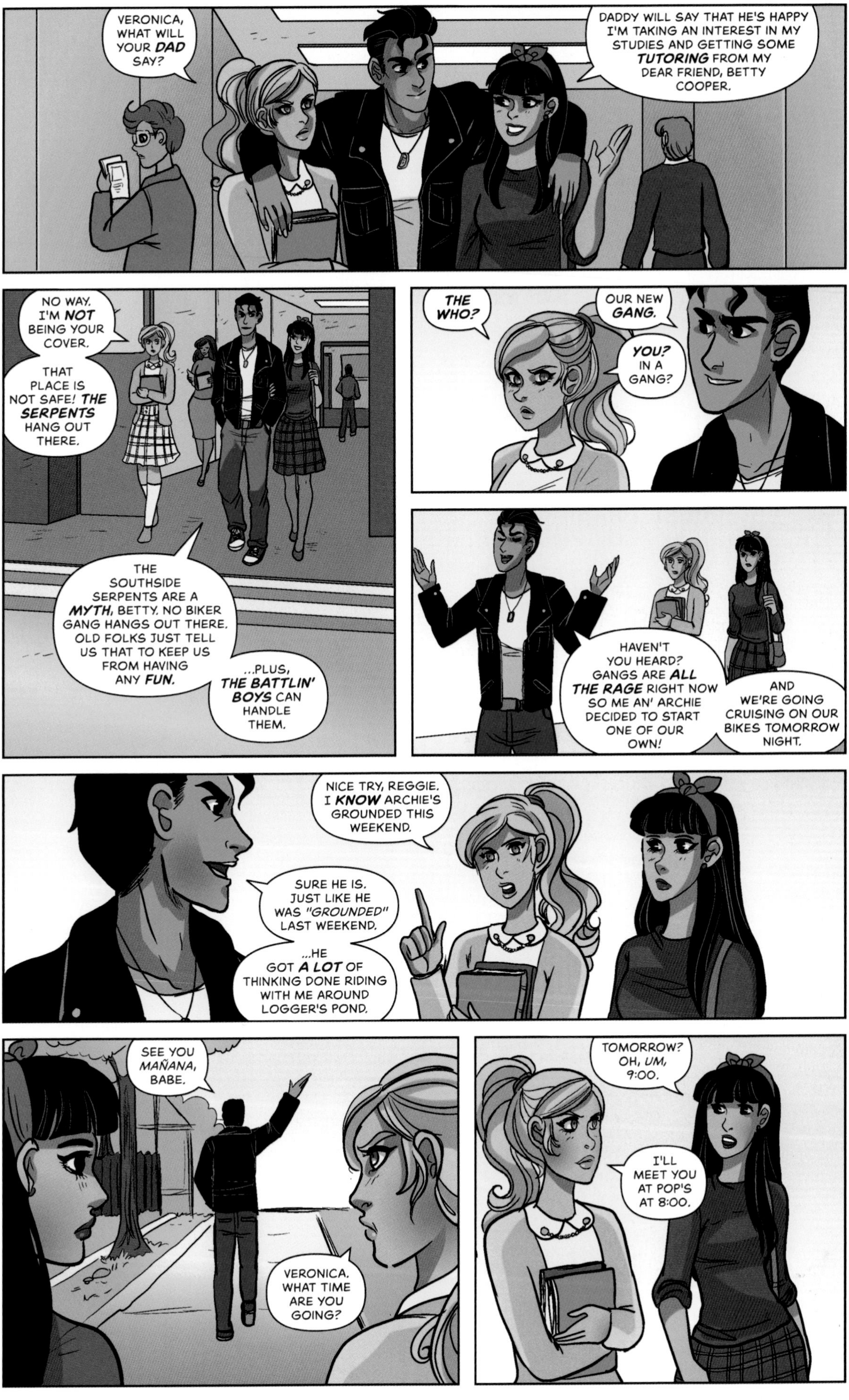
VERONICA, WHAT WILL YOUR DAD SAY?
DADDY WILL SAY THAT HE'S HAPPY I'M TAKING AN INTEREST IN MY STUDIES AND GETTING SOME TUTORING FROM MY DEAR FRIEND, BETTY COOPER.
NO WAY. I'M NOT BEING YOUR COVER.
THAT PLACE IS NOT SAFE! THE SERPENTS HANG OUT THERE.
THE SOUTHSIDE SERPENTS ARE A MYTH, BETTY. NO BIKER GANG HANGS OUT THERE. OLD FOLKS JUST TELL US THAT TO KEEP US FROM HAVING ANY FUN.
...PLUS, THE BATTLIN' BOYS CAN HANDLE THEM.
THE WHO?
OUR NEW GANG.
YOU? IN A GANG?
HAVEN'T YOU HEARD? GANGS ARE ALL THE RAGE RIGHT NOW SO ME AN' ARCHIE DECIDED TO START ONE OF OUR OWN!
AND WE'RE GOING CRUISING ON OUR BIKES TOMORROW NIGHT.
NICE TRY, REGGIE. I KNOW ARCHIE'S GROUNDED THIS WEEKEND.
SURE HE IS. JUST LIKE HE WAS "GROUNDED" LAST WEEKEND.
...HE GOT A LOT OF THINKING DONE RIDING WITH ME AROUND LOGGER'S POND.
SEE YOU MAÑANA, BABE.
VERONICA. WHAT TIME ARE YOU GOING?
TOMORROW? OH, UM, 9:00.
I'LL MEET YOU AT POP'S AT 8:00.

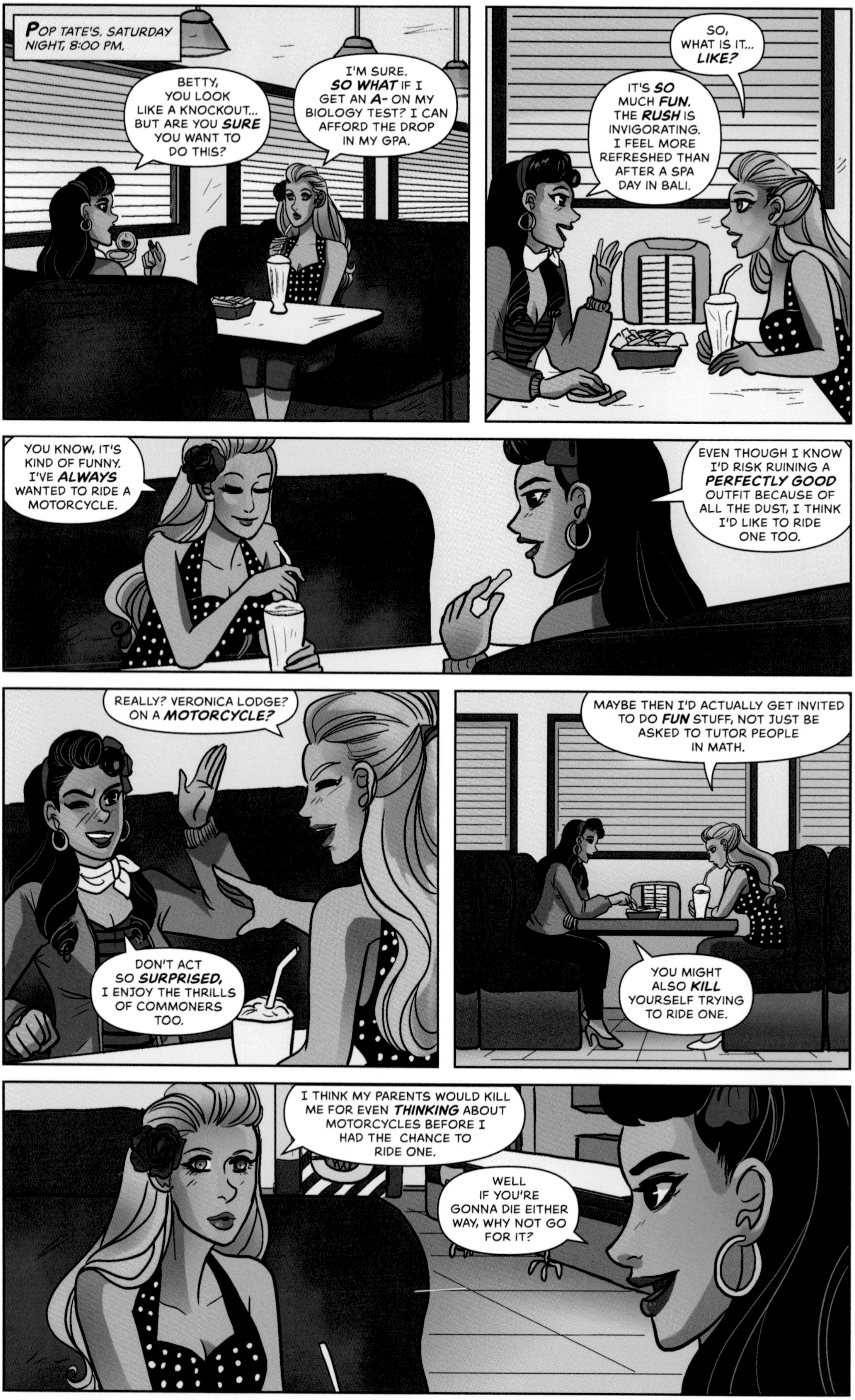
POP TATE'S. SATURDAY NIGHT, 8:00 PM.
BETTY, YOU LOOK LIKE A KNOCKOUT... BUT ARE YOU SURE YOU WANT TO DO THIS?
I'M SURE. SO WHAT IF I GET AN A- ON MY BIOLOGY TEST? I CAN AFFORD THE DROP IN MY GPA.
SO, WHAT IS IT... LIKE?
IT'S SO MUCH FUN. THE RUSH IS INVIGORATING. I FEEL MORE REFRESHED THAN AFTER A SPA DAY IN BALI.
YOU KNOW, IT'S KIND OF FUNNY. I'VE ALWAYS WANTED TO RIDE A MOTORCYCLE.
EVEN THOUGH I KNOW I'D RISK RUINING A PERFECTLY GOOD OUTFIT BECAUSE OF ALL THE DUST, I THINK I'D LIKE TO RIDE ONE TOO.
REALLY? VERONICA LODGE? ON A MOTORCYCLE?
DON'T ACT SO SURPRISED, I ENJOY THE THRILLS OF COMMONERS TOO.
MAYBE THEN I'D ACTUALLY GET INVITED TO DO FUN STUFF, NOT JUST BE ASKED TO TUTOR PEOPLE IN MATH.
YOU MIGHT ALSO KILL YOURSELF TRYING TO RIDE ONE.
I THINK MY PARENTS WOULD KILL ME FOR EVEN THINKING ABOUT MOTORCYCLES BEFORE I HAD THE CHANCE TO RIDE ONE.
WELL IF YOU'RE GONNA DIE EITHER WAY, WHY NOT GO FOR IT?

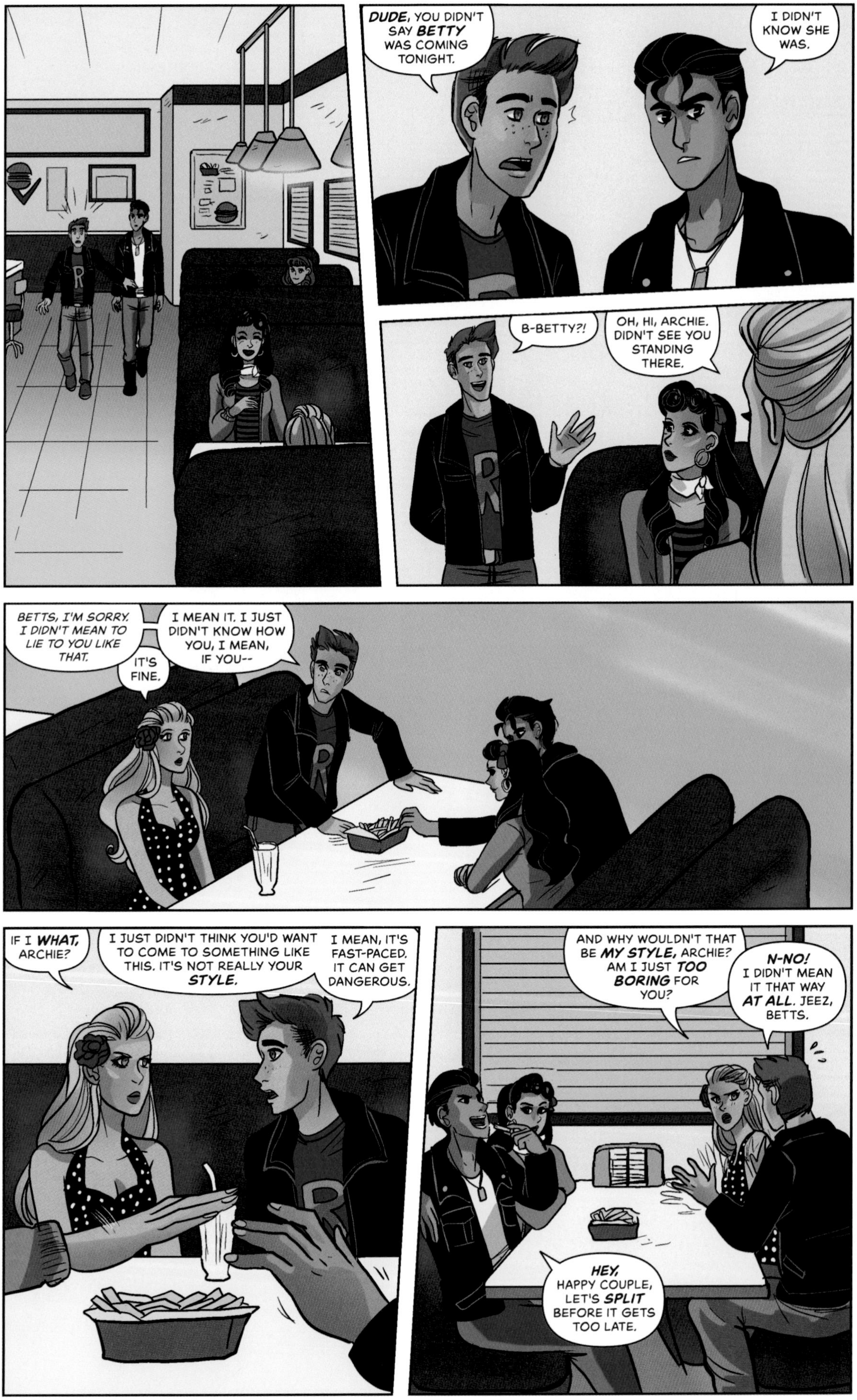

DUDE, YOU DIDN'T SAY BETTY WAS COMING TONIGHT.
I DIDN'T KNOW SHE WAS.
B-BETTY?!
OH, HI, ARCHIE. DIDN'T SEE YOU STANDING THERE.
BETTS, I'M SORRY. I DIDN'T MEAN TO LIE TO YOU LIKE THAT.
IT'S FINE.
I MEAN IT. I JUST DIDN'T KNOW HOW YOU, I MEAN, IF YOU--
IF I WHAT, ARCHIE?
I JUST DIDN'T THINK YOU'D WANT TO COME TO SOMETHING LIKE THIS. IT'S NOT REALLY YOUR STYLE.
I MEAN, IT'S FAST-PACED. IT CAN GET DANGEROUS.
AND WHY WOULDN'T THAT BE MY STYLE, ARCHIE? AM I JUST TOO BORING FOR YOU?
N-NO! I DIDN'T MEAN IT THAT WAY AT ALL. JEEZ, BETTS.
HEY, HAPPY COUPLE, LET'S SPLIT BEFORE IT GETS TOO LATE.

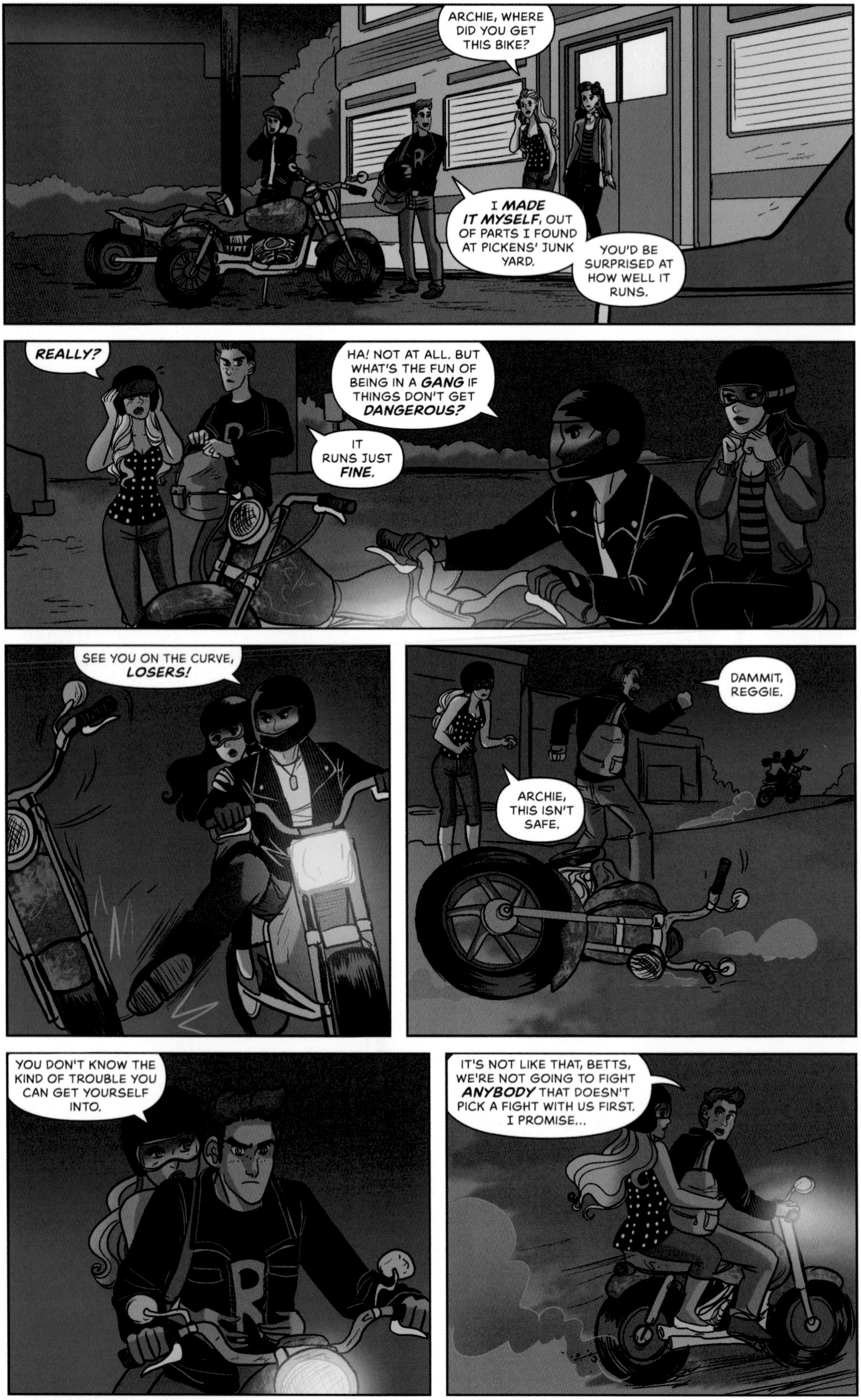

ARCHIE, WHERE DID YOU GET THIS BIKE?
I MADE IT MYSELF, OUT OF PARTS I FOUND AT PICKENS' JUNK YARD.
YOU'D BE SURPRISED AT HOW WELL IT RUNS.
REALLY?
HA! NOT AT ALL. BUT WHAT'S THE FUN OF BEING IN A GANG IF THINGS DON'T GET DANGEROUS?
IT RUNS JUST FINE.
SEE YOU ON THE CURVE, LOSERS!
DAMMIT, REGGIE.
ARCHIE, THIS ISN'T SAFE.
YOU DON'T KNOW THE KIND OF TROUBLE YOU CAN GET YOURSELF INTO.
IT'S NOT LIKE THAT, BETTS, WE'RE NOT GOING TO FIGHT ANYBODY THAT DOESN'T PICK A FIGHT WITH US FIRST. I PROMISE...

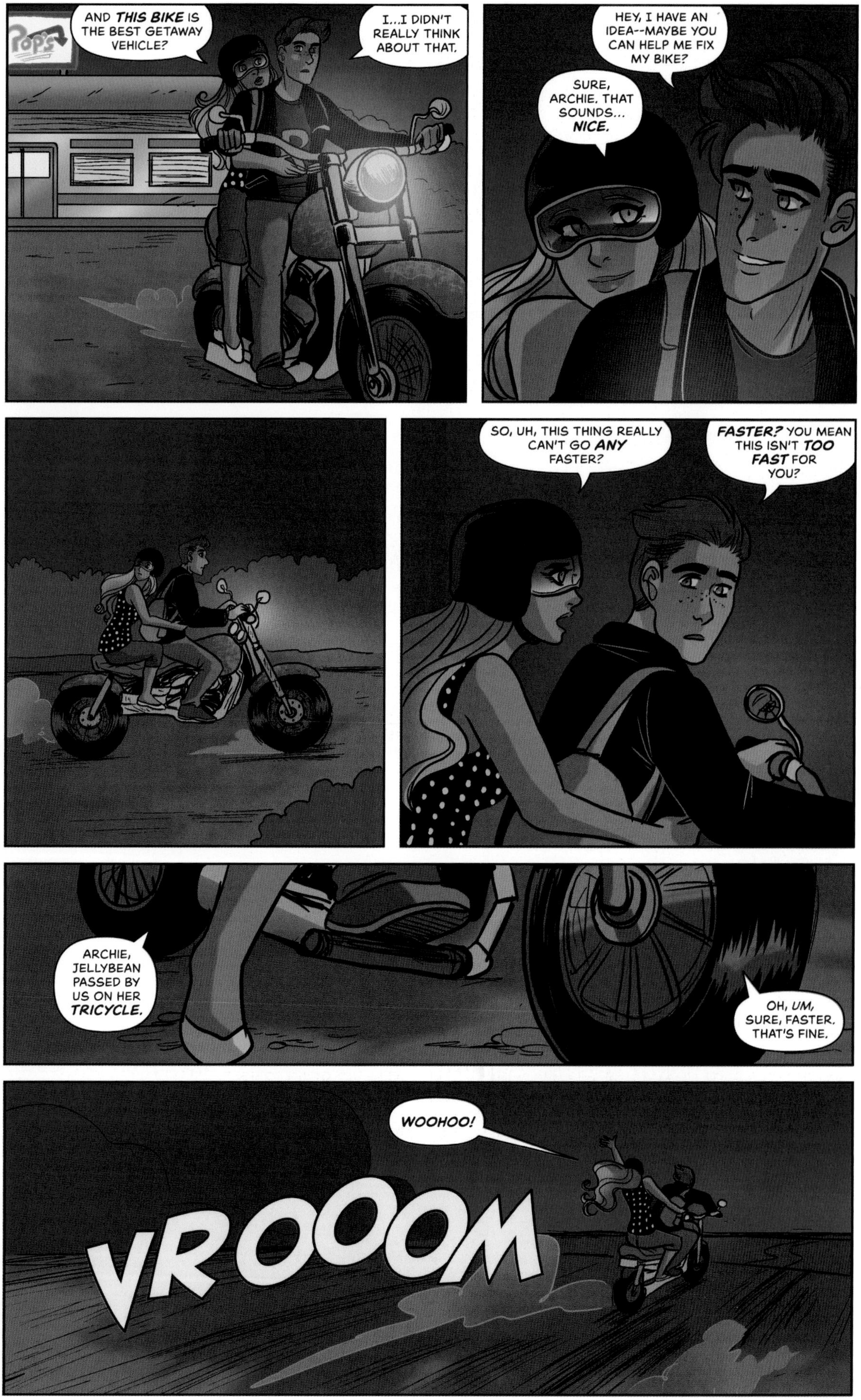
Pop's
AND **THIS BIKE** IS THE BEST GETAWAY VEHICLE?
I...I DIDN'T REALLY THINK ABOUT THAT.
HEY, I HAVE AN IDEA--MAYBE YOU CAN HELP ME FIX MY BIKE?
SURE, ARCHIE. THAT SOUNDS... **NICE.**
SO, UH, THIS THING REALLY CAN'T GO **ANY** FASTER?
FASTER? YOU MEAN THIS ISN'T **TOO FAST** FOR YOU?
ARCHIE, JELLYBEAN PASSED BY US ON HER **TRICYCLE.**
OH, *UM*, SURE, FASTER. THAT'S FINE.
WOOHOO!
VROOOM

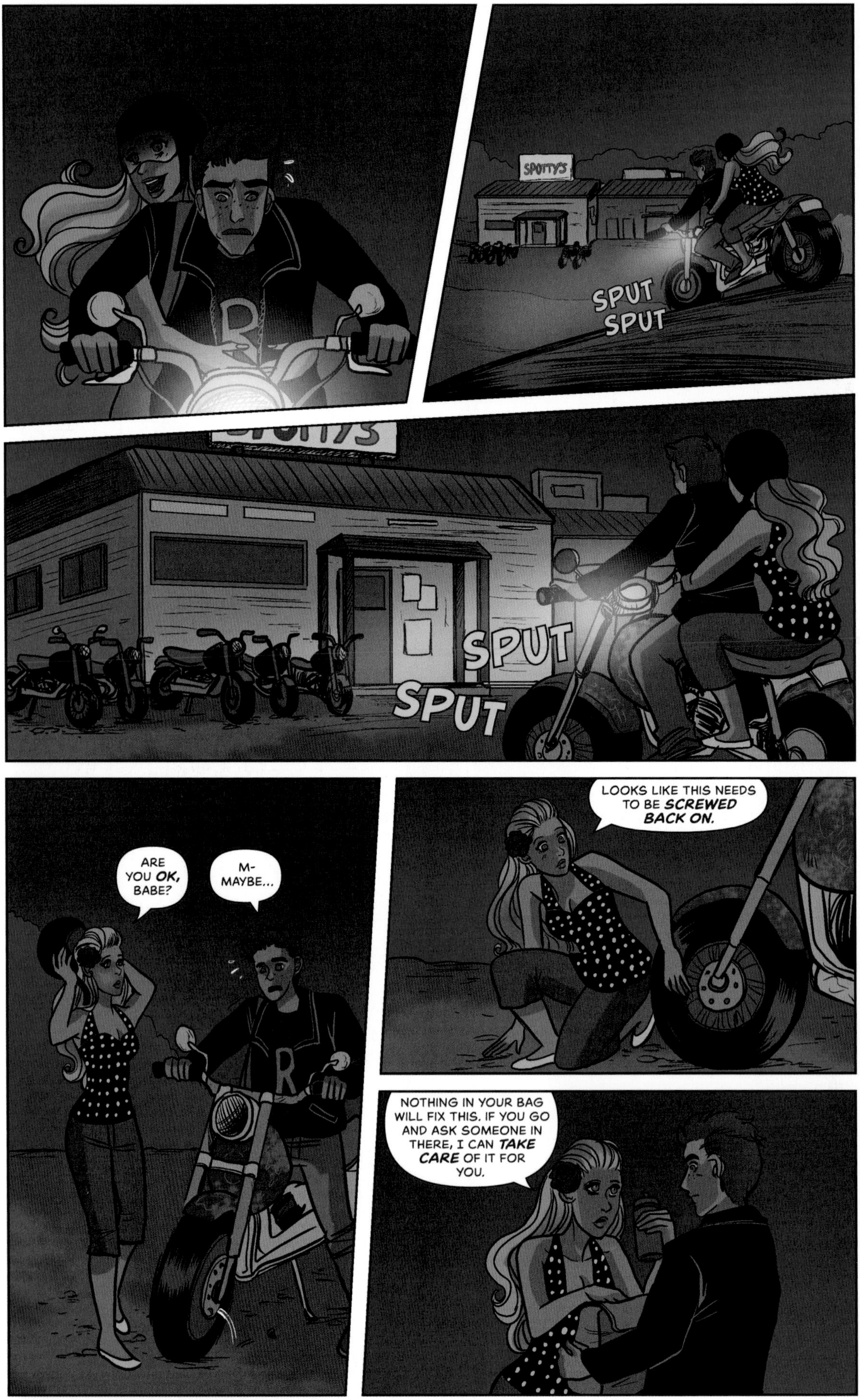
SPOTTY'S
SPUT
SPUT
SPUT
SPUT
ARE YOU **OK,** BABE?
M-MAYBE...
LOOKS LIKE THIS NEEDS TO BE ***SCREWED BACK ON.***
NOTHING IN YOUR BAG WILL FIX THIS. IF YOU GO AND ASK SOMEONE IN THERE, I CAN ***TAKE CARE*** OF IT FOR YOU.

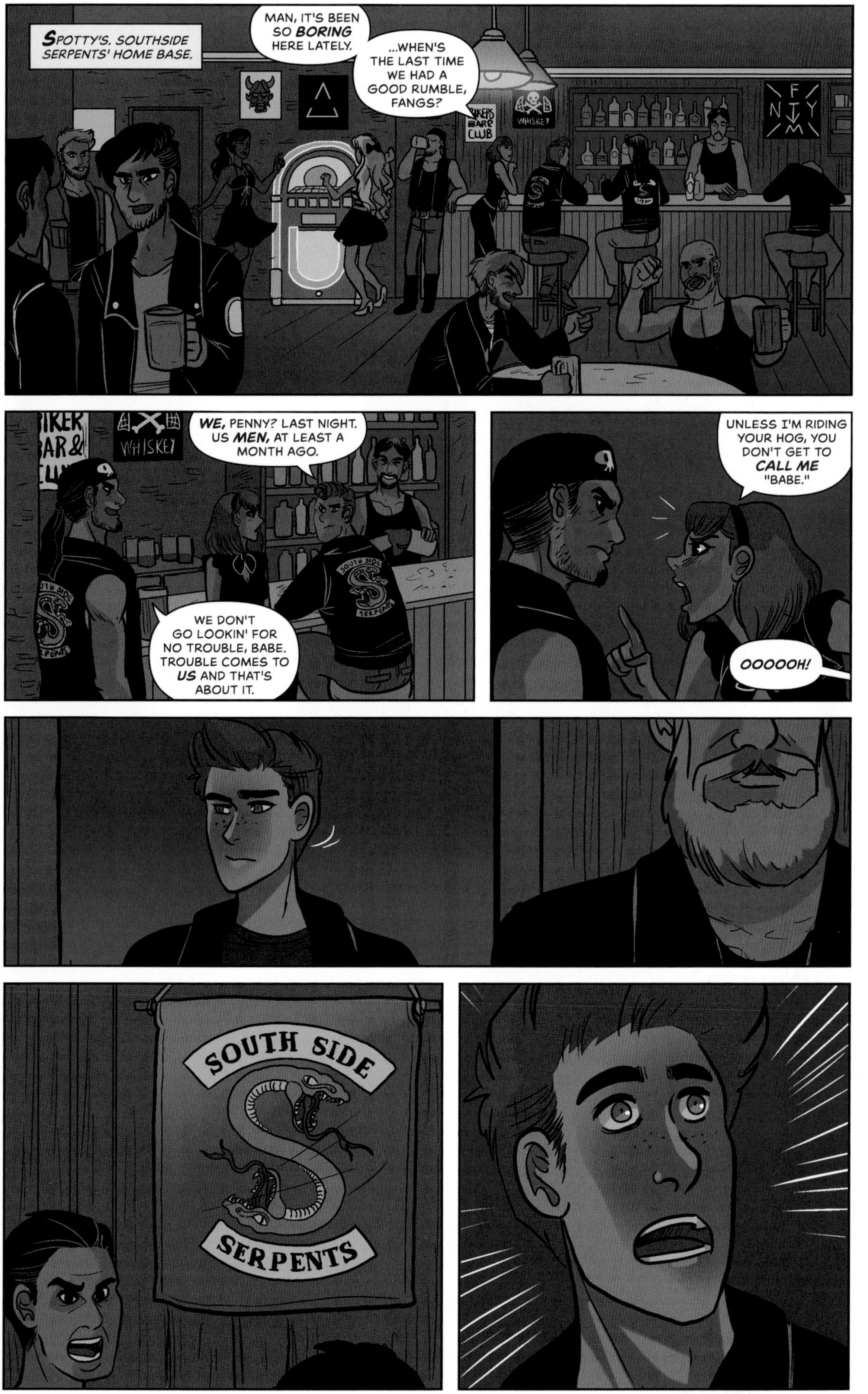

SPOTTY'S, SOUTHSIDE SERPENTS' HOME BASE.
MAN, IT'S BEEN SO BORING HERE LATELY.
...WHEN'S THE LAST TIME WE HAD A GOOD RUMBLE, FANGS?
WHISKEY
WE, PENNY? LAST NIGHT. US MEN, AT LEAST A MONTH AGO.
WE DON'T GO LOOKIN' FOR NO TROUBLE, BABE. TROUBLE COMES TO US AND THAT'S ABOUT IT.
UNLESS I'M RIDING YOUR HOG, YOU DON'T GET TO CALL ME "BABE."
OOOOOH!
SOUTH SIDE
SERPENTS

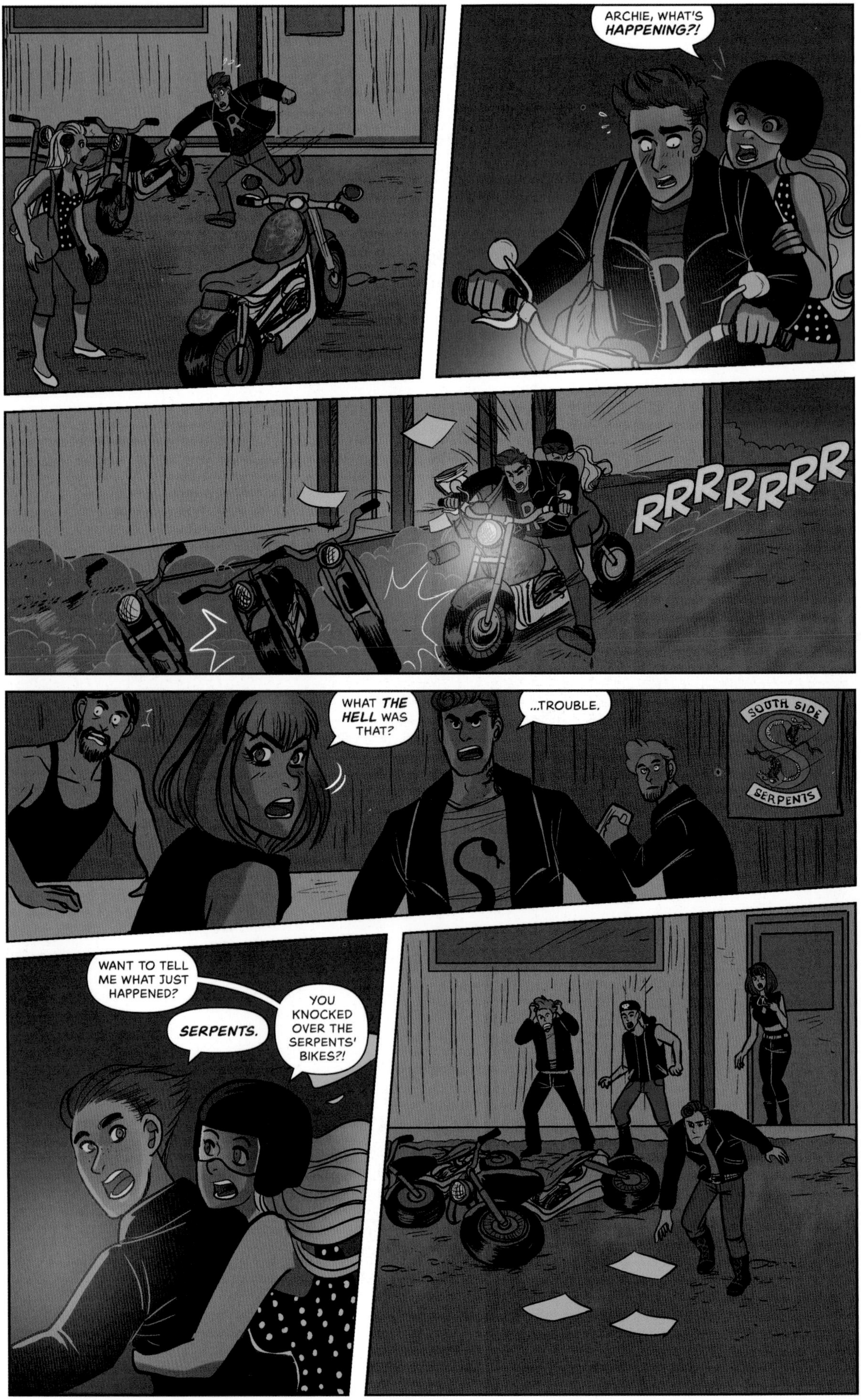
ARCHIE, WHAT'S HAPPENING?!
RRRRRRR
WHAT THE HELL WAS THAT?
...TROUBLE.
SOUTH SIDE SERPENTS
WANT TO TELL ME WHAT JUST HAPPENED?
SERPENTS.
YOU KNOCKED OVER THE SERPENTS' BIKES?!

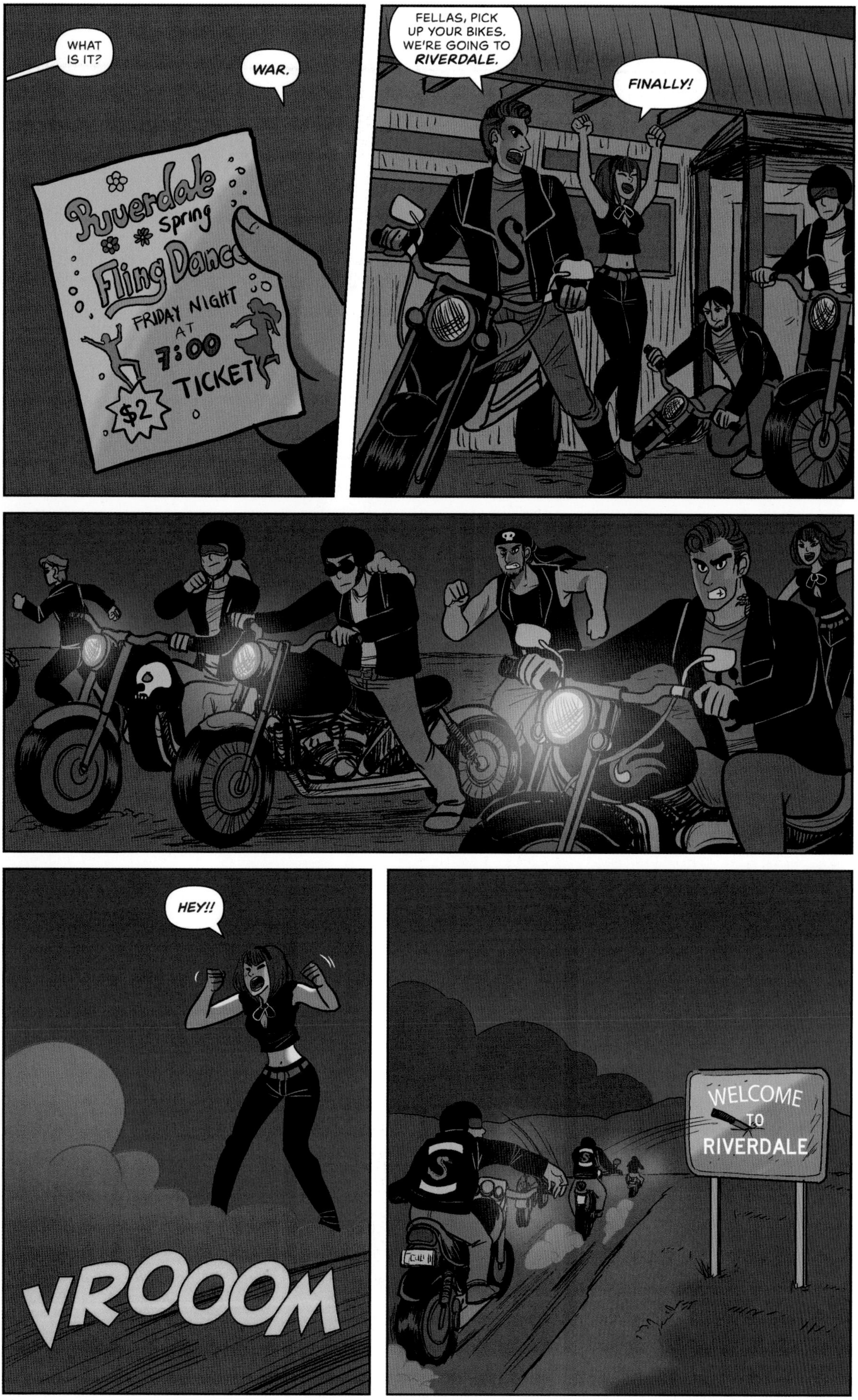
WHAT IS IT?
WAR.
Riverdale Spring Fling Dance
FRIDAY NIGHT AT 7:00
$2 TICKET
FELLAS, PICK UP YOUR BIKES. WE'RE GOING TO RIVERDALE.
FINALLY!
HEY!!
VROOOM
WELCOME TO RIVERDALE

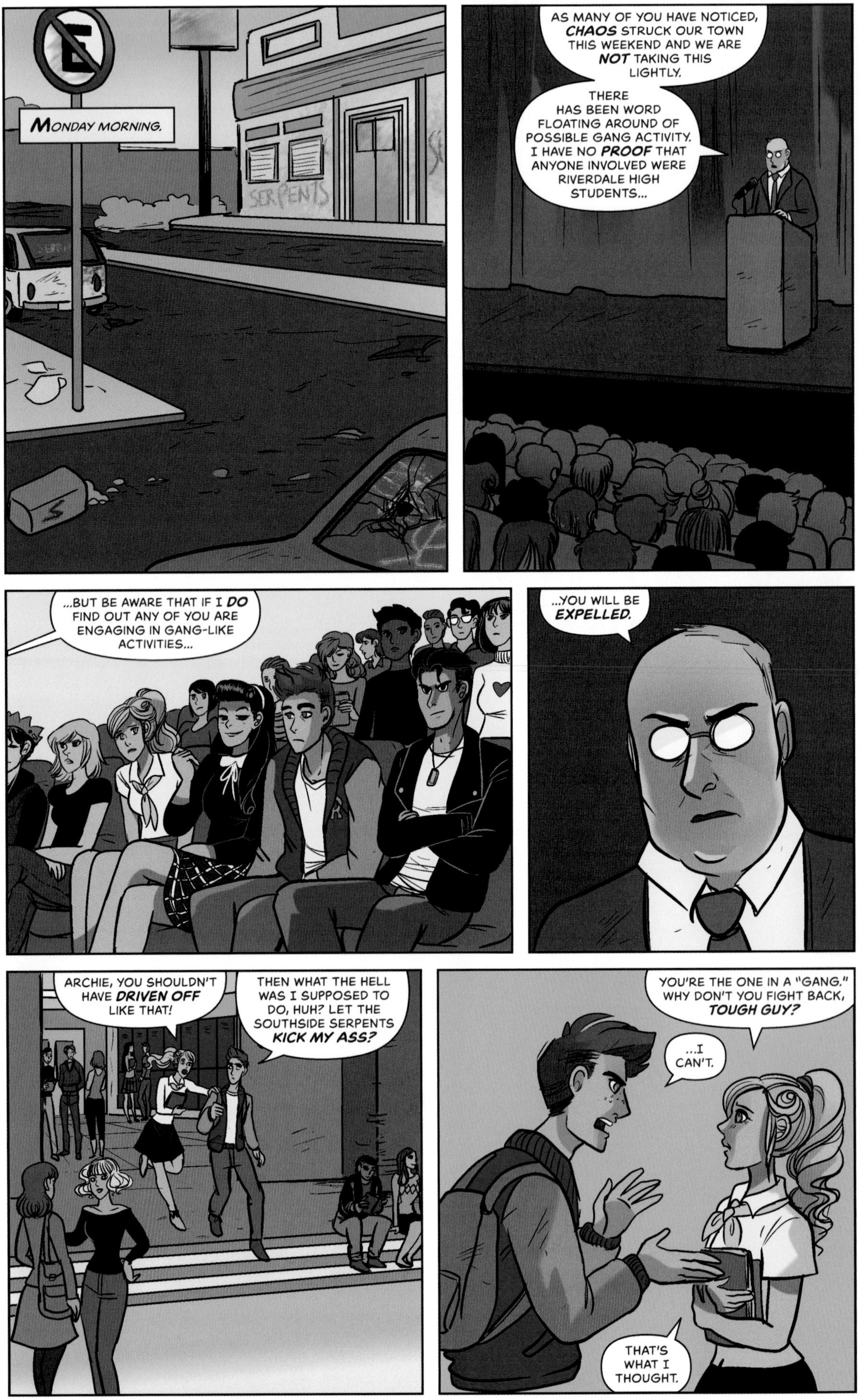
MONDAY MORNING.
SERPENTS
AS MANY OF YOU HAVE NOTICED, CHAOS STRUCK OUR TOWN THIS WEEKEND AND WE ARE NOT TAKING THIS LIGHTLY.
THERE HAS BEEN WORD FLOATING AROUND OF POSSIBLE GANG ACTIVITY. I HAVE NO PROOF THAT ANYONE INVOLVED WERE RIVERDALE HIGH STUDENTS...
...BUT BE AWARE THAT IF I DO FIND OUT ANY OF YOU ARE ENGAGING IN GANG-LIKE ACTIVITIES...
...YOU WILL BE EXPELLED.
ARCHIE, YOU SHOULDN'T HAVE DRIVEN OFF LIKE THAT!
THEN WHAT THE HELL WAS I SUPPOSED TO DO, HUH? LET THE SOUTHSIDE SERPENTS KICK MY ASS?
YOU'RE THE ONE IN A "GANG." WHY DON'T YOU FIGHT BACK, TOUGH GUY?
...I CAN'T.
THAT'S WHAT I THOUGHT.

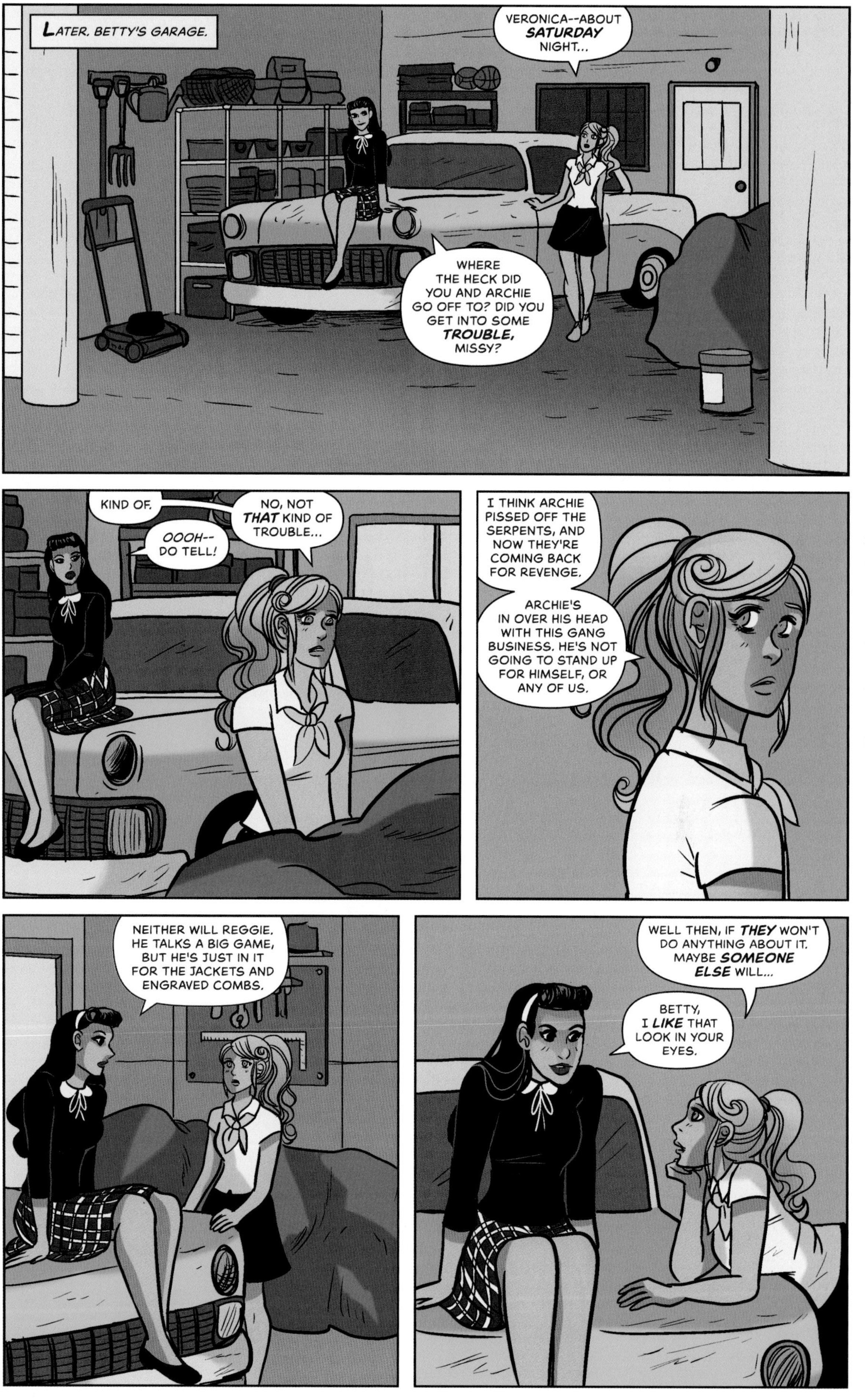
LATER. BETTY'S GARAGE.
VERONICA--ABOUT SATURDAY NIGHT...
WHERE THE HECK DID YOU AND ARCHIE GO OFF TO? DID YOU GET INTO SOME TROUBLE, MISSY?
NO, NOT THAT KIND OF TROUBLE...
KIND OF.
OOOH-- DO TELL!
I THINK ARCHIE PISSED OFF THE SERPENTS, AND NOW THEY'RE COMING BACK FOR REVENGE.
ARCHIE'S IN OVER HIS HEAD WITH THIS GANG BUSINESS. HE'S NOT GOING TO STAND UP FOR HIMSELF, OR ANY OF US.
NEITHER WILL REGGIE. HE TALKS A BIG GAME, BUT HE'S JUST IN IT FOR THE JACKETS AND ENGRAVED COMBS.
WELL THEN, IF THEY WON'T DO ANYTHING ABOUT IT. MAYBE SOMEONE ELSE WILL...
BETTY, I LIKE THAT LOOK IN YOUR EYES.

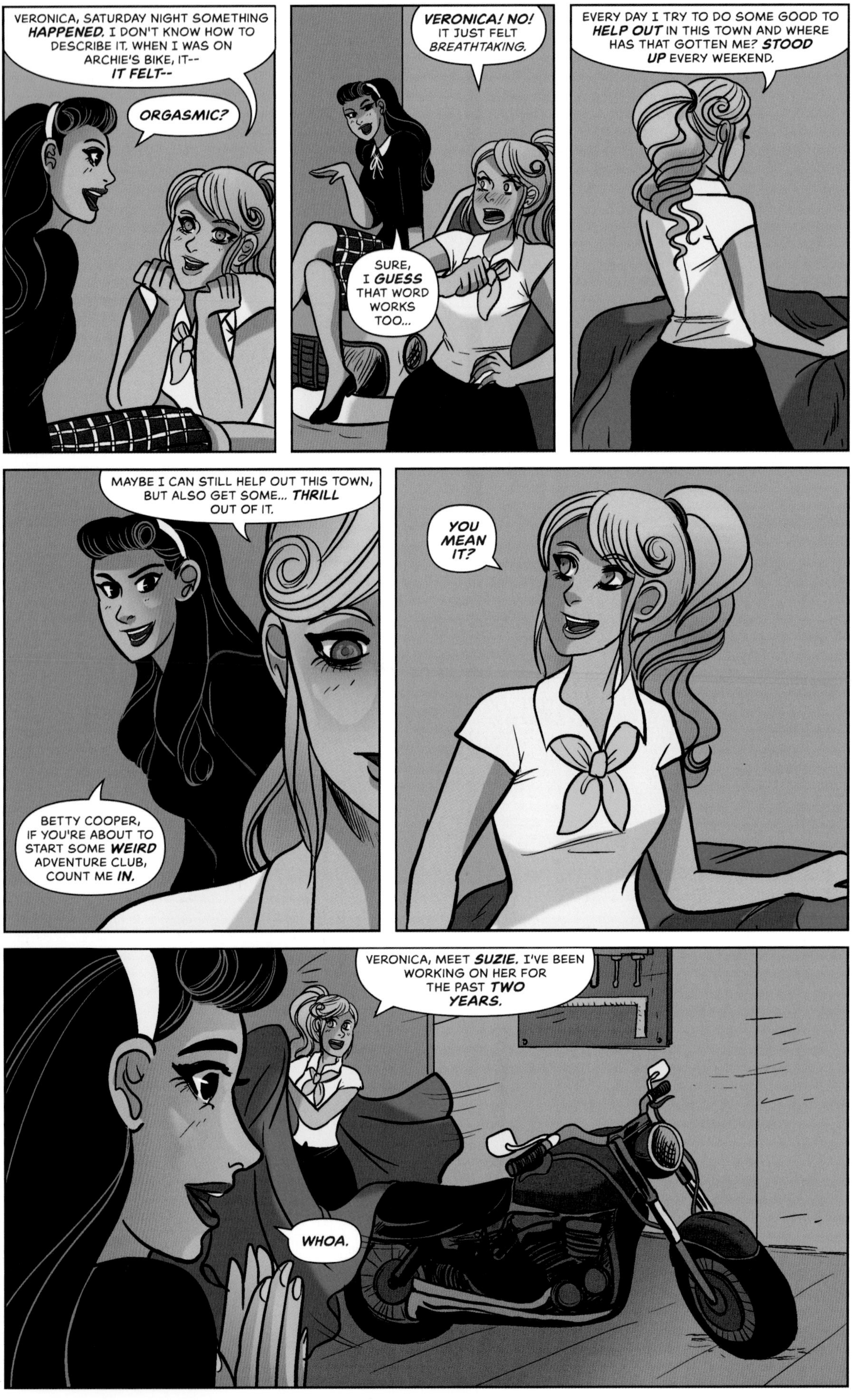

VERONICA, SATURDAY NIGHT SOMETHING **HAPPENED.** I DON'T KNOW HOW TO DESCRIBE IT. WHEN I WAS ON ARCHIE'S BIKE, IT-- **IT FELT--**
ORGASMIC?
VERONICA! NO! IT JUST FELT *BREATHTAKING.*
SURE, I **GUESS** THAT WORD WORKS TOO...
EVERY DAY I TRY TO DO SOME GOOD TO **HELP OUT** IN THIS TOWN AND WHERE HAS THAT GOTTEN ME? **STOOD UP** EVERY WEEKEND.
MAYBE I CAN STILL HELP OUT THIS TOWN, BUT ALSO GET SOME... **THRILL** OUT OF IT.
BETTY COOPER, IF YOU'RE ABOUT TO START SOME **WEIRD** ADVENTURE CLUB, COUNT ME **IN.**
YOU MEAN IT?
VERONICA, MEET **SUZIE.** I'VE BEEN WORKING ON HER FOR THE PAST **TWO YEARS.**
WHOA.

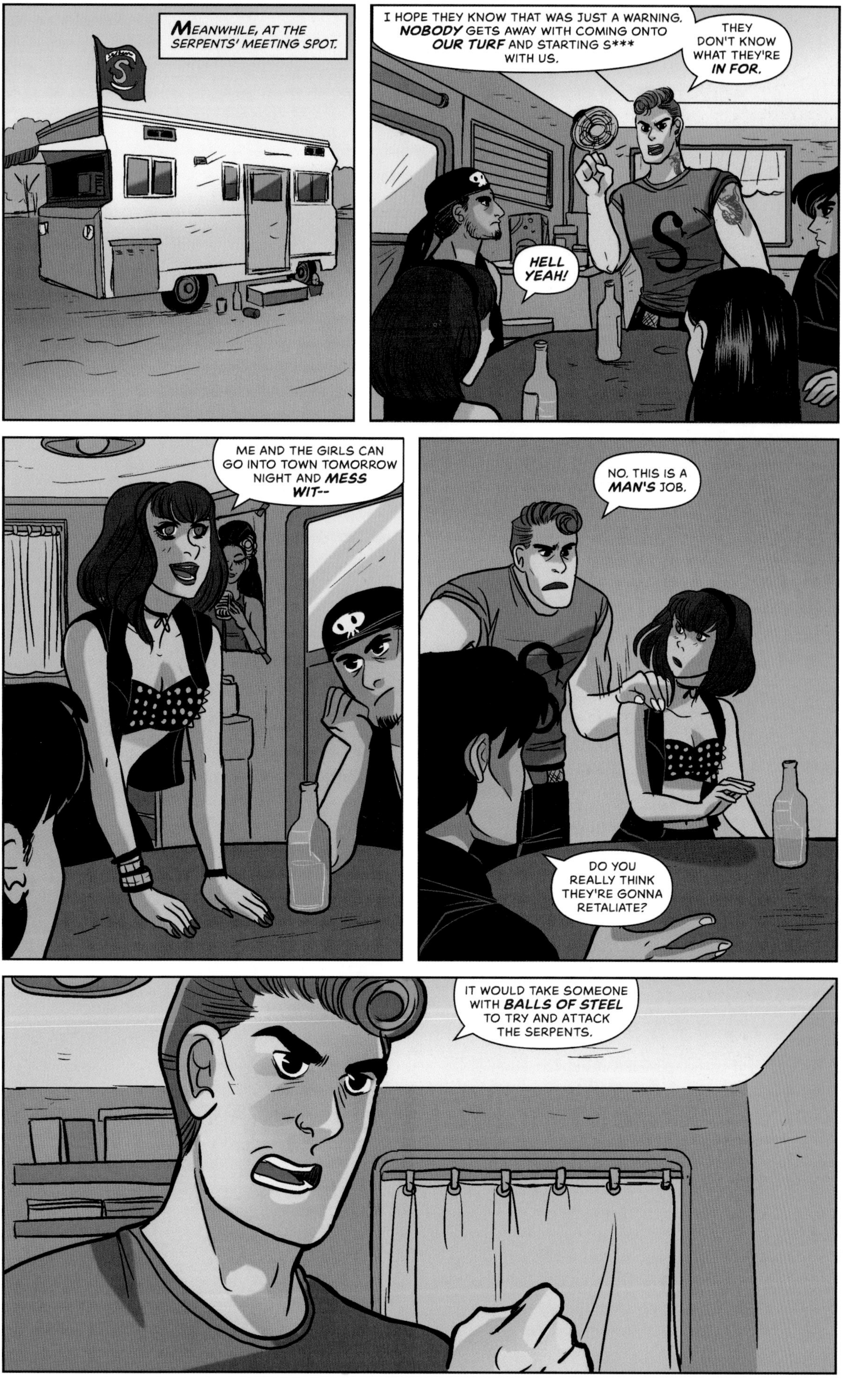
MEANWHILE, AT THE SERPENTS' MEETING SPOT.
I HOPE THEY KNOW THAT WAS JUST A WARNING. NOBODY GETS AWAY WITH COMING ONTO OUR TURF AND STARTING S*** WITH US.
THEY DON'T KNOW WHAT THEY'RE IN FOR.
HELL YEAH!
ME AND THE GIRLS CAN GO INTO TOWN TOMORROW NIGHT AND MESS WIT--
NO. THIS IS A MAN'S JOB.
DO YOU REALLY THINK THEY'RE GONNA RETALIATE?
IT WOULD TAKE SOMEONE WITH BALLS OF STEEL TO TRY AND ATTACK THE SERPENTS.

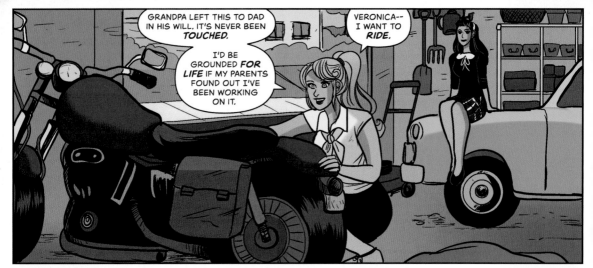

GRANDPA LEFT THIS TO DAD IN HIS WILL, IT'S NEVER BEEN *TOUCHED*.

I'D BE GROUNDED *FOR LIFE* IF MY PARENTS FOUND OUT I'VE BEEN WORKING ON IT.

VERONICA-- I WANT TO *RIDE*.

DO YOU EVEN KNOW HOW?

I THINK I CAN GET THE HANG OF IT. PLUS, YOU SAID YOU WANTED TO LEARN, TOO.

LEARN? HONEY, I NEVER TOLD YOU THIS, BUT-- I *ALREADY* KNOW HOW.

REALLY?! THEN LET'S TAKE ON THE SERPENTS.

US TWO? KICK THE ASSES OF A DANGEROUS *BIKER GANG*, REALLY, BETTY?

WE CAN'T DO IT ALONE. WE'RE GONNA NEED *STRENGTH IN NUMBERS*.

BUT VERONICA, YOU KNOW OUR BOYFRIENDS ARE *NEVER* GOING TO STEP UP AND FIGHT.

...WHO THE HELL SAID ANYTHING ABOUT *BOYS?*

to be continued...

Chapter Two

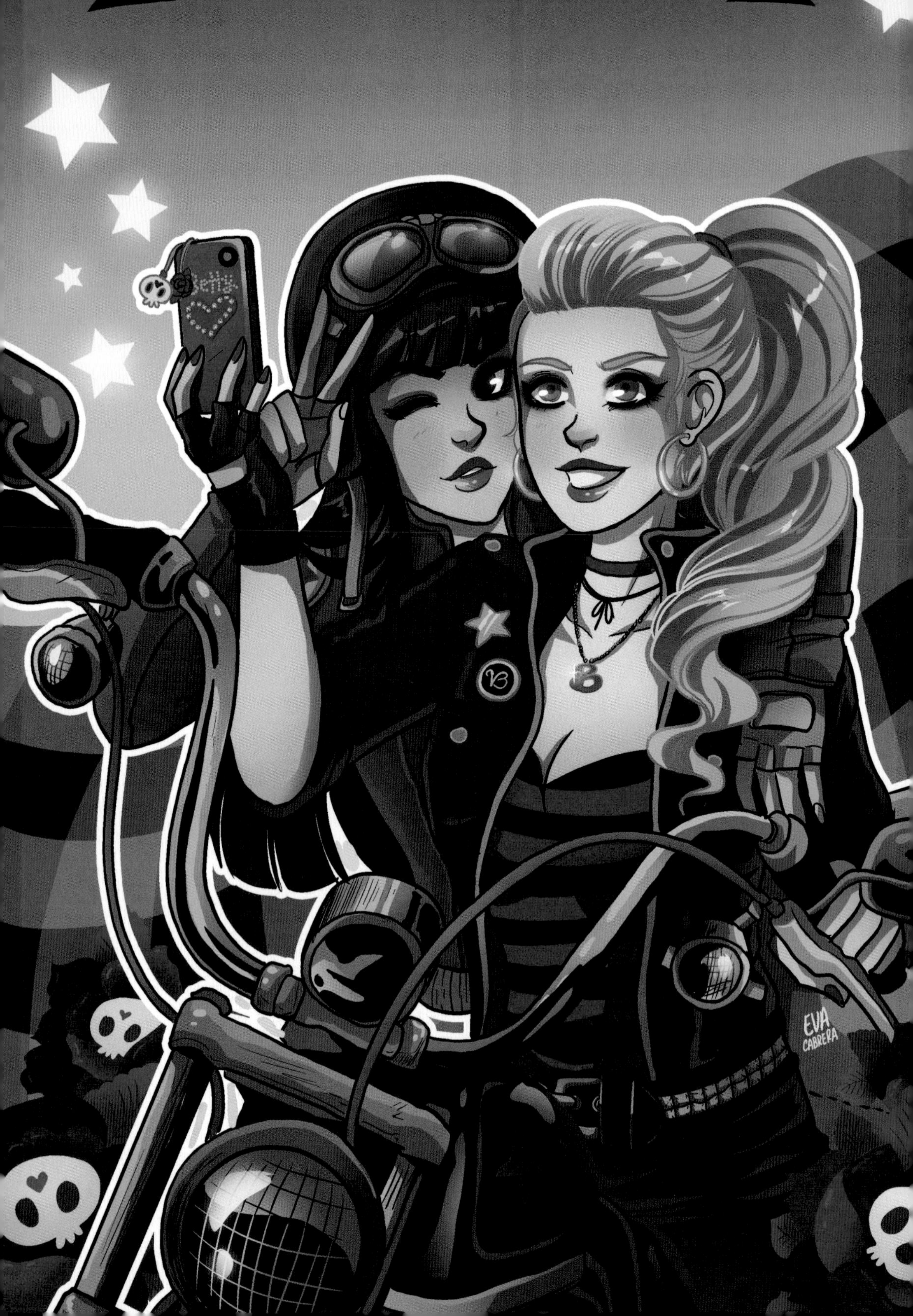
EVA CABRERA

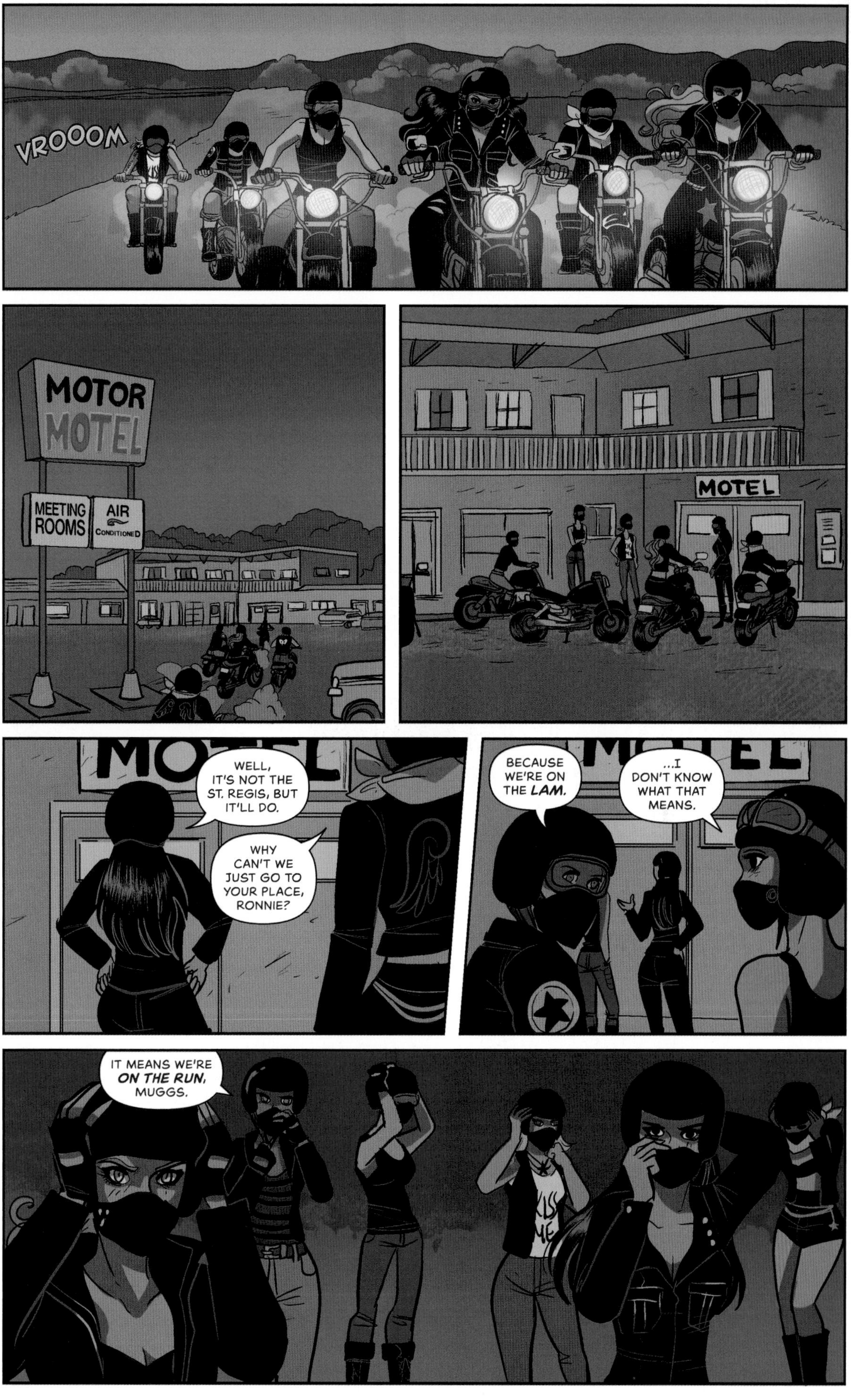
VROOOM
MOTOR MOTEL
MEETING ROOMS
AIR CONDITIONED
MOTEL
WELL, IT'S NOT THE ST. REGIS, BUT IT'LL DO.
WHY CAN'T WE JUST GO TO YOUR PLACE, RONNIE?
BECAUSE WE'RE ON THE LAM.
...I DON'T KNOW WHAT THAT MEANS.
IT MEANS WE'RE ON THE RUN, MUGGS.

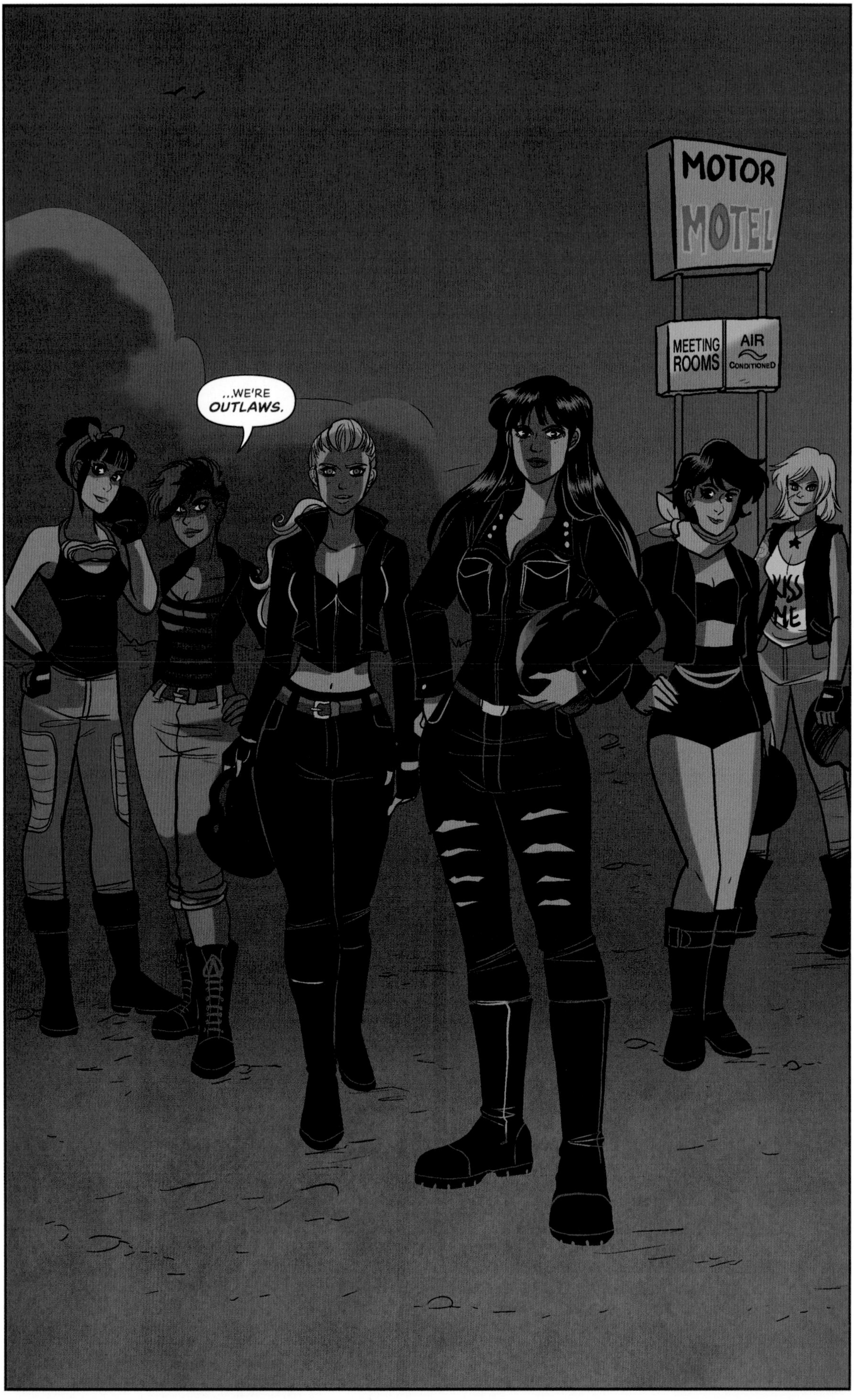
...WE'RE OUTLAWS.
MOTOR MOTEL
MEETING ROOMS
AIR CONDITIONED

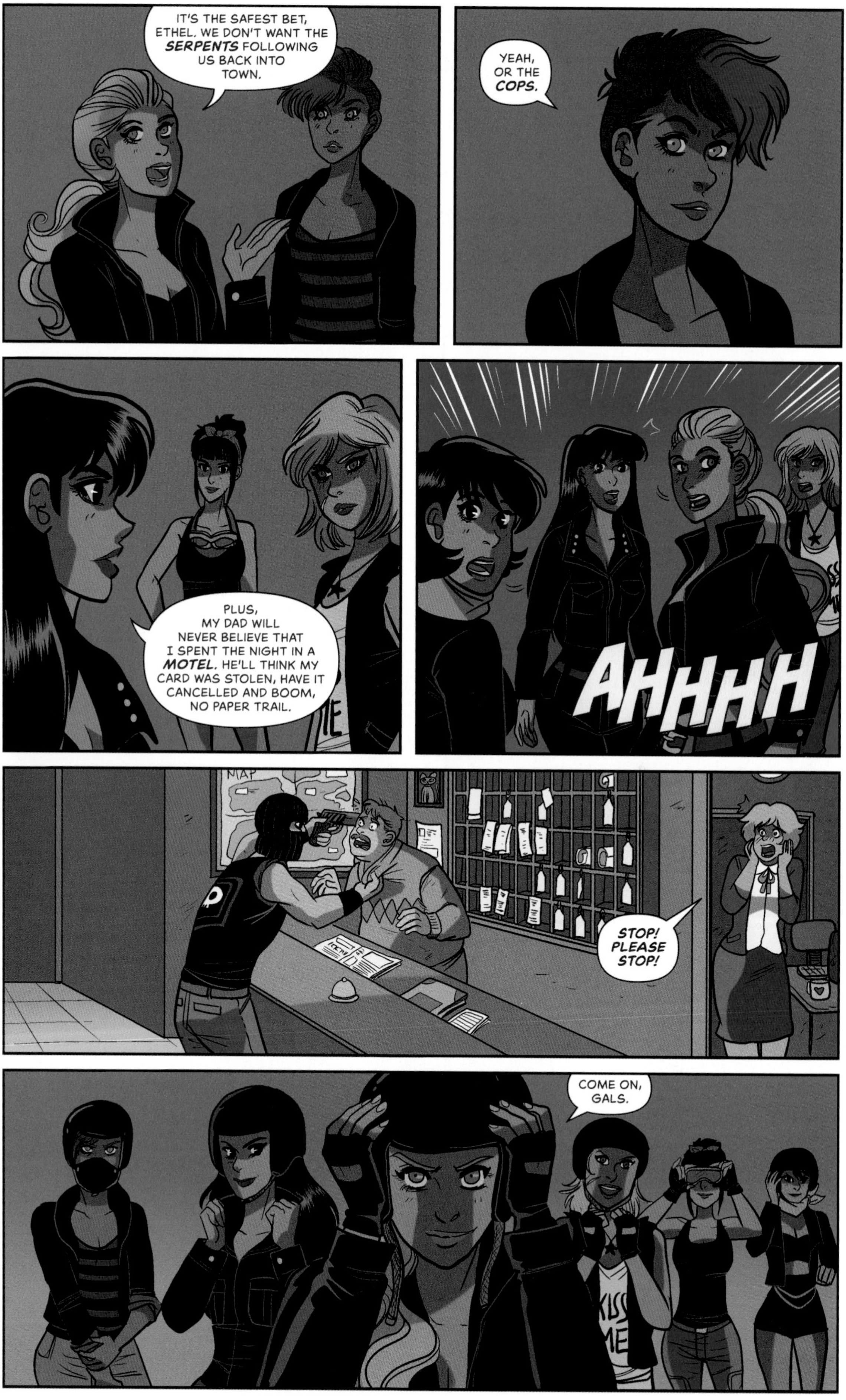

IT'S THE SAFEST BET, ETHEL. WE DON'T WANT THE SERPENTS FOLLOWING US BACK INTO TOWN.
YEAH, OR THE COPS.
PLUS, MY DAD WILL NEVER BELIEVE THAT I SPENT THE NIGHT IN A MOTEL. HE'LL THINK MY CARD WAS STOLEN, HAVE IT CANCELLED AND BOOM, NO PAPER TRAIL.
AHHHH
MAP
STOP! PLEASE STOP!
COME ON, GALS.
KISS ME

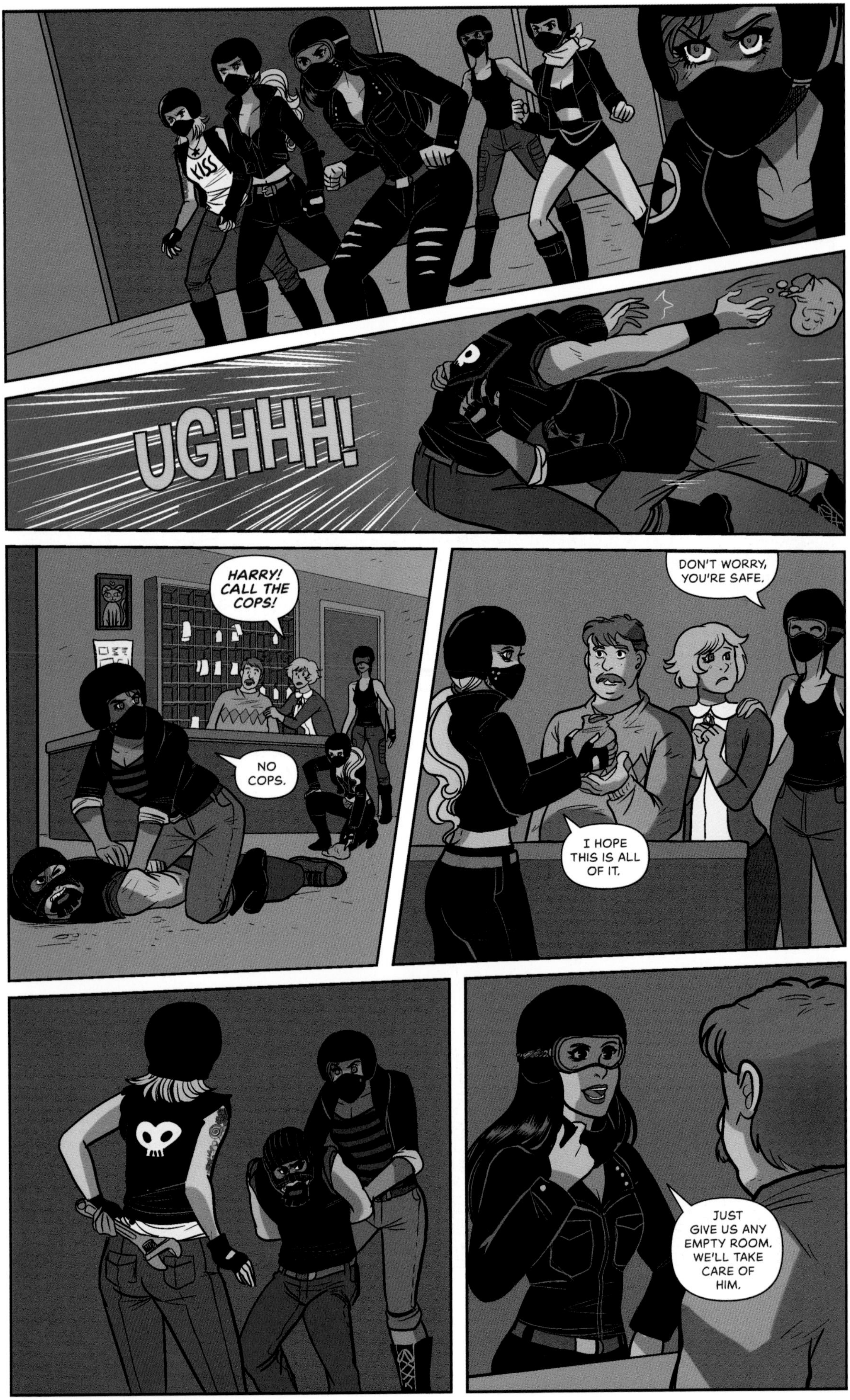
UGHHH!
HARRY! CALL THE COPS!
NO COPS.
DON'T WORRY, YOU'RE SAFE.
I HOPE THIS IS ALL OF IT.
JUST GIVE US ANY EMPTY ROOM. WE'LL TAKE CARE OF HIM.

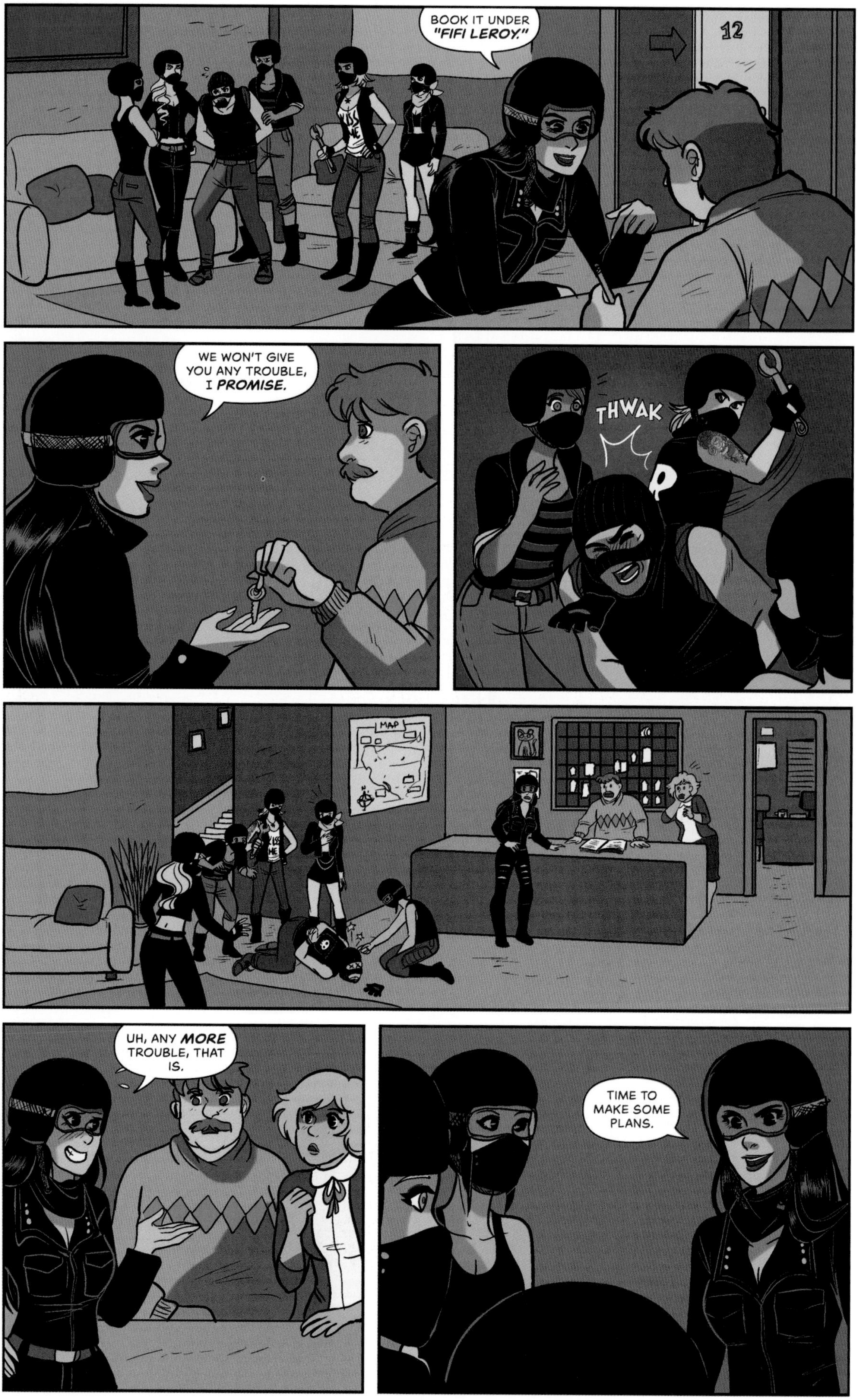
BOOK IT UNDER "FIFI LEROY."
12
WE WON'T GIVE YOU ANY TROUBLE, I PROMISE.
THWAK
MAP
UH, ANY MORE TROUBLE, THAT IS.
TIME TO MAKE SOME PLANS.

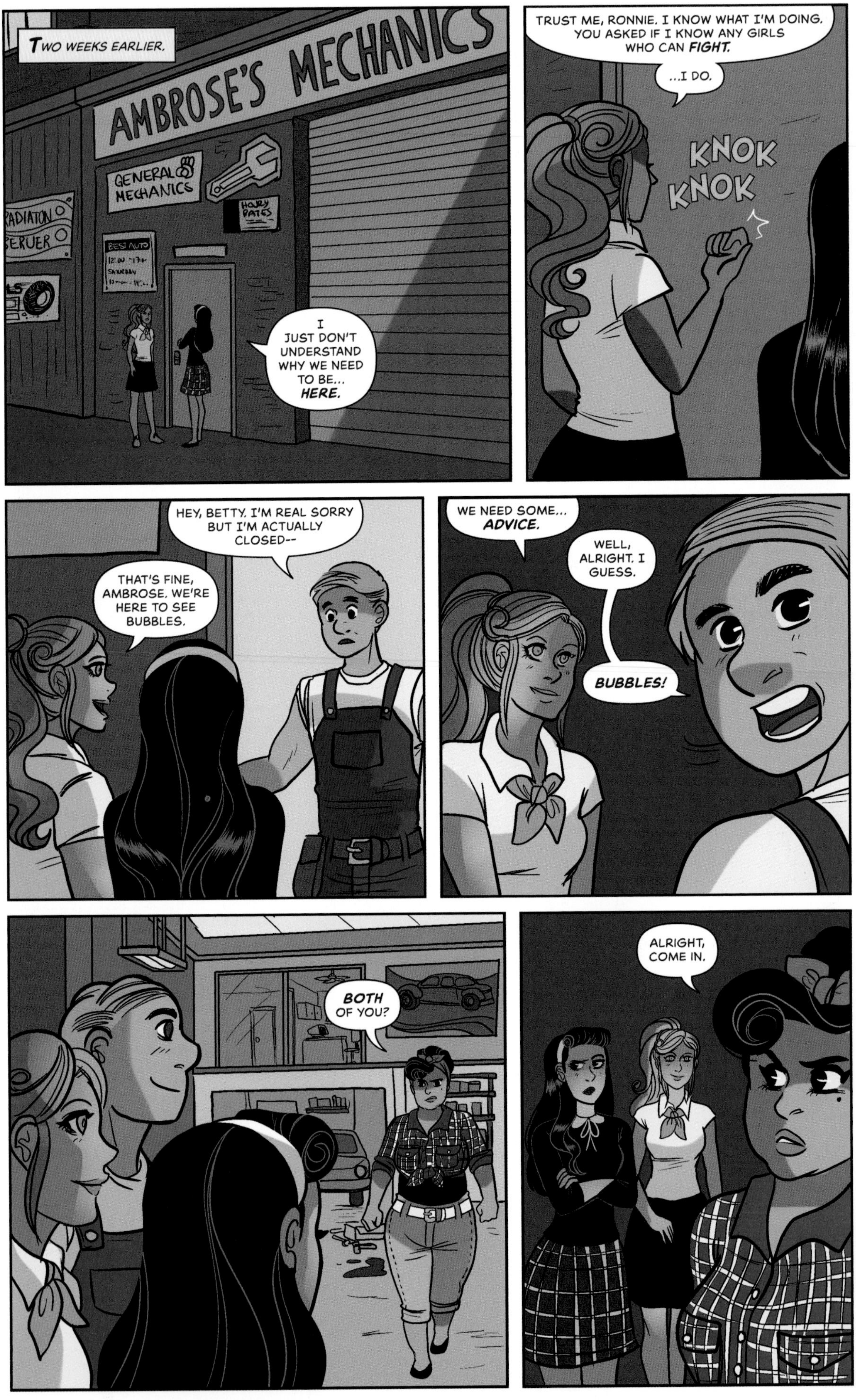
TWO WEEKS EARLIER.
AMBROSE'S MECHANICS
GENERAL MECHANICS
I JUST DON'T UNDERSTAND WHY WE NEED TO BE... HERE.
TRUST ME, RONNIE. I KNOW WHAT I'M DOING. YOU ASKED IF I KNOW ANY GIRLS WHO CAN FIGHT.
...I DO.
KNOK KNOK
HEY, BETTY. I'M REAL SORRY BUT I'M ACTUALLY CLOSED--
THAT'S FINE, AMBROSE. WE'RE HERE TO SEE BUBBLES.
WE NEED SOME... ADVICE.
WELL, ALRIGHT. I GUESS.
BUBBLES!
BOTH OF YOU?
ALRIGHT, COME IN.

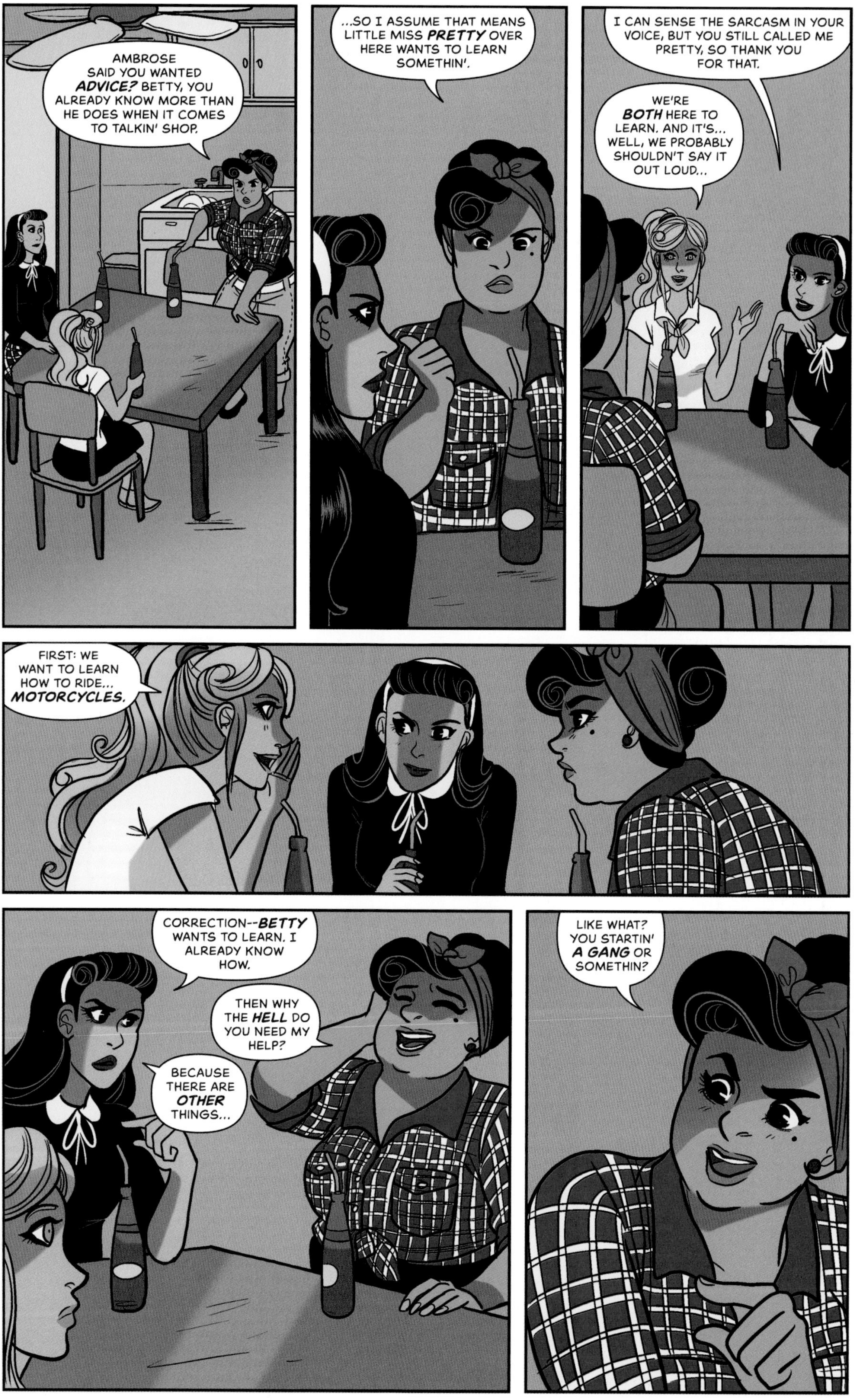
AMBROSE SAID YOU WANTED ADVICE? BETTY, YOU ALREADY KNOW MORE THAN HE DOES WHEN IT COMES TO TALKIN' SHOP.
...SO I ASSUME THAT MEANS LITTLE MISS PRETTY OVER HERE WANTS TO LEARN SOMETHIN'.
I CAN SENSE THE SARCASM IN YOUR VOICE, BUT YOU STILL CALLED ME PRETTY, SO THANK YOU FOR THAT.
WE'RE BOTH HERE TO LEARN. AND IT'S... WELL, WE PROBABLY SHOULDN'T SAY IT OUT LOUD...
FIRST: WE WANT TO LEARN HOW TO RIDE... MOTORCYCLES.
CORRECTION--BETTY WANTS TO LEARN. I ALREADY KNOW HOW.
THEN WHY THE HELL DO YOU NEED MY HELP?
BECAUSE THERE ARE OTHER THINGS...
LIKE WHAT? YOU STARTIN' A GANG OR SOMETHIN?

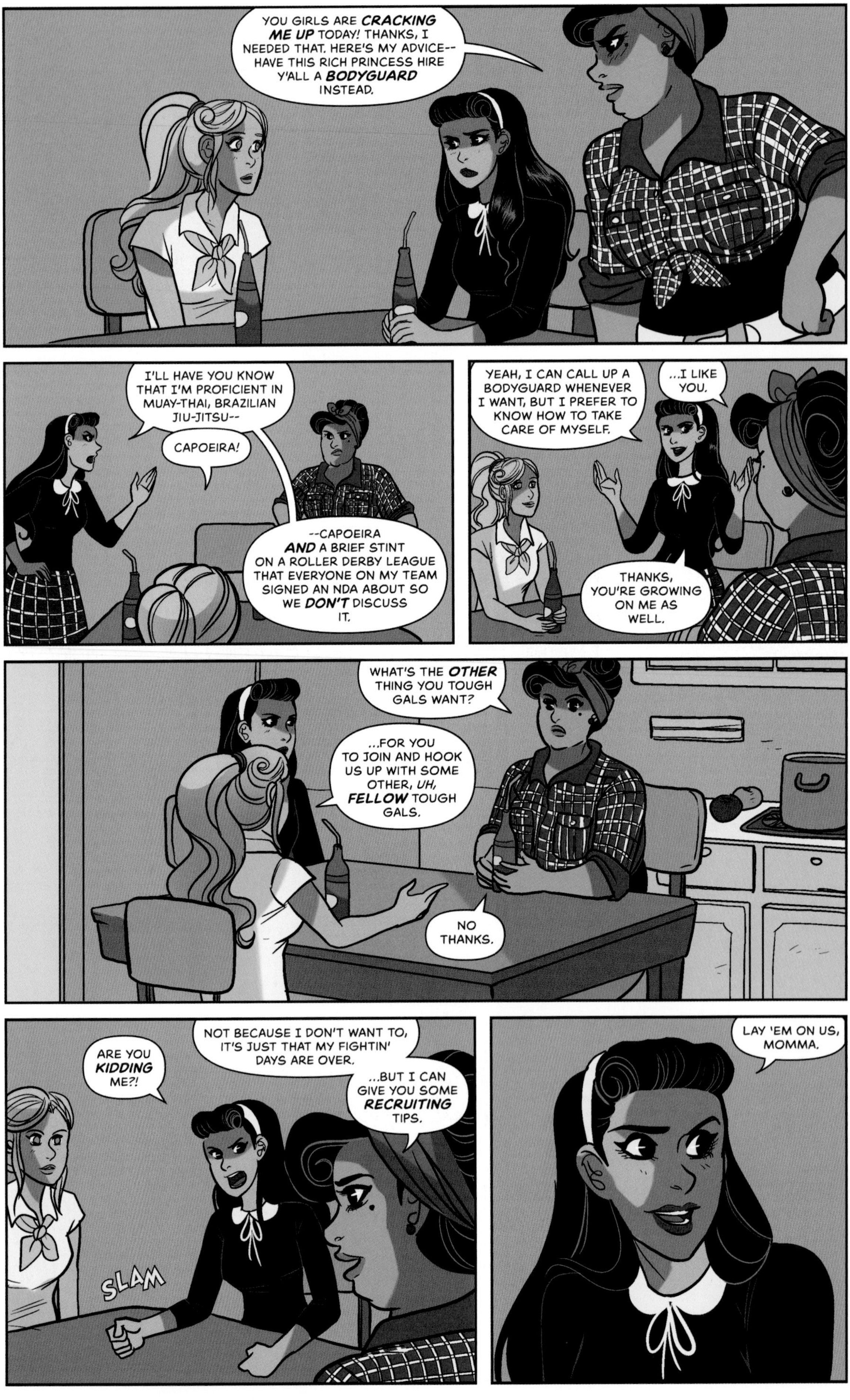
YOU GIRLS ARE **CRACKING ME UP** TODAY! THANKS, I NEEDED THAT. HERE'S MY ADVICE-- HAVE THIS RICH PRINCESS HIRE Y'ALL A **BODYGUARD** INSTEAD.
I'LL HAVE YOU KNOW THAT I'M PROFICIENT IN MUAY-THAI, BRAZILIAN JIU-JITSU--
CAPOEIRA!
--CAPOEIRA **AND** A BRIEF STINT ON A ROLLER DERBY LEAGUE THAT EVERYONE ON MY TEAM SIGNED AN NDA ABOUT SO WE **DON'T** DISCUSS IT.
YEAH, I CAN CALL UP A BODYGUARD WHENEVER I WANT, BUT I PREFER TO KNOW HOW TO TAKE CARE OF MYSELF.
...I LIKE YOU.
THANKS, YOU'RE GROWING ON ME AS WELL.
WHAT'S THE **OTHER** THING YOU TOUGH GALS WANT?
...FOR YOU TO JOIN AND HOOK US UP WITH SOME OTHER, *UH*, **FELLOW** TOUGH GALS.
NO THANKS.
ARE YOU **KIDDING** ME?!
NOT BECAUSE I DON'T WANT TO, IT'S JUST THAT MY FIGHTIN' DAYS ARE OVER.
...BUT I CAN GIVE YOU SOME **RECRUITING** TIPS.
SLAM
LAY 'EM ON US, MOMMA.

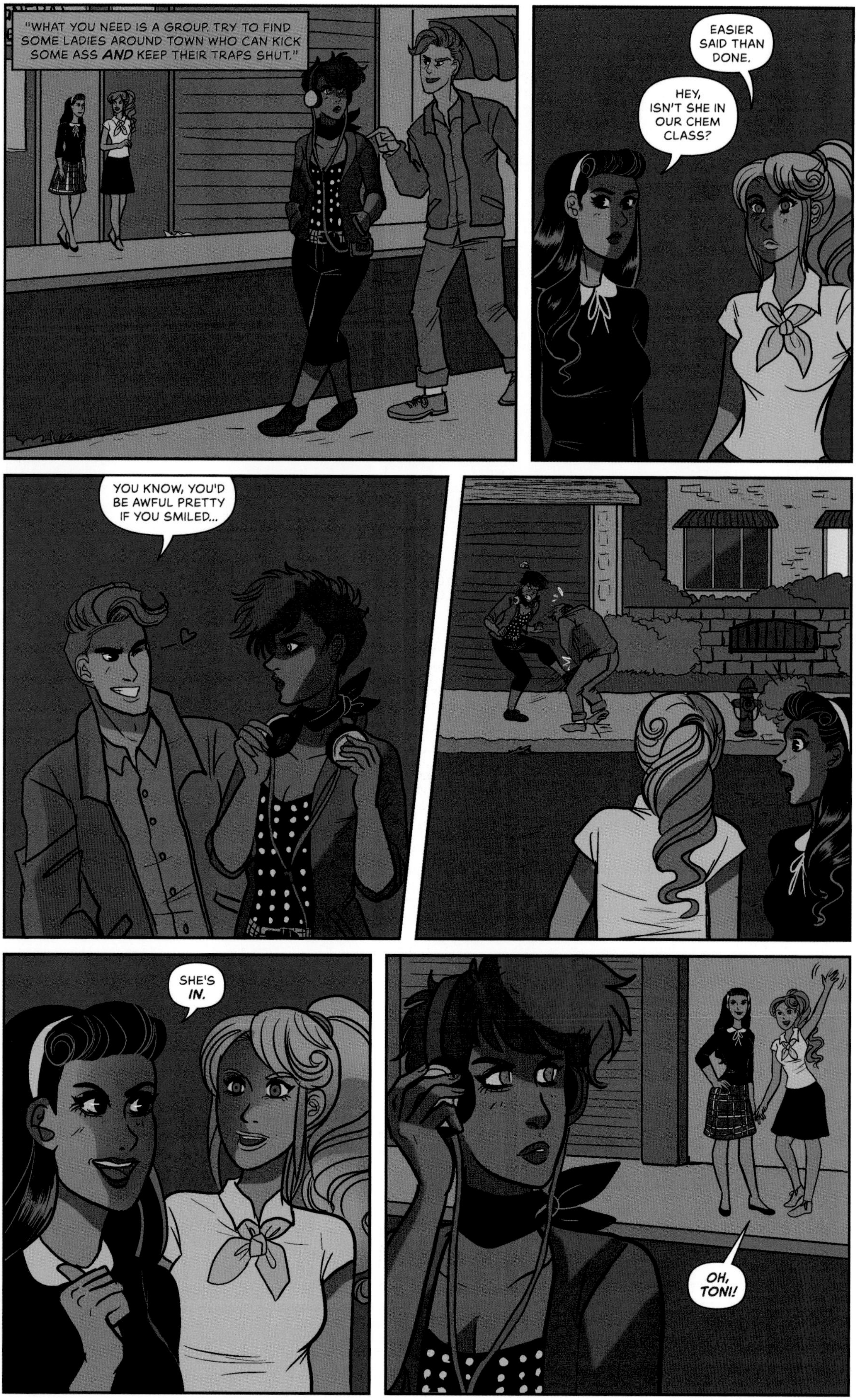
"WHAT YOU NEED IS A GROUP. TRY TO FIND SOME LADIES AROUND TOWN WHO CAN KICK SOME ASS AND KEEP THEIR TRAPS SHUT."
EASIER SAID THAN DONE.
HEY, ISN'T SHE IN OUR CHEM CLASS?
YOU KNOW, YOU'D BE AWFUL PRETTY IF YOU SMILED...
SHE'S IN.
OH, TONI!

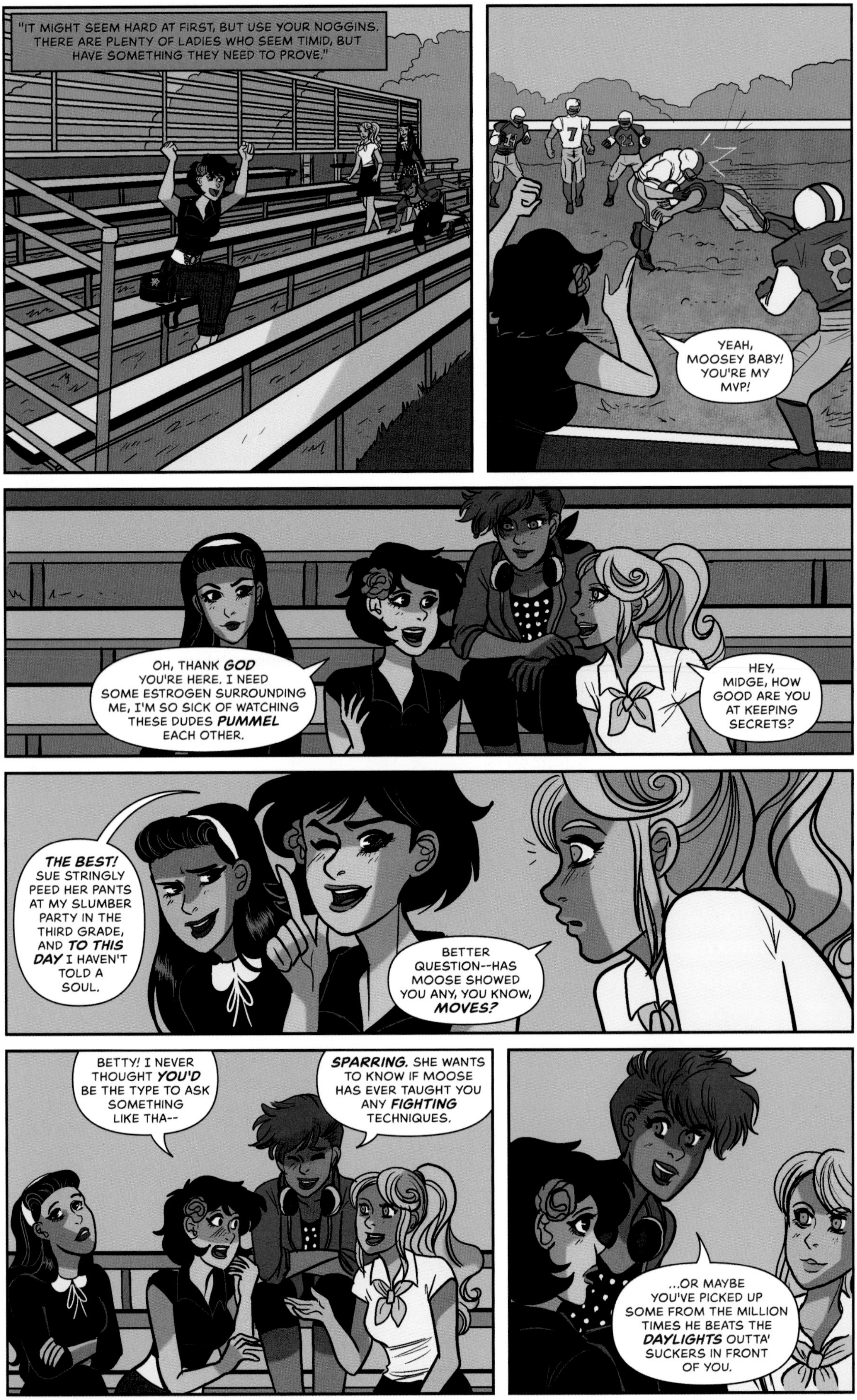
"IT MIGHT SEEM HARD AT FIRST, BUT USE YOUR NOGGINS. THERE ARE PLENTY OF LADIES WHO SEEM TIMID, BUT HAVE SOMETHING THEY NEED TO PROVE."
YEAH, MOOSEY BABY! YOU'RE MY MVP!
OH, THANK GOD YOU'RE HERE. I NEED SOME ESTROGEN SURROUNDING ME, I'M SO SICK OF WATCHING THESE DUDES PUMMEL EACH OTHER.
HEY, MIDGE, HOW GOOD ARE YOU AT KEEPING SECRETS?
THE BEST! SUE STRINGLY PEED HER PANTS AT MY SLUMBER PARTY IN THE THIRD GRADE, AND TO THIS DAY I HAVEN'T TOLD A SOUL.
BETTER QUESTION--HAS MOOSE SHOWED YOU ANY, YOU KNOW, MOVES?
BETTY! I NEVER THOUGHT YOU'D BE THE TYPE TO ASK SOMETHING LIKE THA--
SPARRING. SHE WANTS TO KNOW IF MOOSE HAS EVER TAUGHT YOU ANY FIGHTING TECHNIQUES.
...OR MAYBE YOU'VE PICKED UP SOME FROM THE MILLION TIMES HE BEATS THE DAYLIGHTS OUTTA' SUCKERS IN FRONT OF YOU.

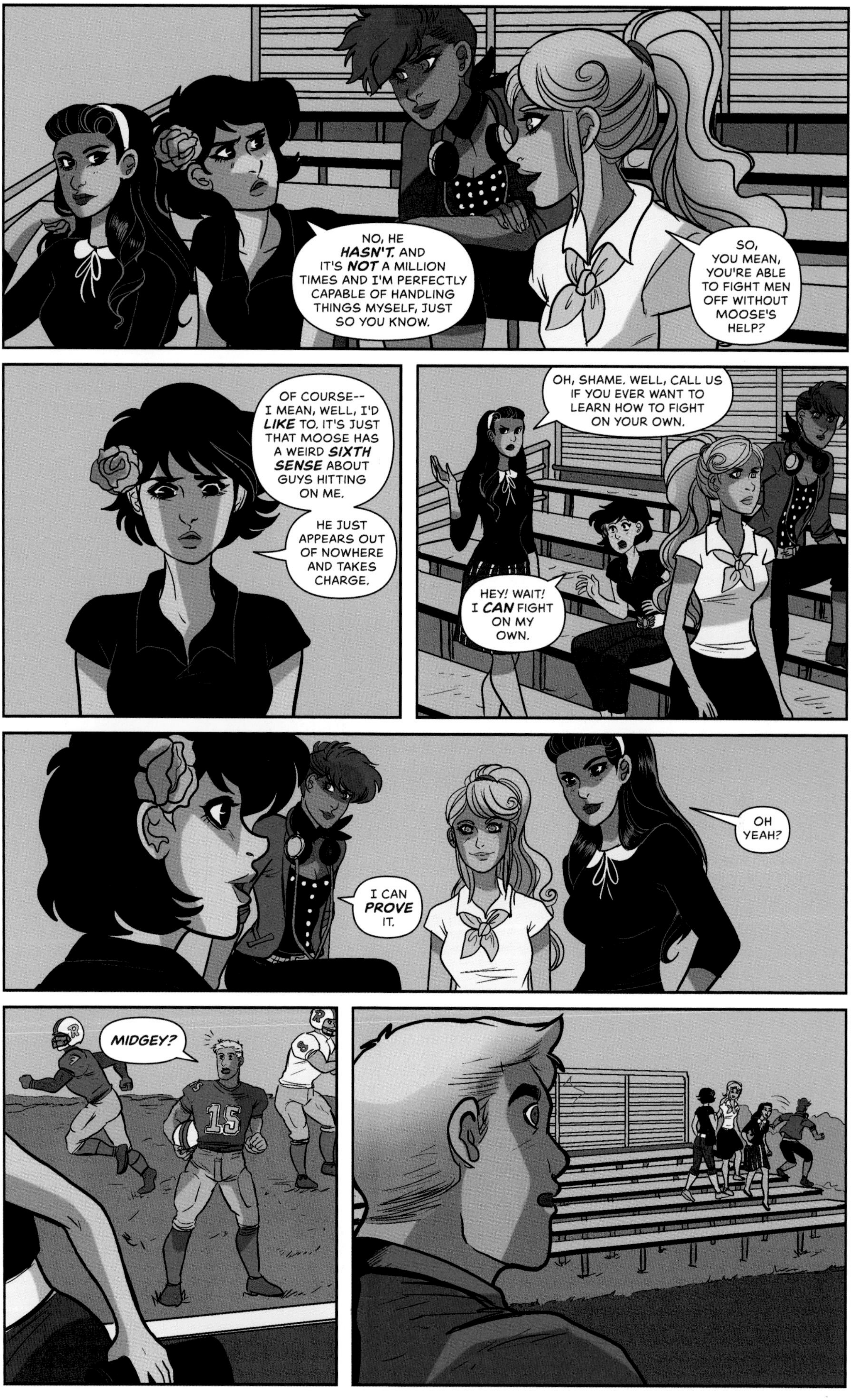

NO, HE HASN'T. AND IT'S NOT A MILLION TIMES AND I'M PERFECTLY CAPABLE OF HANDLING THINGS MYSELF, JUST SO YOU KNOW.
SO, YOU MEAN, YOU'RE ABLE TO FIGHT MEN OFF WITHOUT MOOSE'S HELP?
OF COURSE-- I MEAN, WELL, I'D LIKE TO. IT'S JUST THAT MOOSE HAS A WEIRD SIXTH SENSE ABOUT GUYS HITTING ON ME.
HE JUST APPEARS OUT OF NOWHERE AND TAKES CHARGE.
OH, SHAME. WELL, CALL US IF YOU EVER WANT TO LEARN HOW TO FIGHT ON YOUR OWN.
HEY! WAIT! I CAN FIGHT ON MY OWN.
I CAN PROVE IT.
OH YEAH?
MIDGEY?

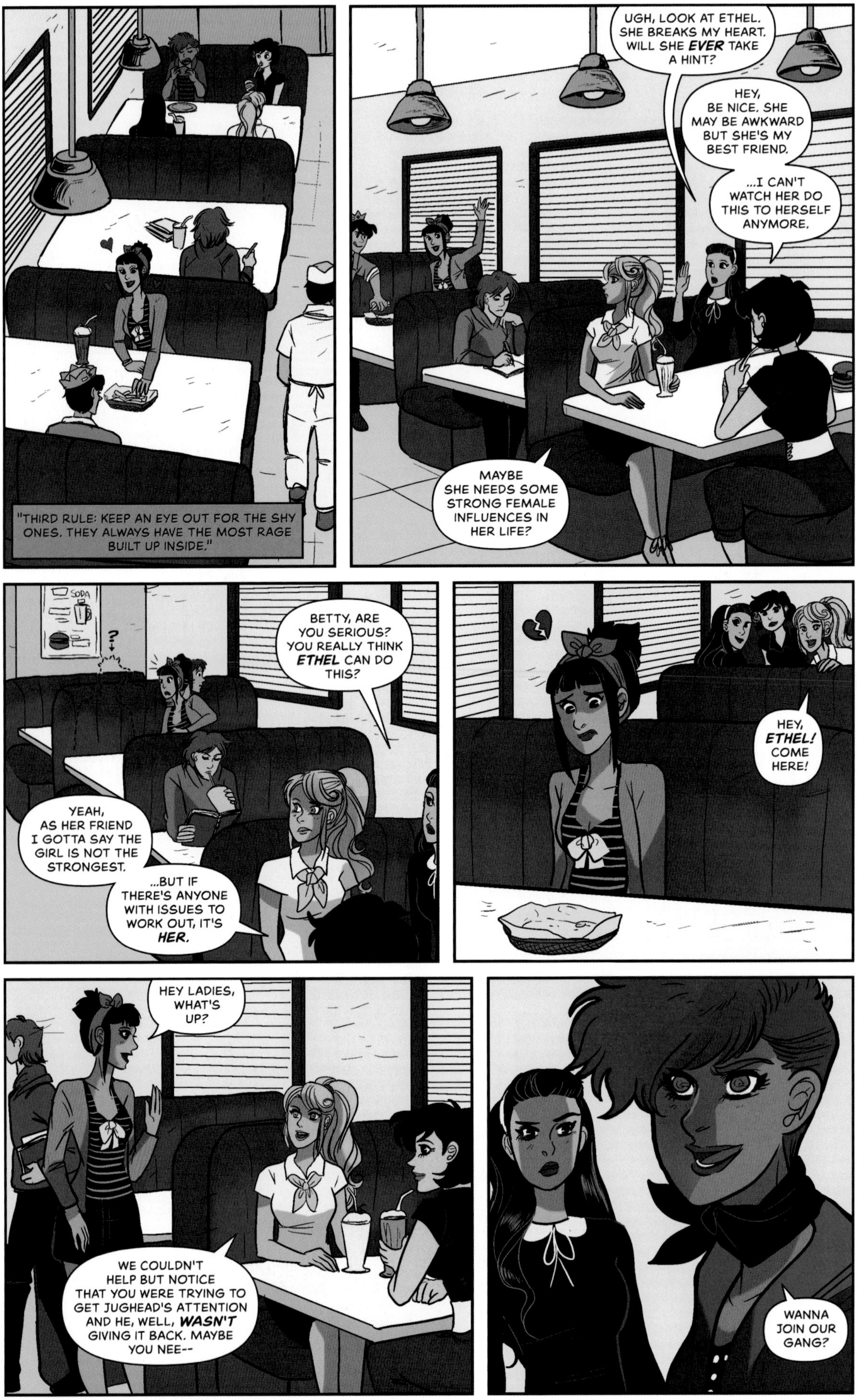
"THIRD RULE: KEEP AN EYE OUT FOR THE SHY ONES. THEY ALWAYS HAVE THE MOST RAGE BUILT UP INSIDE."
UGH, LOOK AT ETHEL. SHE BREAKS MY HEART. WILL SHE EVER TAKE A HINT?
HEY, BE NICE. SHE MAY BE AWKWARD BUT SHE'S MY BEST FRIEND.
...I CAN'T WATCH HER DO THIS TO HERSELF ANYMORE.
MAYBE SHE NEEDS SOME STRONG FEMALE INFLUENCES IN HER LIFE?
SODA
?
BETTY, ARE YOU SERIOUS? YOU REALLY THINK ETHEL CAN DO THIS?
YEAH, AS HER FRIEND I GOTTA SAY THE GIRL IS NOT THE STRONGEST.
...BUT IF THERE'S ANYONE WITH ISSUES TO WORK OUT, IT'S HER.
HEY, ETHEL! COME HERE!
HEY LADIES, WHAT'S UP?
WE COULDN'T HELP BUT NOTICE THAT YOU WERE TRYING TO GET JUGHEAD'S ATTENTION AND HE, WELL, WASN'T GIVING IT BACK. MAYBE YOU NEE--
WANNA JOIN OUR GANG?

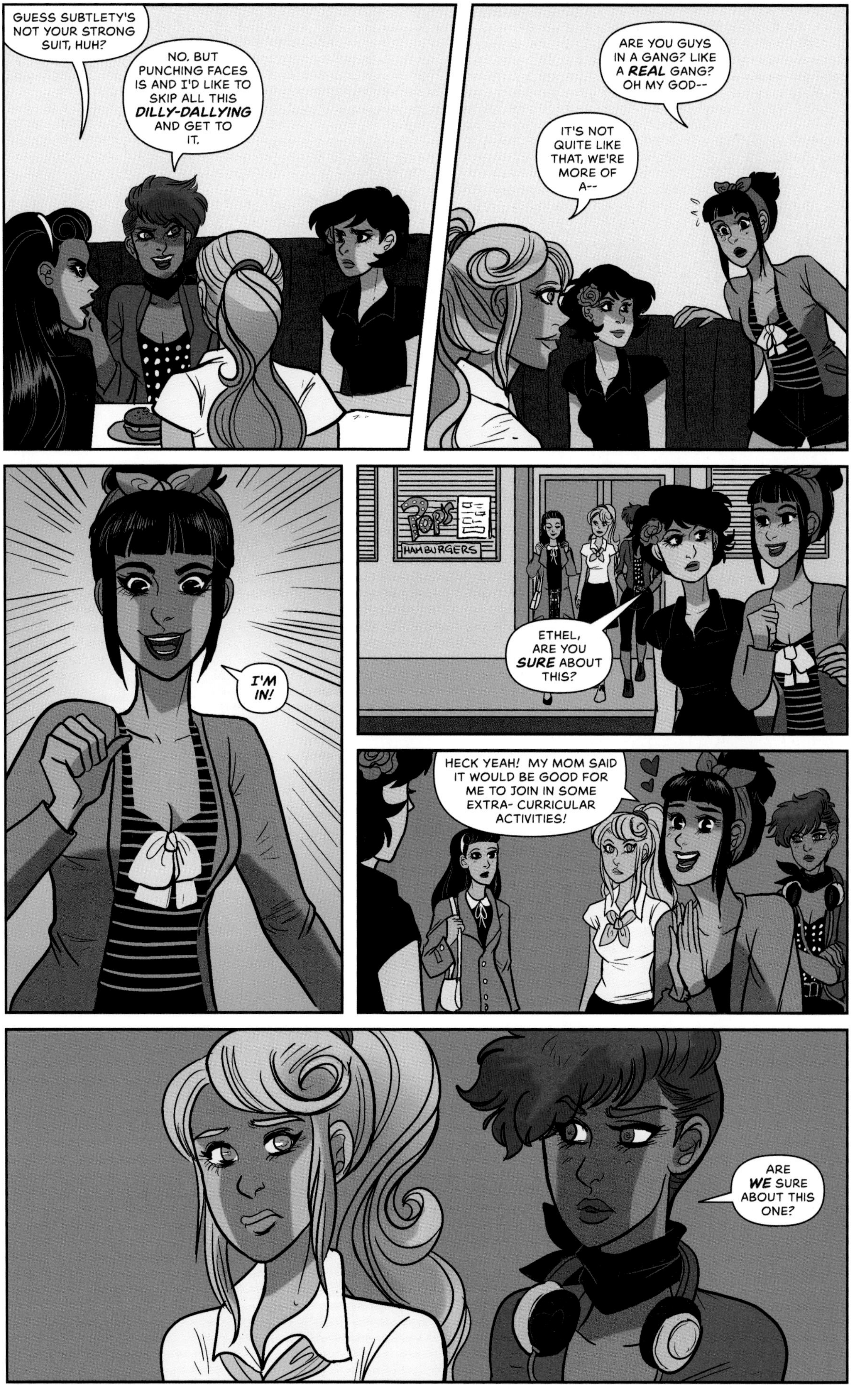
GUESS SUBTLETY'S NOT YOUR STRONG SUIT, HUH?
NO. BUT PUNCHING FACES IS AND I'D LIKE TO SKIP ALL THIS DILLY-DALLYING AND GET TO IT.
ARE YOU GUYS IN A GANG? LIKE A REAL GANG? OH MY GOD--
IT'S NOT QUITE LIKE THAT, WE'RE MORE OF A--
I'M IN!
POP'S
HAMBURGERS
ETHEL, ARE YOU SURE ABOUT THIS?
HECK YEAH! MY MOM SAID IT WOULD BE GOOD FOR ME TO JOIN IN SOME EXTRA- CURRICULAR ACTIVITIES!
ARE WE SURE ABOUT THIS ONE?

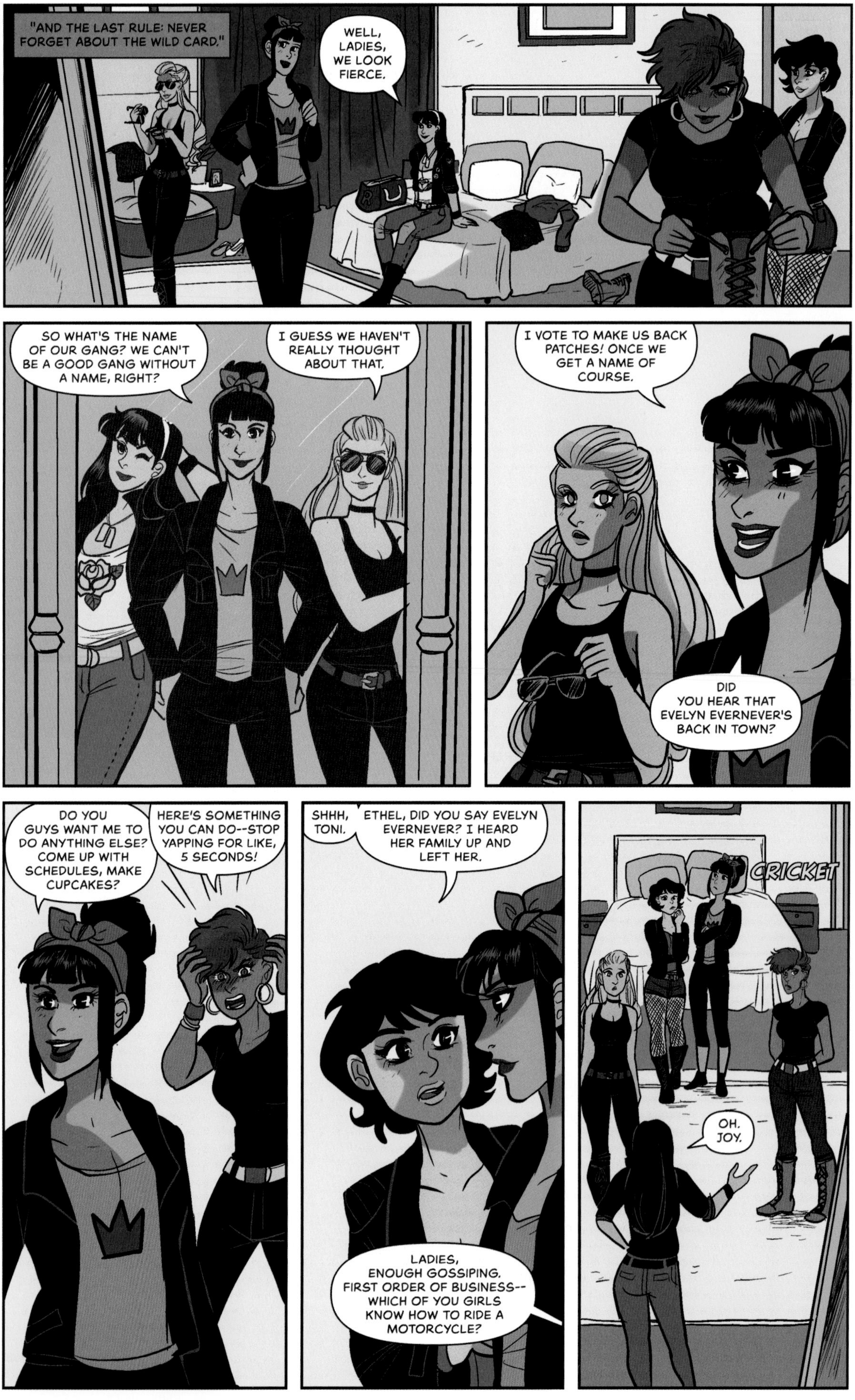
"AND THE LAST RULE: NEVER FORGET ABOUT THE WILD CARD."
WELL, LADIES, WE LOOK FIERCE.
SO WHAT'S THE NAME OF OUR GANG? WE CAN'T BE A GOOD GANG WITHOUT A NAME, RIGHT?
I GUESS WE HAVEN'T REALLY THOUGHT ABOUT THAT.
I VOTE TO MAKE US BACK PATCHES! ONCE WE GET A NAME OF COURSE.
DID YOU HEAR THAT EVELYN EVERNEVER'S BACK IN TOWN?
DO YOU GUYS WANT ME TO DO ANYTHING ELSE? COME UP WITH SCHEDULES, MAKE CUPCAKES?
HERE'S SOMETHING YOU CAN DO--STOP YAPPING FOR LIKE, 5 SECONDS!
SHHH, TONI.
ETHEL, DID YOU SAY EVELYN EVERNEVER? I HEARD HER FAMILY UP AND LEFT HER.
LADIES, ENOUGH GOSSIPING. FIRST ORDER OF BUSINESS--WHICH OF YOU GIRLS KNOW HOW TO RIDE A MOTORCYCLE?
CRICKET
OH. JOY.

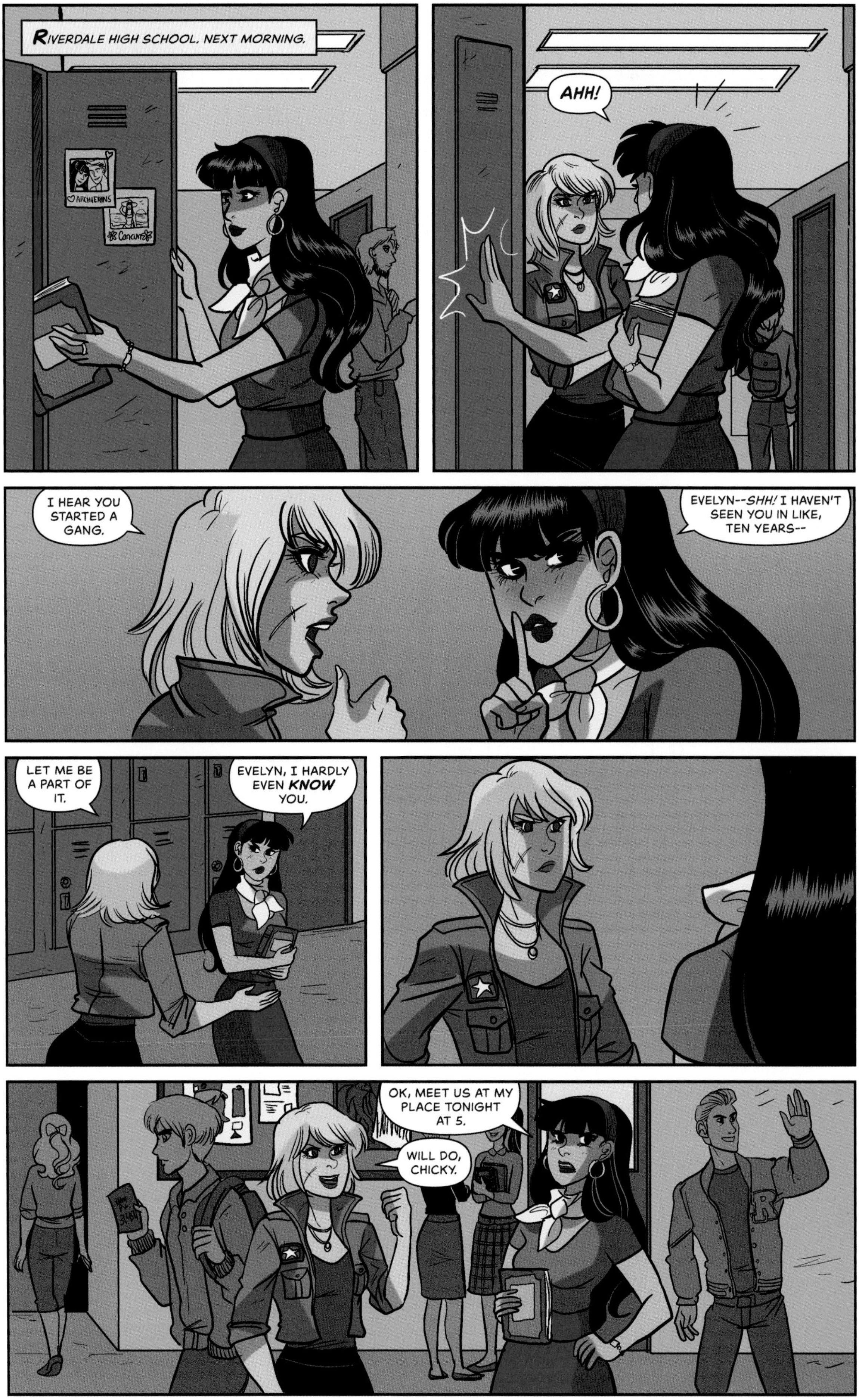
RIVERDALE HIGH SCHOOL, NEXT MORNING.
AHH!
I HEAR YOU STARTED A GANG.
EVELYN--SHH! I HAVEN'T SEEN YOU IN LIKE, TEN YEARS--
LET ME BE A PART OF IT.
EVELYN, I HARDLY EVEN KNOW YOU.
OK, MEET US AT MY PLACE TONIGHT AT 5.
WILL DO, CHICKY.

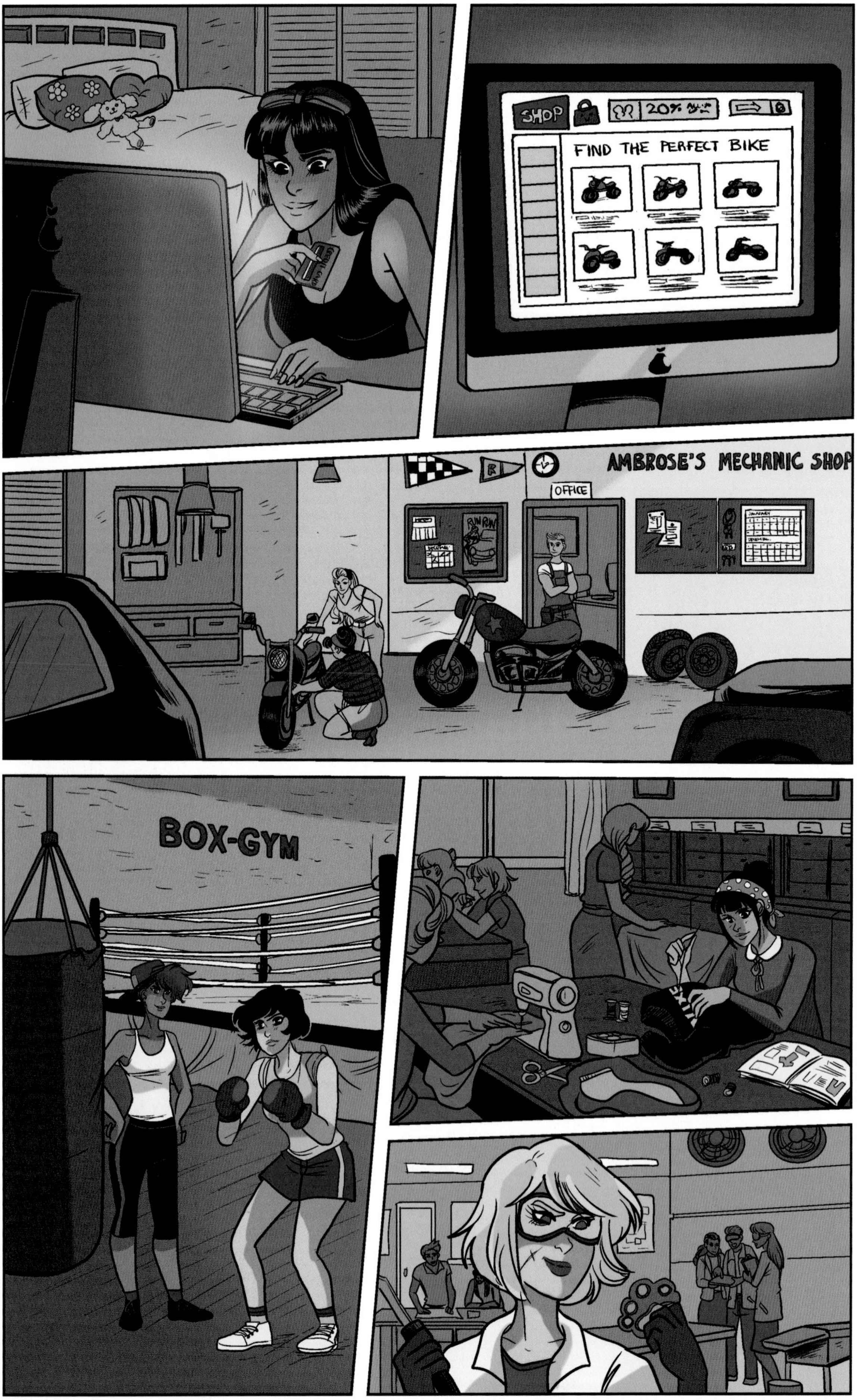
SHOP
20%
FIND THE PERFECT BIKE
AMBROSE'S MECHANIC SHOP
OFFICE
BOX-GYM

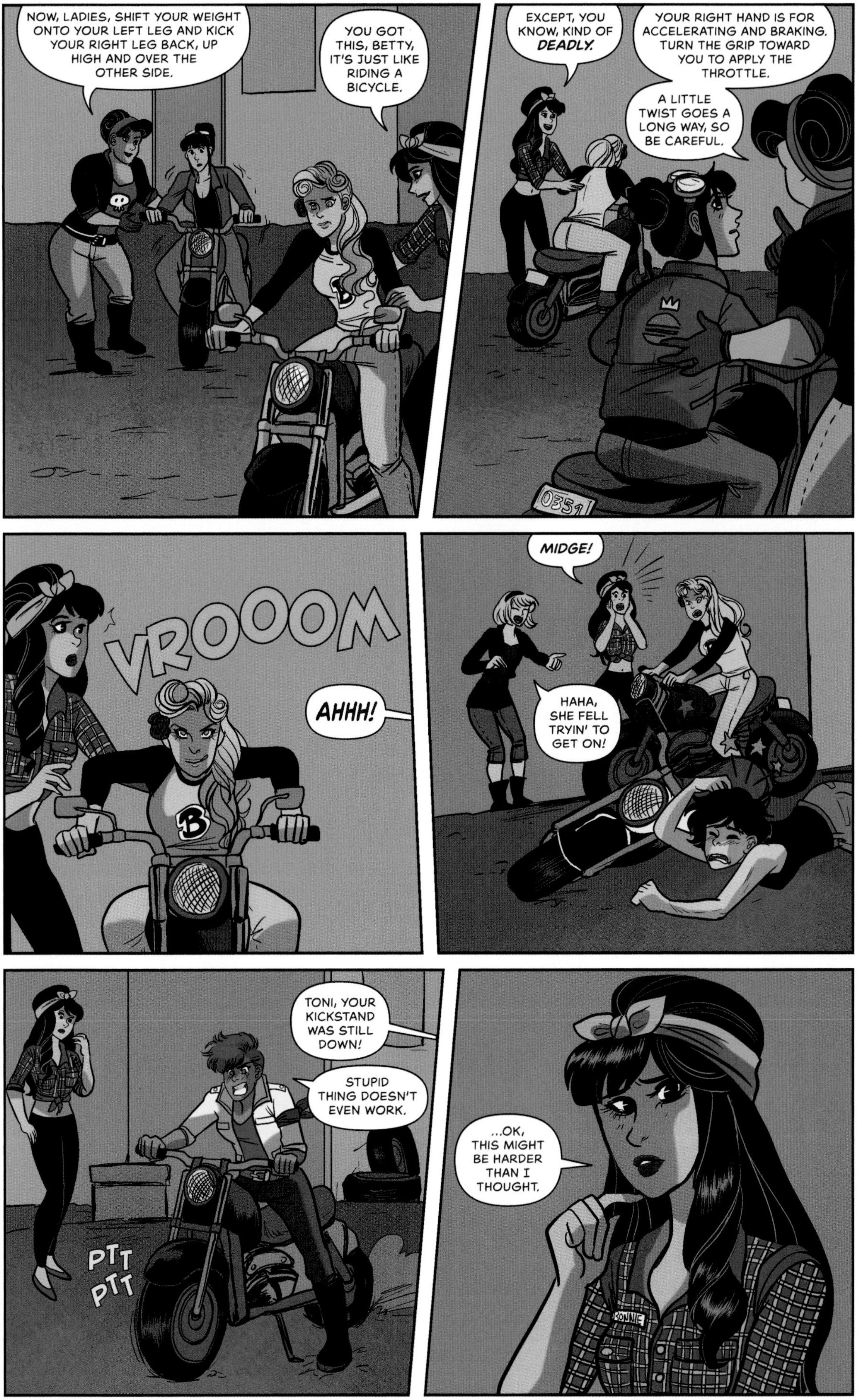
NOW, LADIES, SHIFT YOUR WEIGHT ONTO YOUR LEFT LEG AND KICK YOUR RIGHT LEG BACK, UP HIGH AND OVER THE OTHER SIDE.
YOU GOT THIS, BETTY, IT'S JUST LIKE RIDING A BICYCLE.
EXCEPT, YOU KNOW, KIND OF *DEADLY.*
YOUR RIGHT HAND IS FOR ACCELERATING AND BRAKING. TURN THE GRIP TOWARD YOU TO APPLY THE THROTTLE.
A LITTLE TWIST GOES A LONG WAY, SO BE CAREFUL.
VROOOM
AHHH!
MIDGE!
HAHA, SHE FELL TRYIN' TO GET ON!
TONI, YOUR KICKSTAND WAS STILL DOWN!
STUPID THING DOESN'T EVEN WORK.
PTT PTT
...OK, THIS MIGHT BE HARDER THAN I THOUGHT.

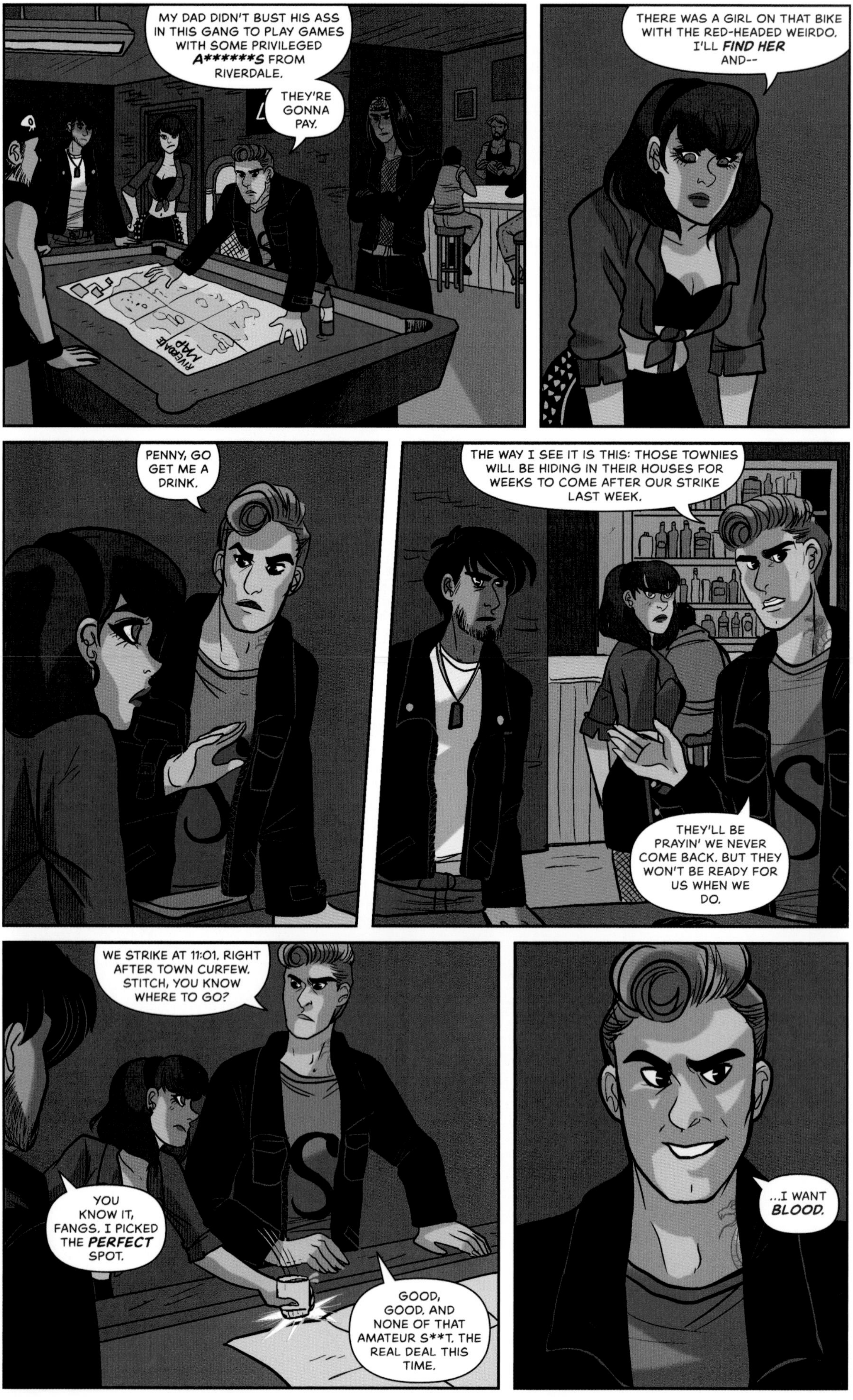
MY DAD DIDN'T BUST HIS ASS IN THIS GANG TO PLAY GAMES WITH SOME PRIVILEGED A******S FROM RIVERDALE.
THEY'RE GONNA PAY.
RIVERDALE MAP
THERE WAS A GIRL ON THAT BIKE WITH THE RED-HEADED WEIRDO. I'LL FIND HER AND--
PENNY, GO GET ME A DRINK.
THE WAY I SEE IT IS THIS: THOSE TOWNIES WILL BE HIDING IN THEIR HOUSES FOR WEEKS TO COME AFTER OUR STRIKE LAST WEEK.
THEY'LL BE PRAYIN' WE NEVER COME BACK, BUT THEY WON'T BE READY FOR US WHEN WE DO.
WE STRIKE AT 11:01, RIGHT AFTER TOWN CURFEW. STITCH, YOU KNOW WHERE TO GO?
YOU KNOW IT, FANGS. I PICKED THE PERFECT SPOT.
GOOD, GOOD, AND NONE OF THAT AMATEUR S**T, THE REAL DEAL THIS TIME.
...I WANT BLOOD.

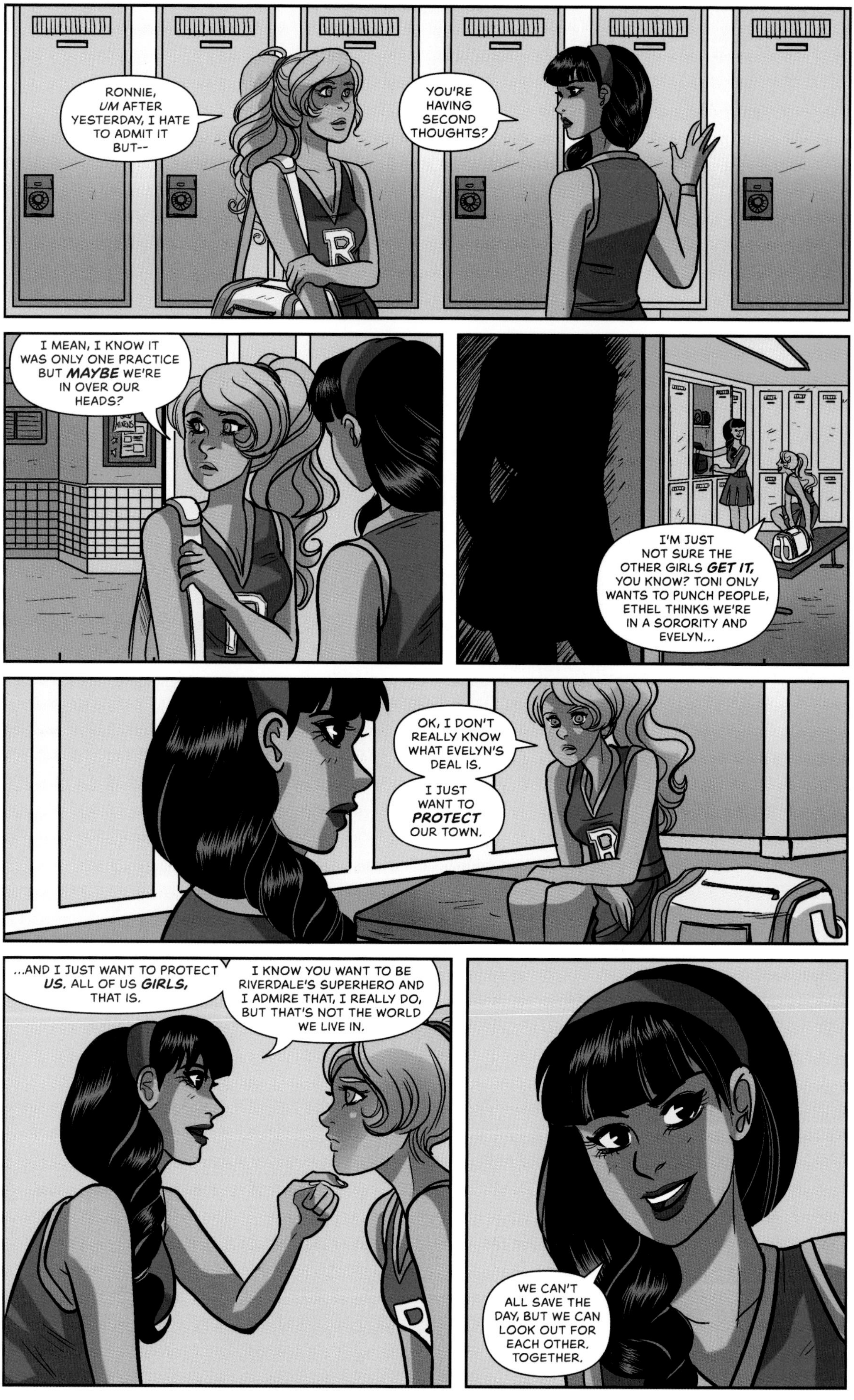
RONNIE, *UM* AFTER YESTERDAY, I HATE TO ADMIT IT BUT--
YOU'RE HAVING SECOND THOUGHTS?
I MEAN, I KNOW IT WAS ONLY ONE PRACTICE BUT **MAYBE** WE'RE IN OVER OUR HEADS?
I'M JUST NOT SURE THE OTHER GIRLS ***GET IT,*** YOU KNOW? TONI ONLY WANTS TO PUNCH PEOPLE, ETHEL THINKS WE'RE IN A SORORITY AND EVELYN...
OK, I DON'T REALLY KNOW WHAT EVELYN'S DEAL IS.
I JUST WANT TO ***PROTECT*** OUR TOWN.
...AND I JUST WANT TO PROTECT ***US.*** ALL OF US ***GIRLS,*** THAT IS.
I KNOW YOU WANT TO BE RIVERDALE'S SUPERHERO AND I ADMIRE THAT, I REALLY DO, BUT THAT'S NOT THE WORLD WE LIVE IN.
WE CAN'T ALL SAVE THE DAY, BUT WE CAN LOOK OUT FOR EACH OTHER. TOGETHER.

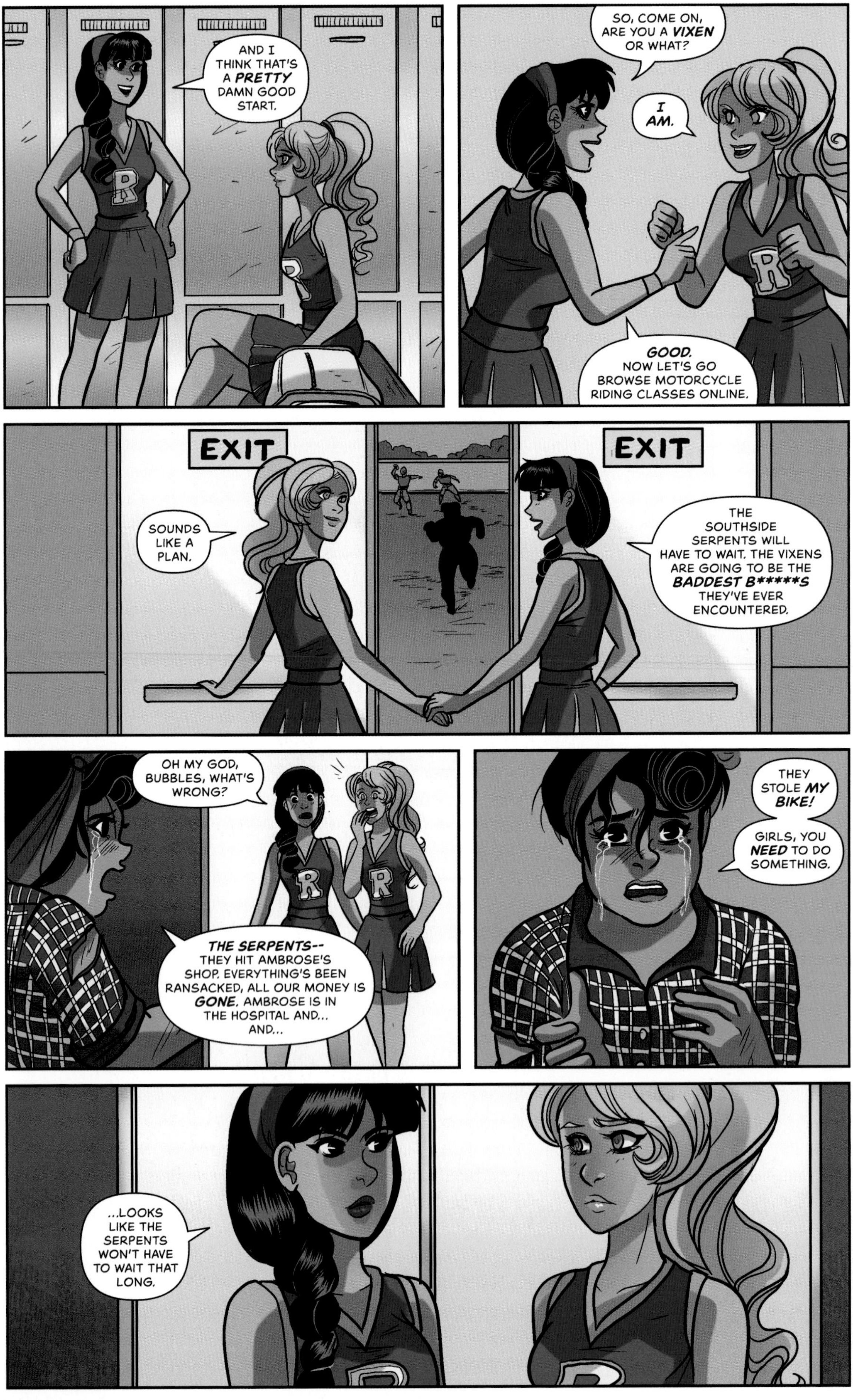
AND I THINK THAT'S A PRETTY DAMN GOOD START.
SO, COME ON, ARE YOU A VIXEN OR WHAT?
I AM.
GOOD. NOW LET'S GO BROWSE MOTORCYCLE RIDING CLASSES ONLINE.
EXIT
EXIT
SOUNDS LIKE A PLAN.
THE SOUTHSIDE SERPENTS WILL HAVE TO WAIT. THE VIXENS ARE GOING TO BE THE BADDEST B*****S THEY'VE EVER ENCOUNTERED.
OH MY GOD, BUBBLES, WHAT'S WRONG?
THE SERPENTS-- THEY HIT AMBROSE'S SHOP. EVERYTHING'S BEEN RANSACKED, ALL OUR MONEY IS GONE. AMBROSE IS IN THE HOSPITAL AND... AND...
THEY STOLE MY BIKE!
GIRLS, YOU NEED TO DO SOMETHING.
...LOOKS LIKE THE SERPENTS WON'T HAVE TO WAIT THAT LONG.

to be continued...

Chapter Three

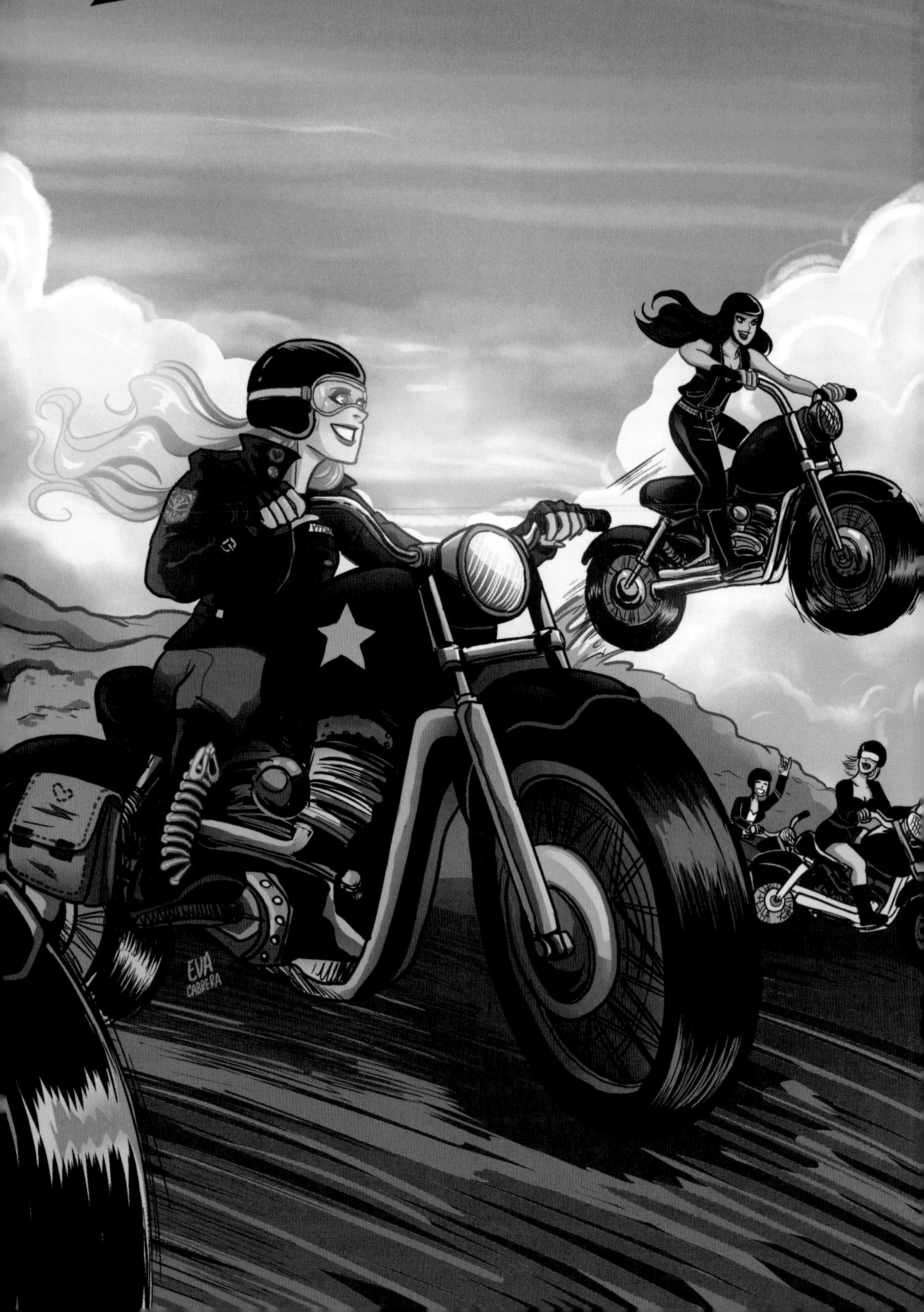
EVA CABRERA

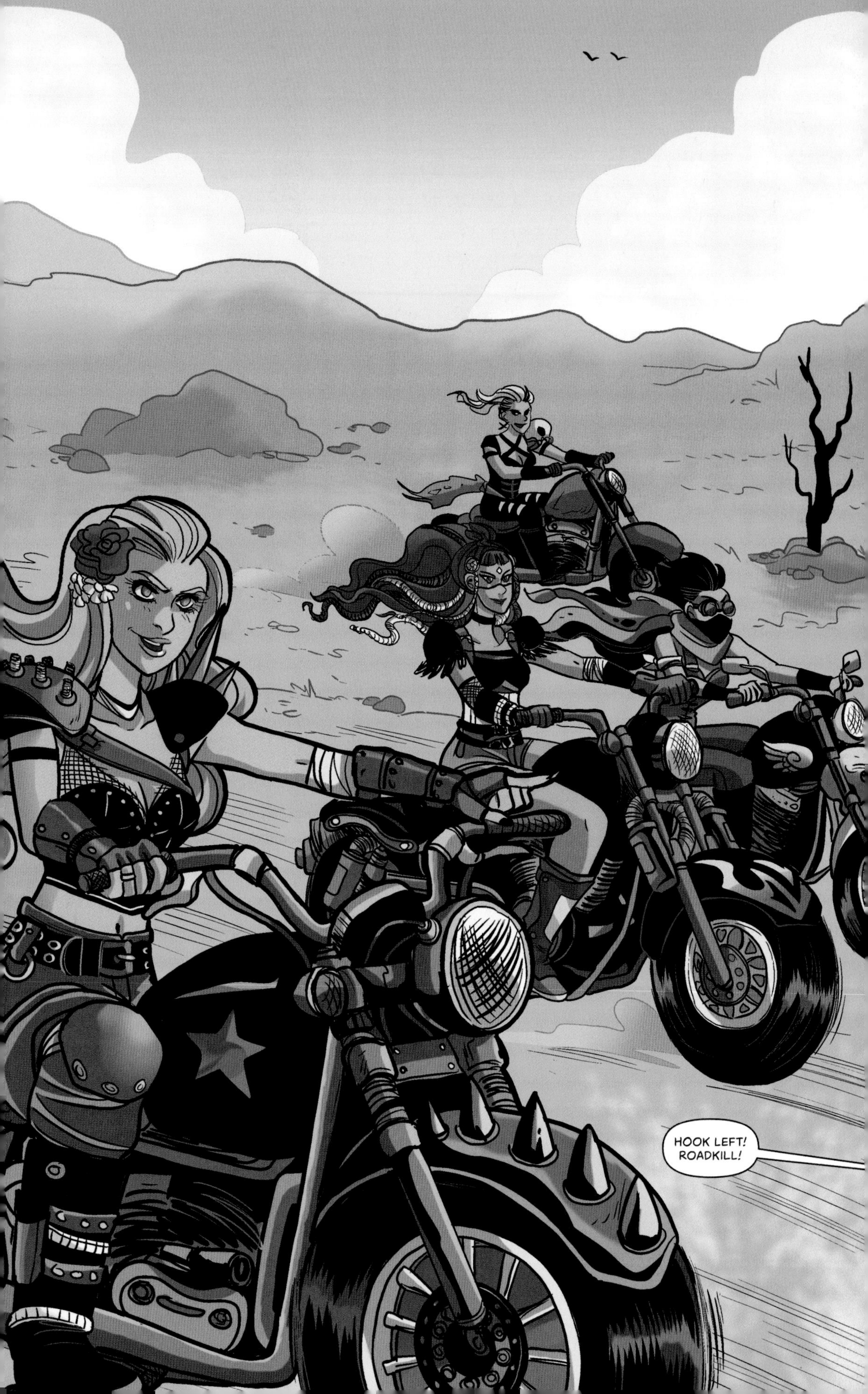
HOOK LEFT!
ROADKILL!

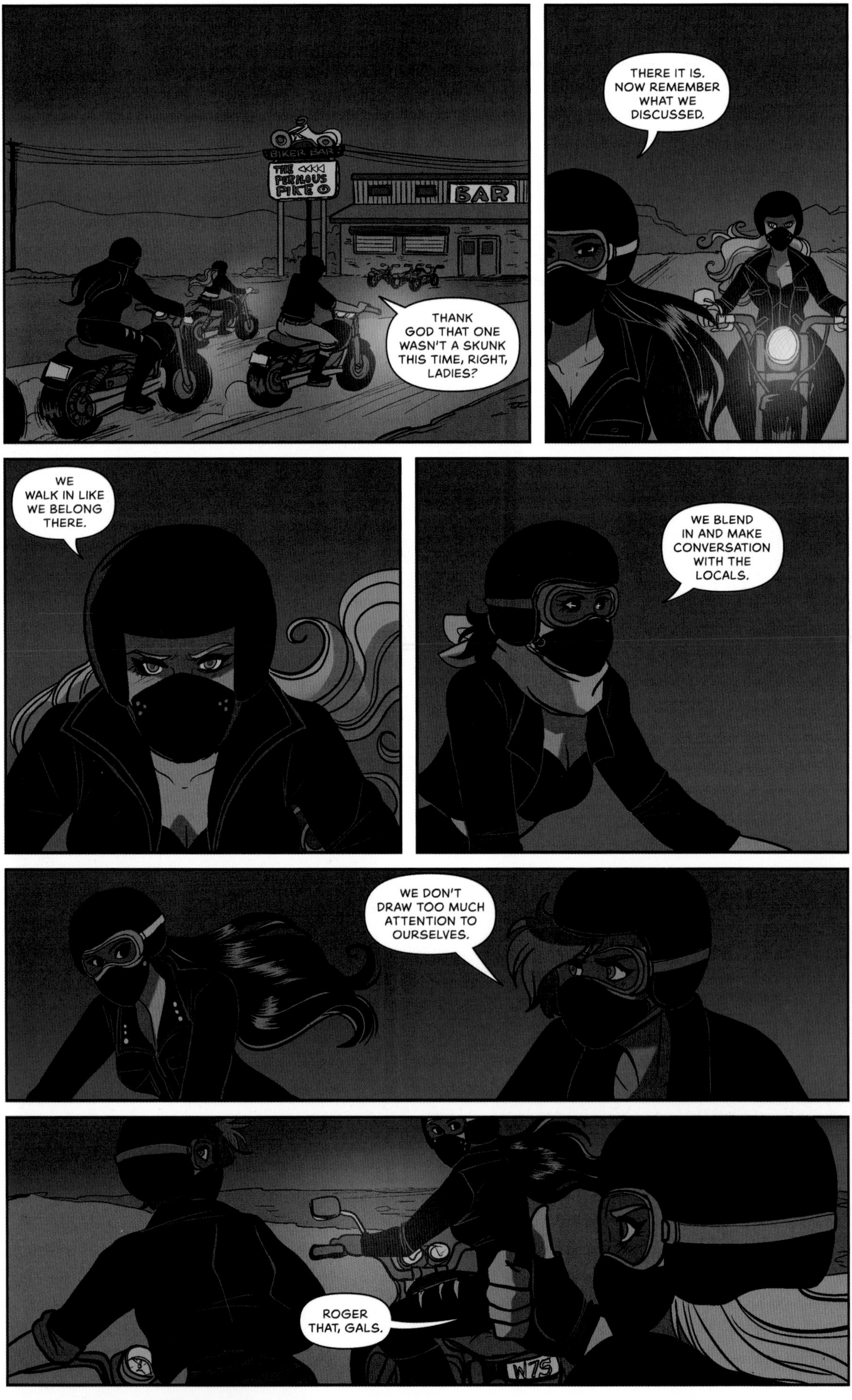
BIKER BAR
THE PERILOUS PIKE
BAR
THANK GOD THAT ONE WASN'T A SKUNK THIS TIME, RIGHT, LADIES?
THERE IT IS. NOW REMEMBER WHAT WE DISCUSSED.
WE WALK IN LIKE WE BELONG THERE.
WE BLEND IN AND MAKE CONVERSATION WITH THE LOCALS.
WE DON'T DRAW TOO MUCH ATTENTION TO OURSELVES.
ROGER THAT, GALS.
W75

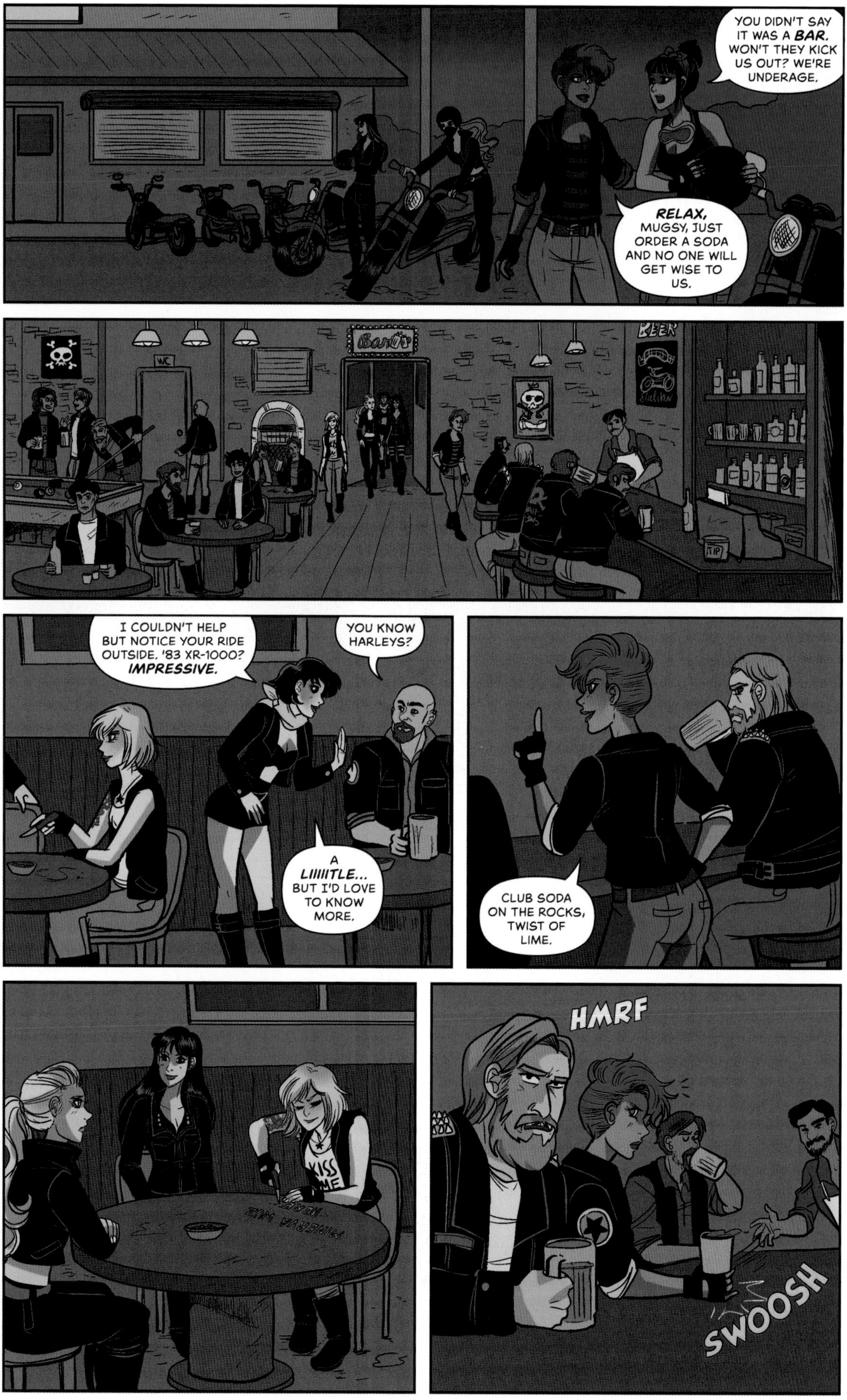
YOU DIDN'T SAY IT WAS A ***BAR.*** WON'T THEY KICK US OUT? WE'RE UNDERAGE.
RELAX, MUGSY, JUST ORDER A SODA AND NO ONE WILL GET WISE TO US.
WC
BEER
TIP
I COULDN'T HELP BUT NOTICE YOUR RIDE OUTSIDE. '83 XR-1000? ***IMPRESSIVE.***
YOU KNOW HARLEYS?
A ***LIIIIITLE...*** BUT I'D LOVE TO KNOW MORE.
CLUB SODA ON THE ROCKS, TWIST OF LIME.
HMRF
SWOOSH

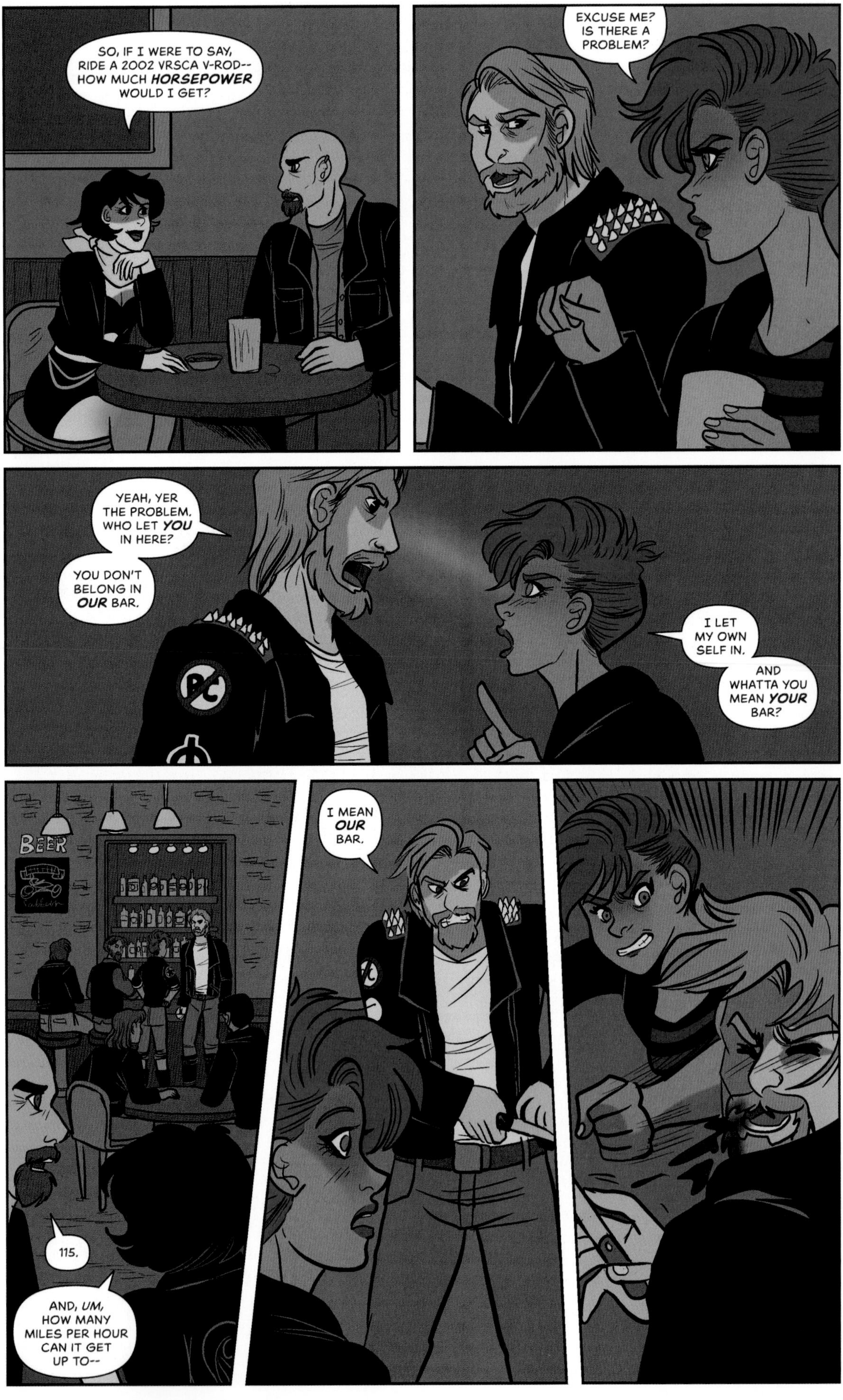
SO, IF I WERE TO SAY, RIDE A 2002 VRSCA V-ROD-- HOW MUCH **HORSEPOWER** WOULD I GET?
EXCUSE ME? IS THERE A PROBLEM?
YEAH, YER THE PROBLEM. WHO LET **YOU** IN HERE?
YOU DON'T BELONG IN **OUR** BAR.
I LET MY OWN SELF IN.
AND WHATTA YOU MEAN **YOUR** BAR?
BEER
115.
AND, *UM*, HOW MANY MILES PER HOUR CAN IT GET UP TO--
I MEAN **OUR** BAR.

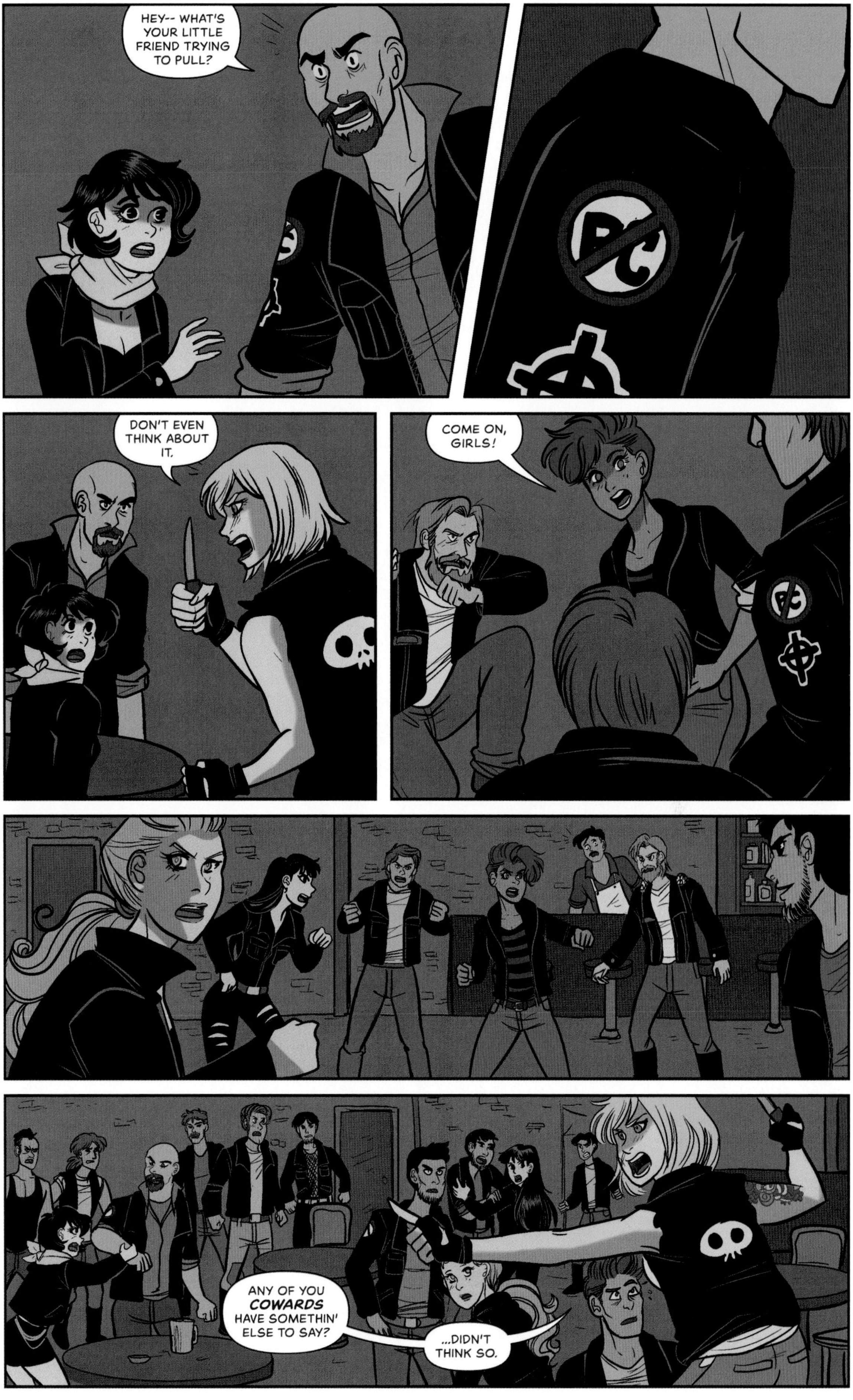
HEY-- WHAT'S YOUR LITTLE FRIEND TRYING TO PULL?
DON'T EVEN THINK ABOUT IT.
COME ON, GIRLS!
ANY OF YOU *COWARDS* HAVE SOMETHIN' ELSE TO SAY?
...DIDN'T THINK SO.

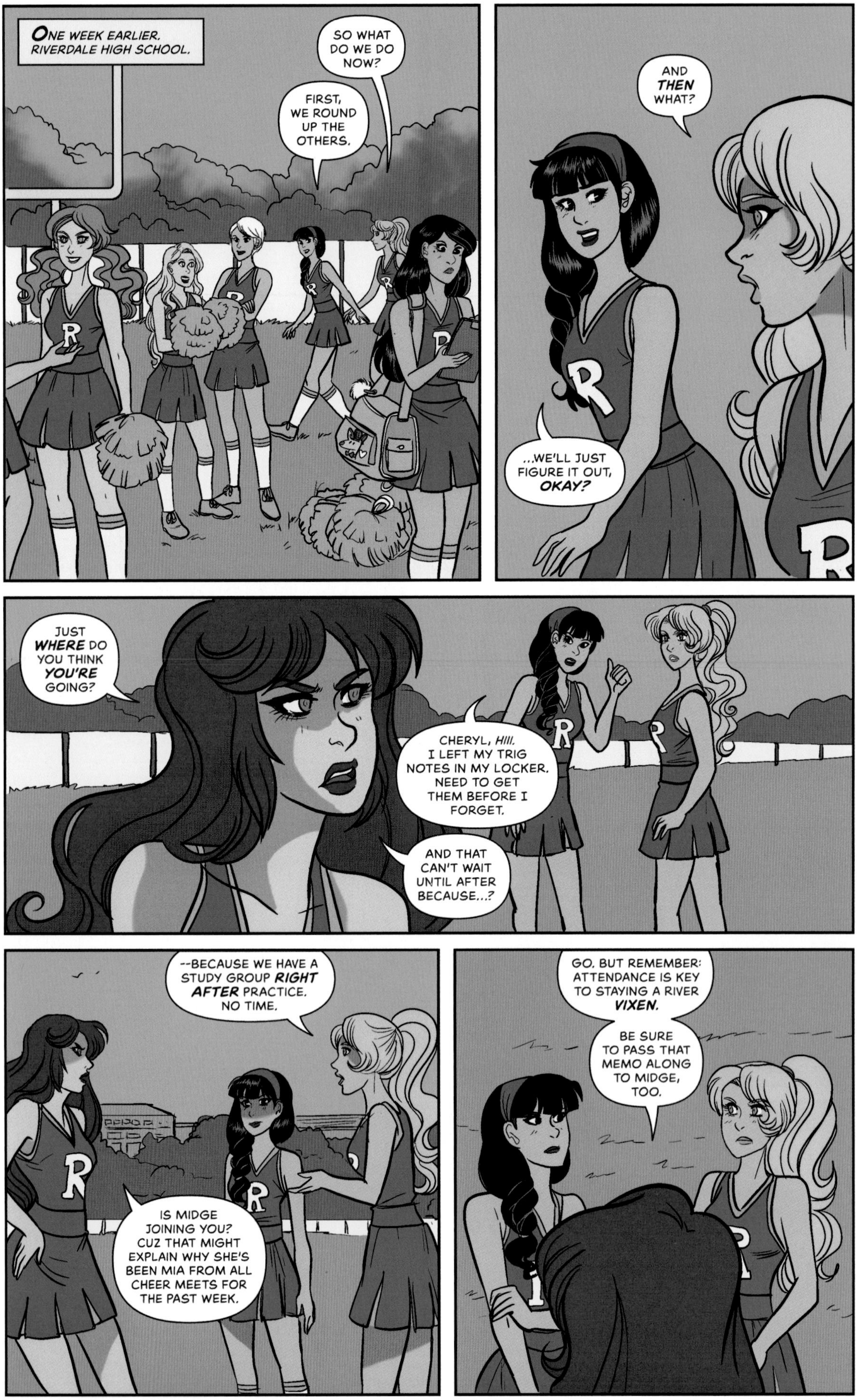
ONE WEEK EARLIER. RIVERDALE HIGH SCHOOL.
SO WHAT DO WE DO NOW?
FIRST, WE ROUND UP THE OTHERS.
AND *THEN* WHAT?
...WE'LL JUST FIGURE IT OUT, *OKAY?*
JUST *WHERE* DO YOU THINK *YOU'RE* GOING?
CHERYL, *HIII.* I LEFT MY TRIG NOTES IN MY LOCKER. NEED TO GET THEM BEFORE I FORGET.
AND THAT CAN'T WAIT UNTIL AFTER BECAUSE...?
--BECAUSE WE HAVE A STUDY GROUP *RIGHT AFTER* PRACTICE. NO TIME.
IS MIDGE JOINING YOU? CUZ THAT MIGHT EXPLAIN WHY SHE'S BEEN MIA FROM ALL CHEER MEETS FOR THE PAST WEEK.
GO, BUT REMEMBER: ATTENDANCE IS KEY TO STAYING A RIVER *VIXEN.*
BE SURE TO PASS THAT MEMO ALONG TO MIDGE, TOO.

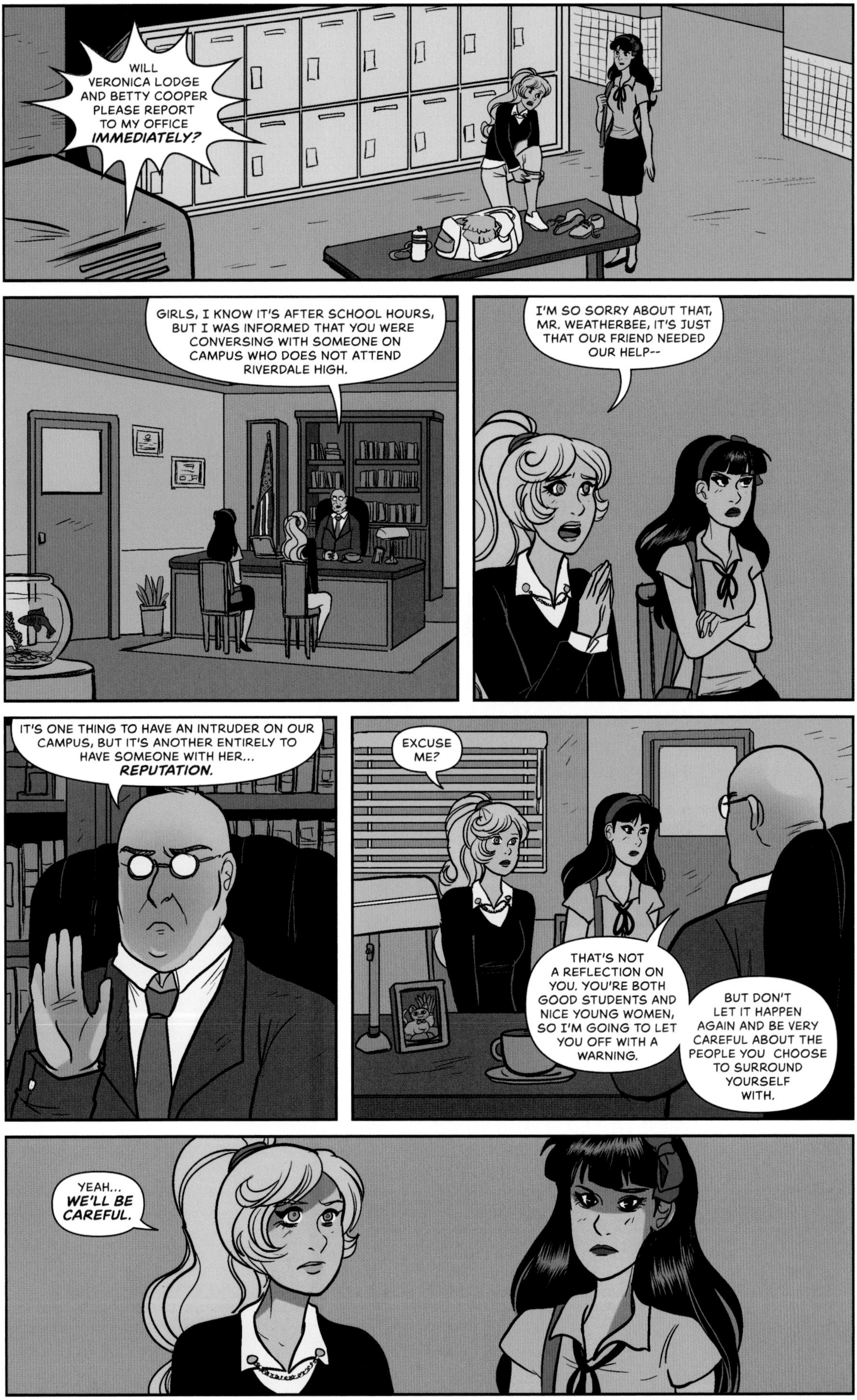
WILL VERONICA LODGE AND BETTY COOPER PLEASE REPORT TO MY OFFICE *IMMEDIATELY?*
GIRLS, I KNOW IT'S AFTER SCHOOL HOURS, BUT I WAS INFORMED THAT YOU WERE CONVERSING WITH SOMEONE ON CAMPUS WHO DOES NOT ATTEND RIVERDALE HIGH.
I'M SO SORRY ABOUT THAT, MR. WEATHERBEE, IT'S JUST THAT OUR FRIEND NEEDED OUR HELP--
IT'S ONE THING TO HAVE AN INTRUDER ON OUR CAMPUS, BUT IT'S ANOTHER ENTIRELY TO HAVE SOMEONE WITH HER... ***REPUTATION.***
EXCUSE ME?
THAT'S NOT A REFLECTION ON YOU. YOU'RE BOTH GOOD STUDENTS AND NICE YOUNG WOMEN, SO I'M GOING TO LET YOU OFF WITH A WARNING.
BUT DON'T LET IT HAPPEN AGAIN AND BE VERY CAREFUL ABOUT THE PEOPLE YOU CHOOSE TO SURROUND YOURSELF WITH.
YEAH... ***WE'LL BE CAREFUL.***

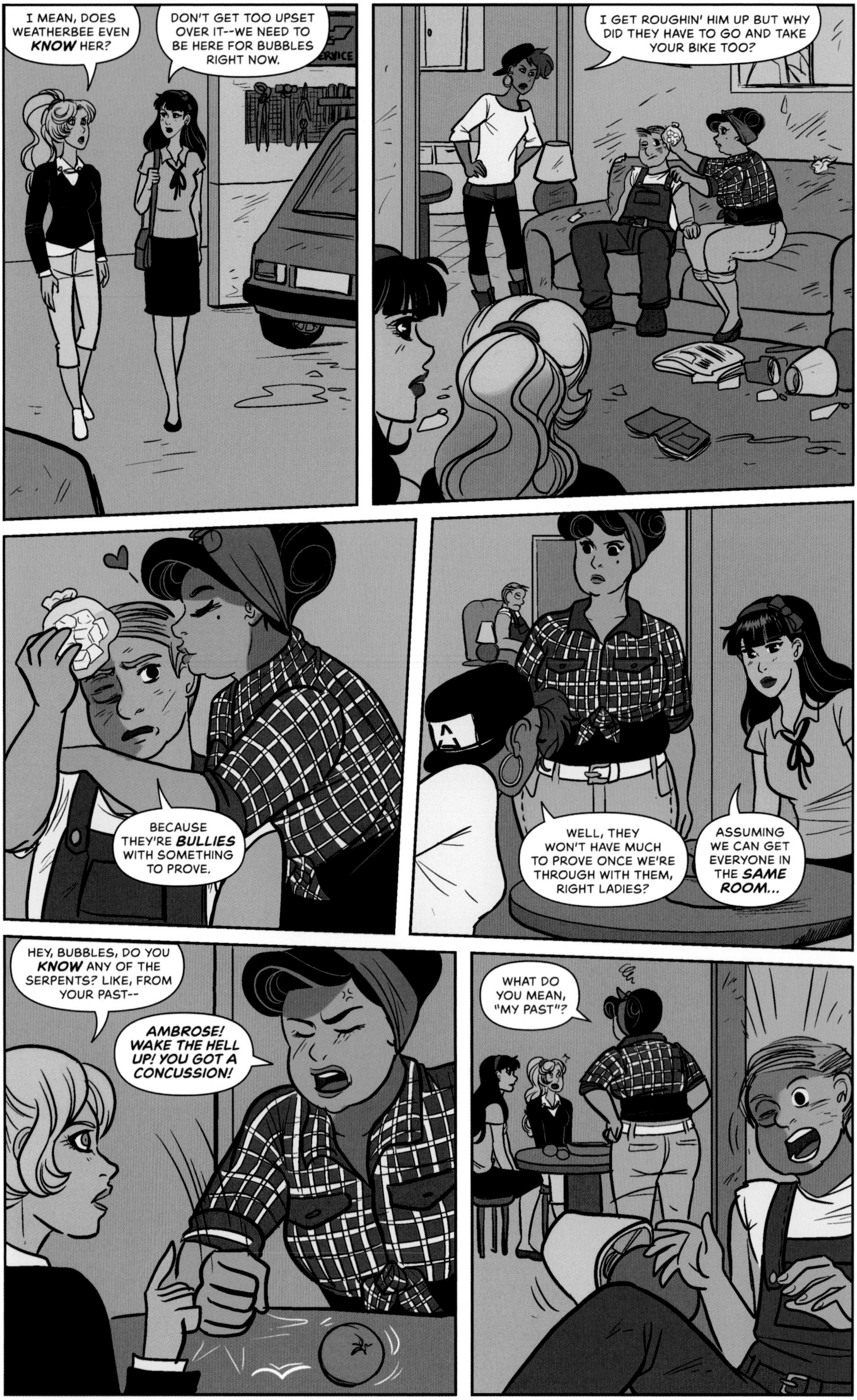
I MEAN, DOES WEATHERBEE EVEN KNOW HER?
DON'T GET TOO UPSET OVER IT--WE NEED TO BE HERE FOR BUBBLES RIGHT NOW.
I GET ROUGHIN' HIM UP BUT WHY DID THEY HAVE TO GO AND TAKE YOUR BIKE TOO?
BECAUSE THEY'RE BULLIES WITH SOMETHING TO PROVE.
WELL, THEY WON'T HAVE MUCH TO PROVE ONCE WE'RE THROUGH WITH THEM, RIGHT LADIES?
ASSUMING WE CAN GET EVERYONE IN THE SAME ROOM...
HEY, BUBBLES, DO YOU KNOW ANY OF THE SERPENTS? LIKE, FROM YOUR PAST--
AMBROSE! WAKE THE HELL UP! YOU GOT A CONCUSSION!
WHAT DO YOU MEAN, "MY PAST"?

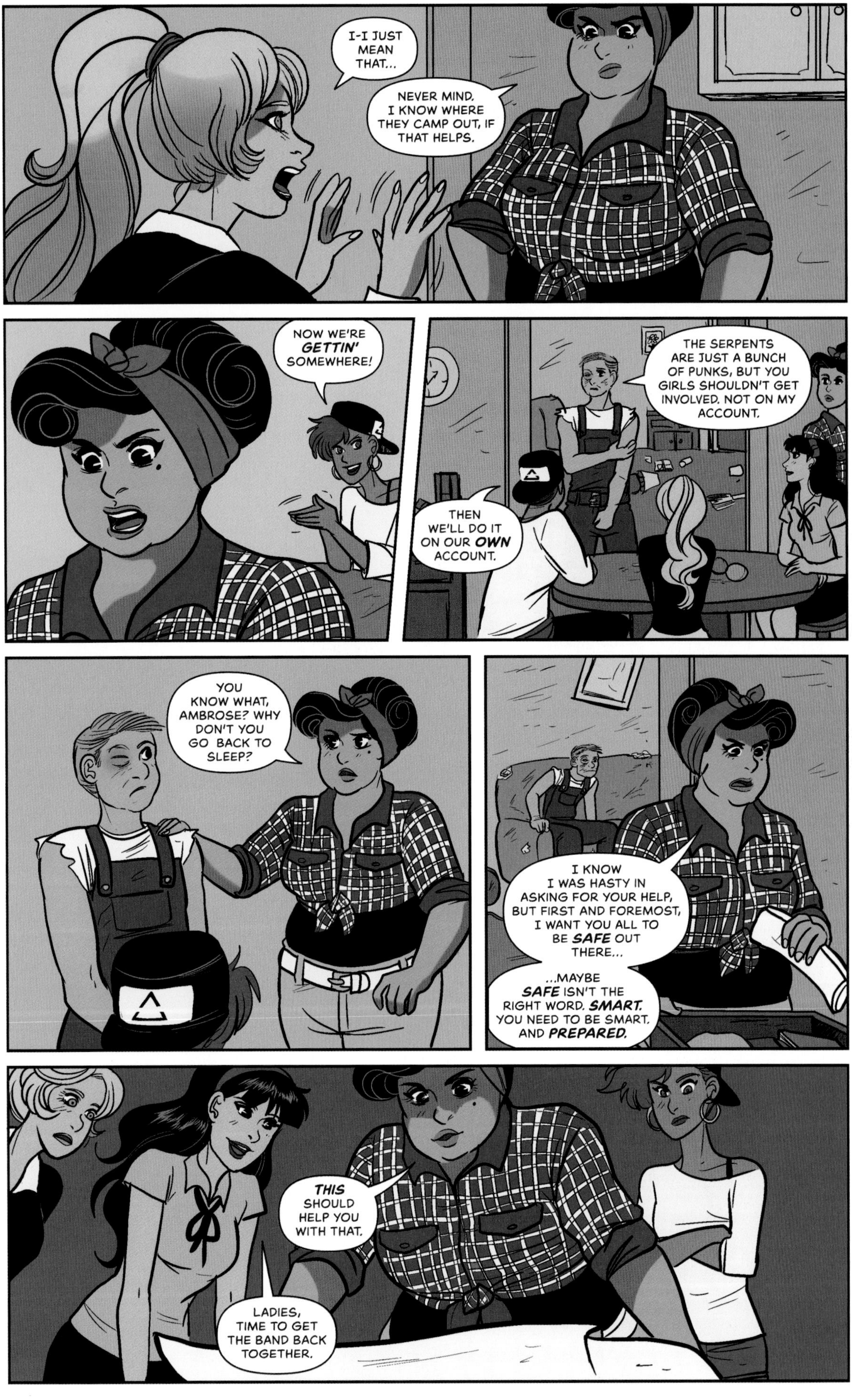
I-I JUST MEAN THAT...
NEVER MIND. I KNOW WHERE THEY CAMP OUT, IF THAT HELPS.
NOW WE'RE GETTIN' SOMEWHERE!
THE SERPENTS ARE JUST A BUNCH OF PUNKS, BUT YOU GIRLS SHOULDN'T GET INVOLVED. NOT ON MY ACCOUNT.
THEN WE'LL DO IT ON OUR OWN ACCOUNT.
YOU KNOW WHAT, AMBROSE? WHY DON'T YOU GO BACK TO SLEEP?
I KNOW I WAS HASTY IN ASKING FOR YOUR HELP, BUT FIRST AND FOREMOST, I WANT YOU ALL TO BE SAFE OUT THERE...
...MAYBE SAFE ISN'T THE RIGHT WORD. SMART. YOU NEED TO BE SMART. AND PREPARED.
THIS SHOULD HELP YOU WITH THAT.
LADIES, TIME TO GET THE BAND BACK TOGETHER.

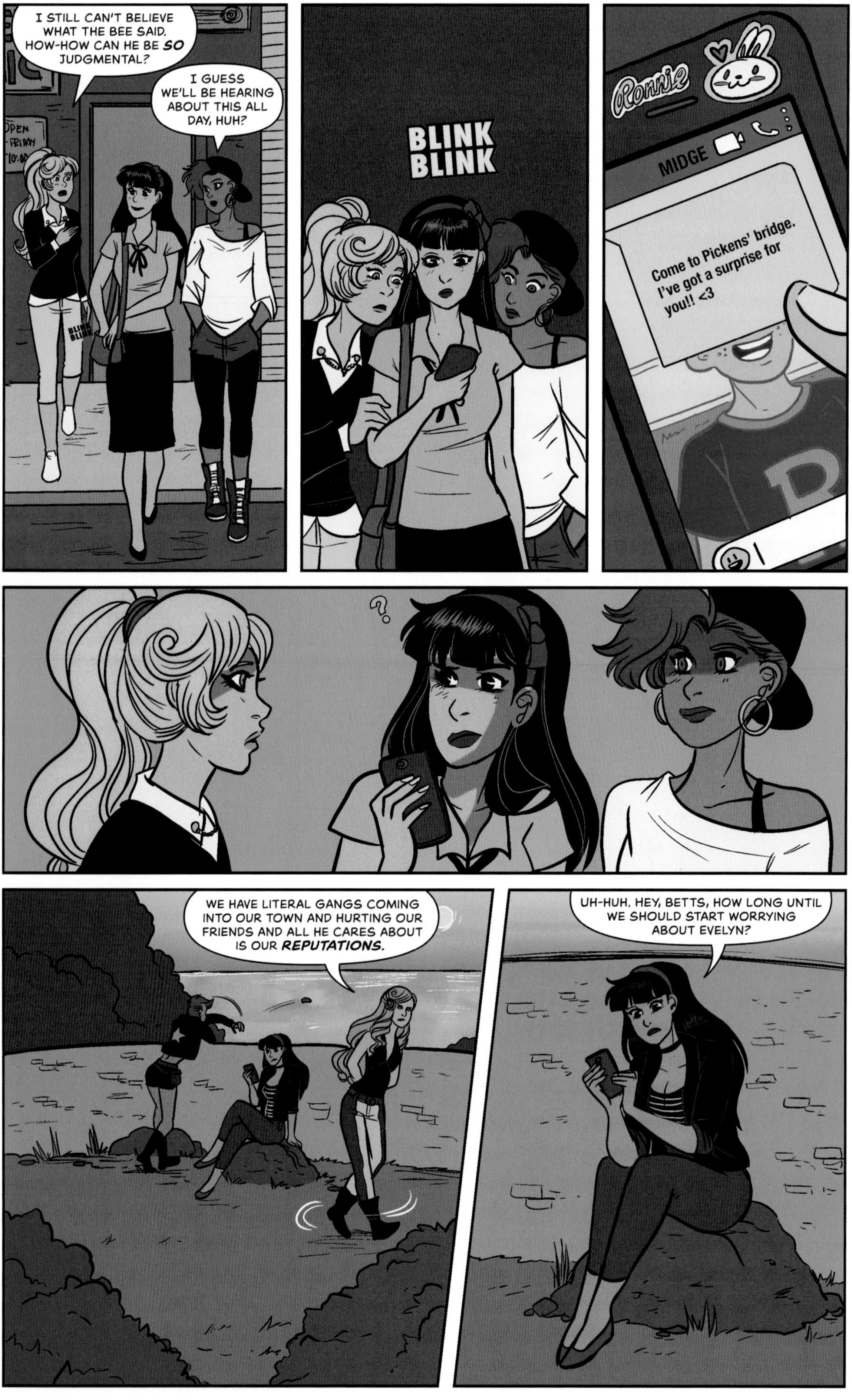
OPEN
FRIDAY
I STILL CAN'T BELIEVE WHAT THE BEE SAID. HOW-HOW CAN HE BE *SO* JUDGMENTAL?
I GUESS WE'LL BE HEARING ABOUT THIS ALL DAY, HUH?
BLINK BLINK
Ronnie
MIDGE
Come to Pickens' bridge. I've got a surprise for you!! <3
?
WE HAVE LITERAL GANGS COMING INTO OUR TOWN AND HURTING OUR FRIENDS AND ALL HE CARES ABOUT IS OUR ***REPUTATIONS.***
UH-HUH. HEY, BETTS, HOW LONG UNTIL WE SHOULD START WORRYING ABOUT EVELYN?

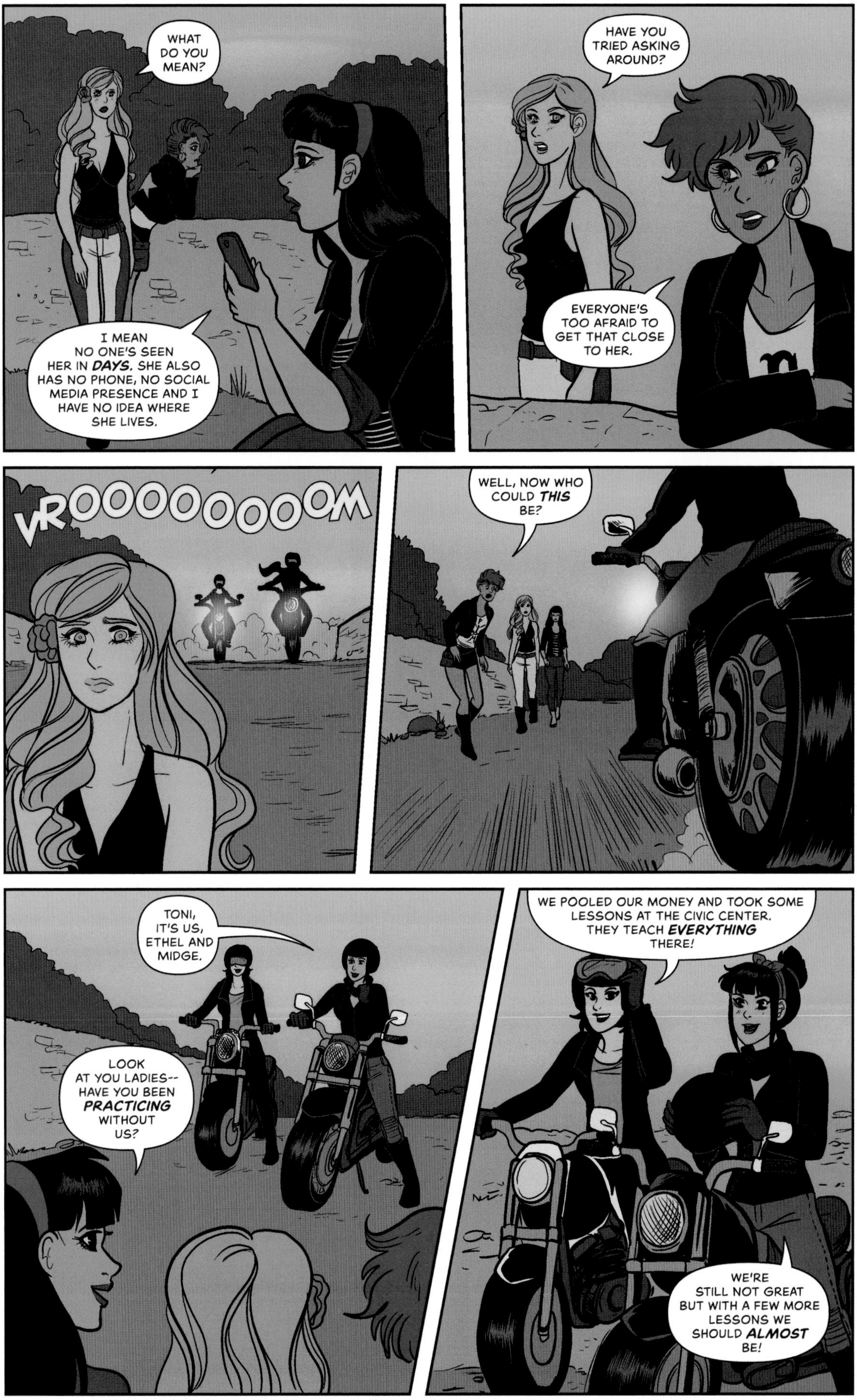
WHAT DO YOU MEAN?
I MEAN NO ONE'S SEEN HER IN *DAYS.* SHE ALSO HAS NO PHONE, NO SOCIAL MEDIA PRESENCE AND I HAVE NO IDEA WHERE SHE LIVES.
HAVE YOU TRIED ASKING AROUND?
EVERYONE'S TOO AFRAID TO GET THAT CLOSE TO HER.
VROOOOOOOOOM
WELL, NOW WHO COULD *THIS* BE?
TONI, IT'S US, ETHEL AND MIDGE.
LOOK AT YOU LADIES-- HAVE YOU BEEN *PRACTICING* WITHOUT US?
WE POOLED OUR MONEY AND TOOK SOME LESSONS AT THE CIVIC CENTER. THEY TEACH *EVERYTHING* THERE!
WE'RE STILL NOT GREAT BUT WITH A FEW MORE LESSONS WE SHOULD *ALMOST* BE!

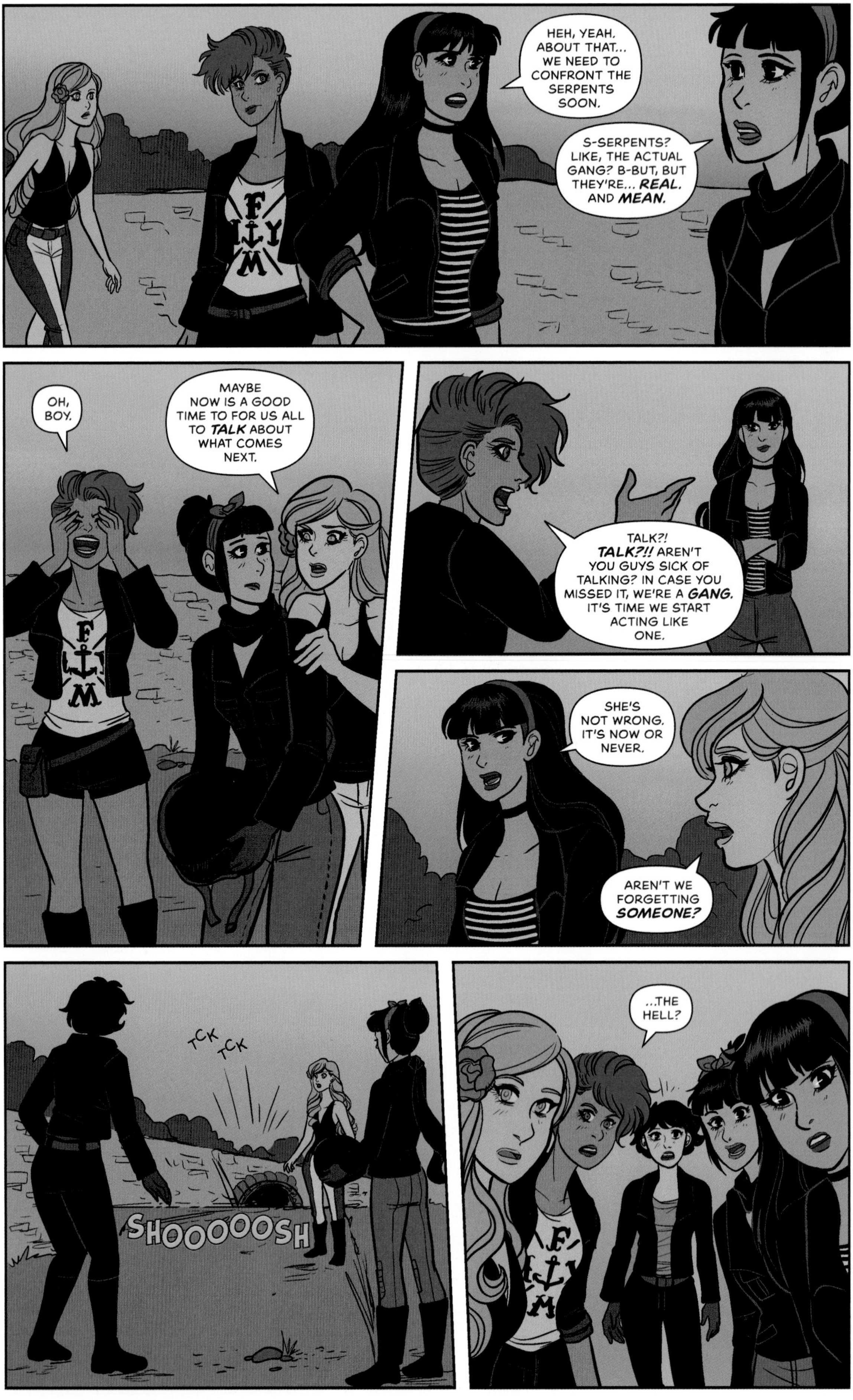
HEH, YEAH, ABOUT THAT... WE NEED TO CONFRONT THE SERPENTS SOON.
S-SERPENTS? LIKE, THE ACTUAL GANG? B-BUT, BUT THEY'RE... **REAL.** AND **MEAN.**
OH, BOY.
MAYBE NOW IS A GOOD TIME TO FOR US ALL TO **TALK** ABOUT WHAT COMES NEXT.
TALK?! **TALK?!!** AREN'T YOU GUYS SICK OF TALKING? IN CASE YOU MISSED IT, WE'RE A **GANG.** IT'S TIME WE START ACTING LIKE ONE.
SHE'S NOT WRONG. IT'S NOW OR NEVER.
AREN'T WE FORGETTING **SOMEONE?**
TCK TCK
SHOOOOOSH
...THE HELL?

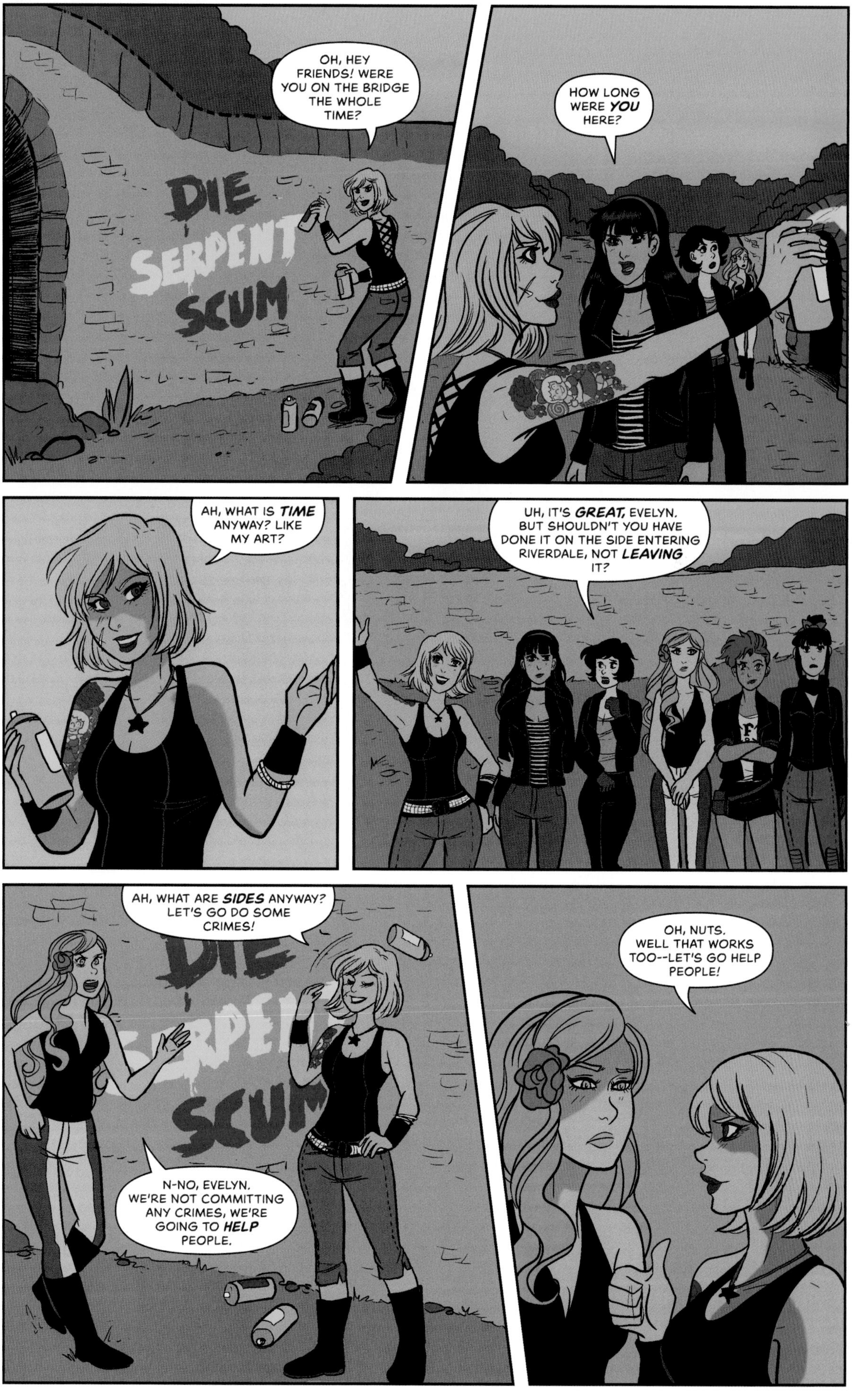
OH, HEY FRIENDS! WERE YOU ON THE BRIDGE THE WHOLE TIME?
DIE SERPENT SCUM
HOW LONG WERE *YOU* HERE?
AH, WHAT IS *TIME* ANYWAY? LIKE MY ART?
UH, IT'S *GREAT,* EVELYN. BUT SHOULDN'T YOU HAVE DONE IT ON THE SIDE ENTERING RIVERDALE, NOT *LEAVING* IT?
AH, WHAT ARE *SIDES* ANYWAY? LET'S GO DO SOME CRIMES!
N-NO, EVELYN. WE'RE NOT COMMITTING ANY CRIMES, WE'RE GOING TO *HELP* PEOPLE.
OH, NUTS. WELL THAT WORKS TOO--LET'S GO HELP PEOPLE!

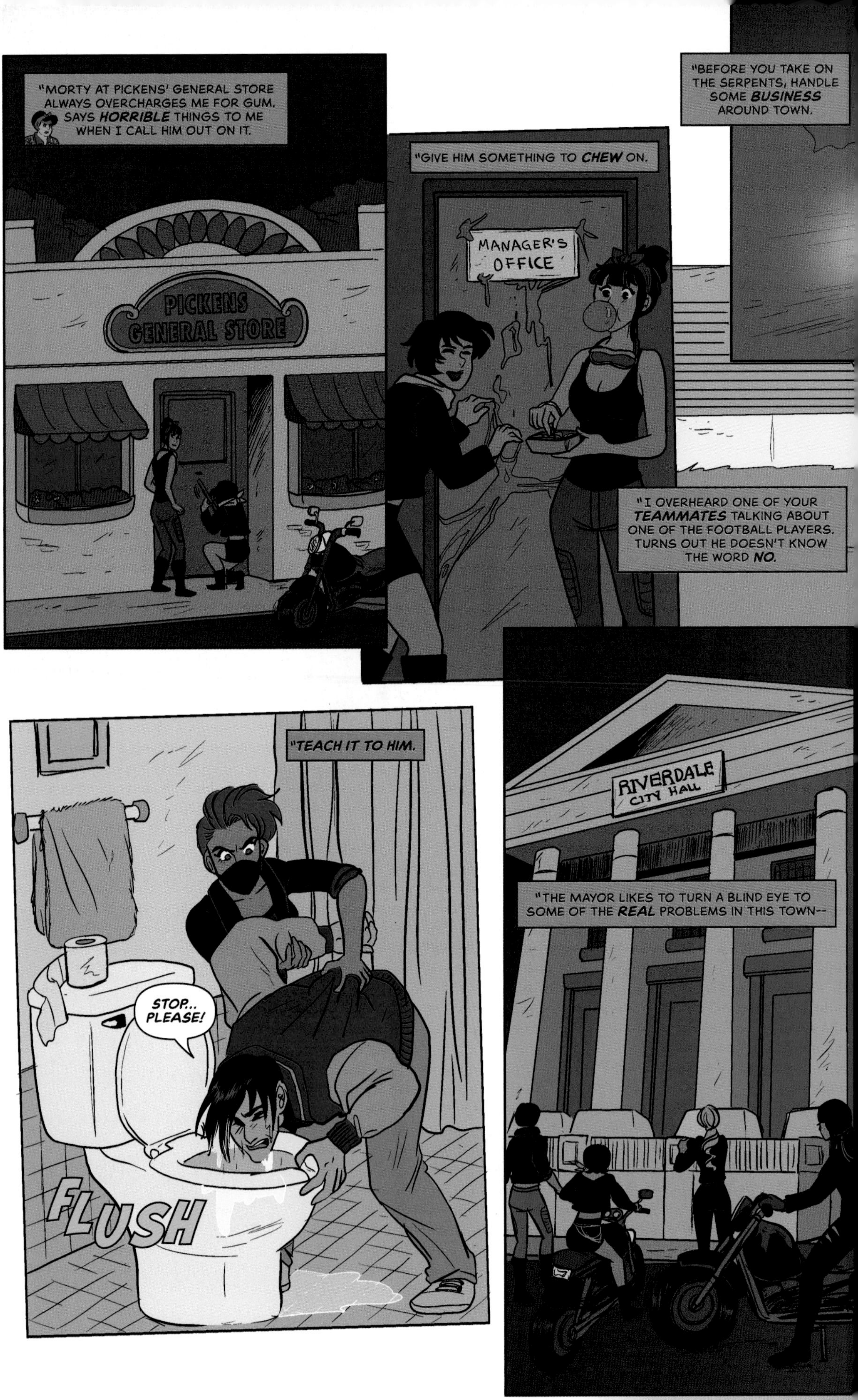
"MORTY AT PICKENS' GENERAL STORE ALWAYS OVERCHARGES ME FOR GUM. SAYS **HORRIBLE** THINGS TO ME WHEN I CALL HIM OUT ON IT.
PICKENS GENERAL STORE
"GIVE HIM SOMETHING TO **CHEW** ON.
MANAGER'S OFFICE
"BEFORE YOU TAKE ON THE SERPENTS, HANDLE SOME **BUSINESS** AROUND TOWN.
"I OVERHEARD ONE OF YOUR **TEAMMATES** TALKING ABOUT ONE OF THE FOOTBALL PLAYERS. TURNS OUT HE DOESN'T KNOW THE WORD **NO.**
"**TEACH IT TO HIM.**
STOP... PLEASE!
FLUSH
RIVERDALE CITY HALL
"THE MAYOR LIKES TO TURN A BLIND EYE TO SOME OF THE **REAL** PROBLEMS IN THIS TOWN--

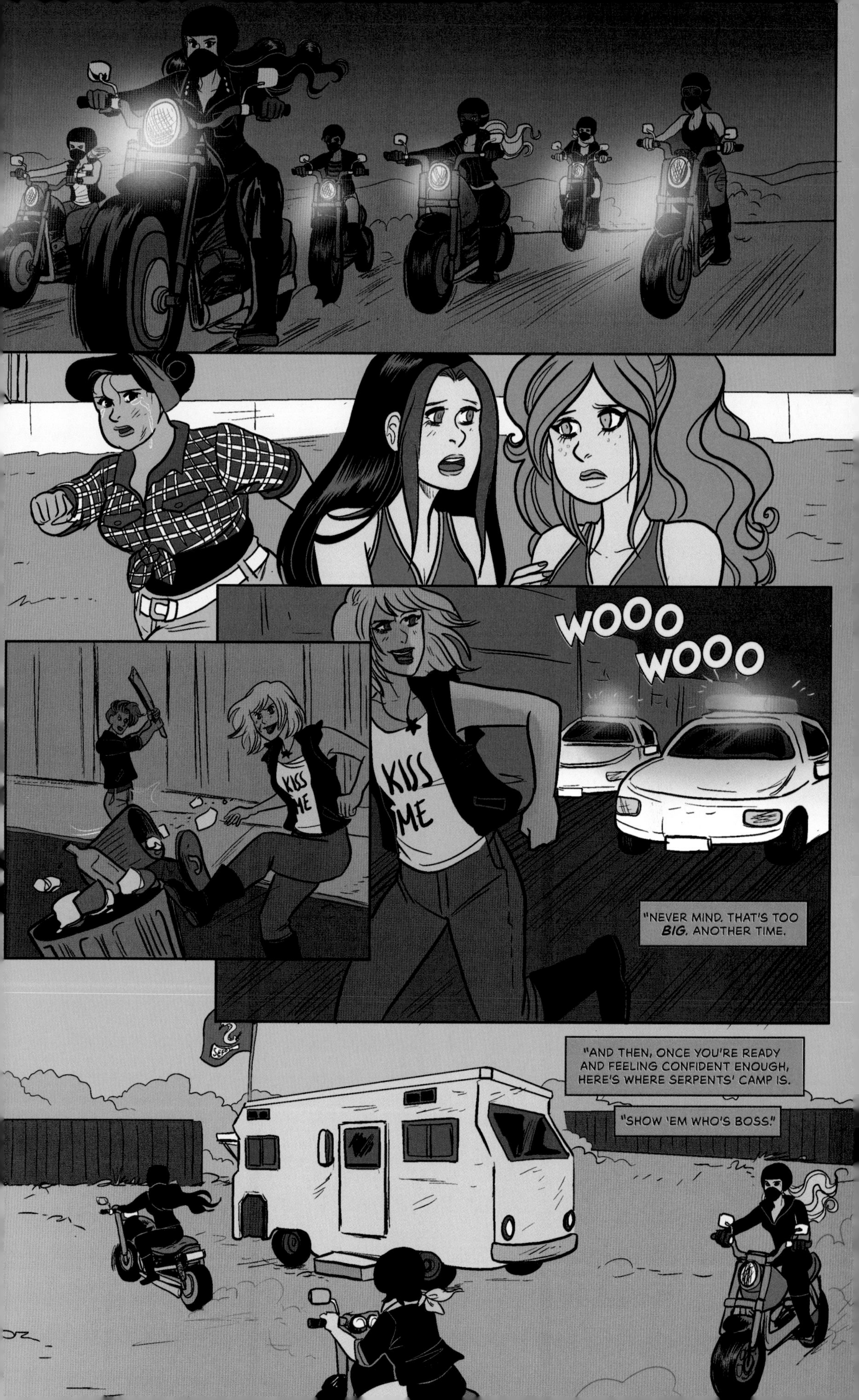
WOOO
WOOO
KISS ME
KISS ME
"NEVER MIND. THAT'S TOO *BIG*. ANOTHER TIME.
"AND THEN, ONCE YOU'RE READY AND FEELING CONFIDENT ENOUGH, HERE'S WHERE SERPENTS' CAMP IS.
"SHOW 'EM WHO'S BOSS."

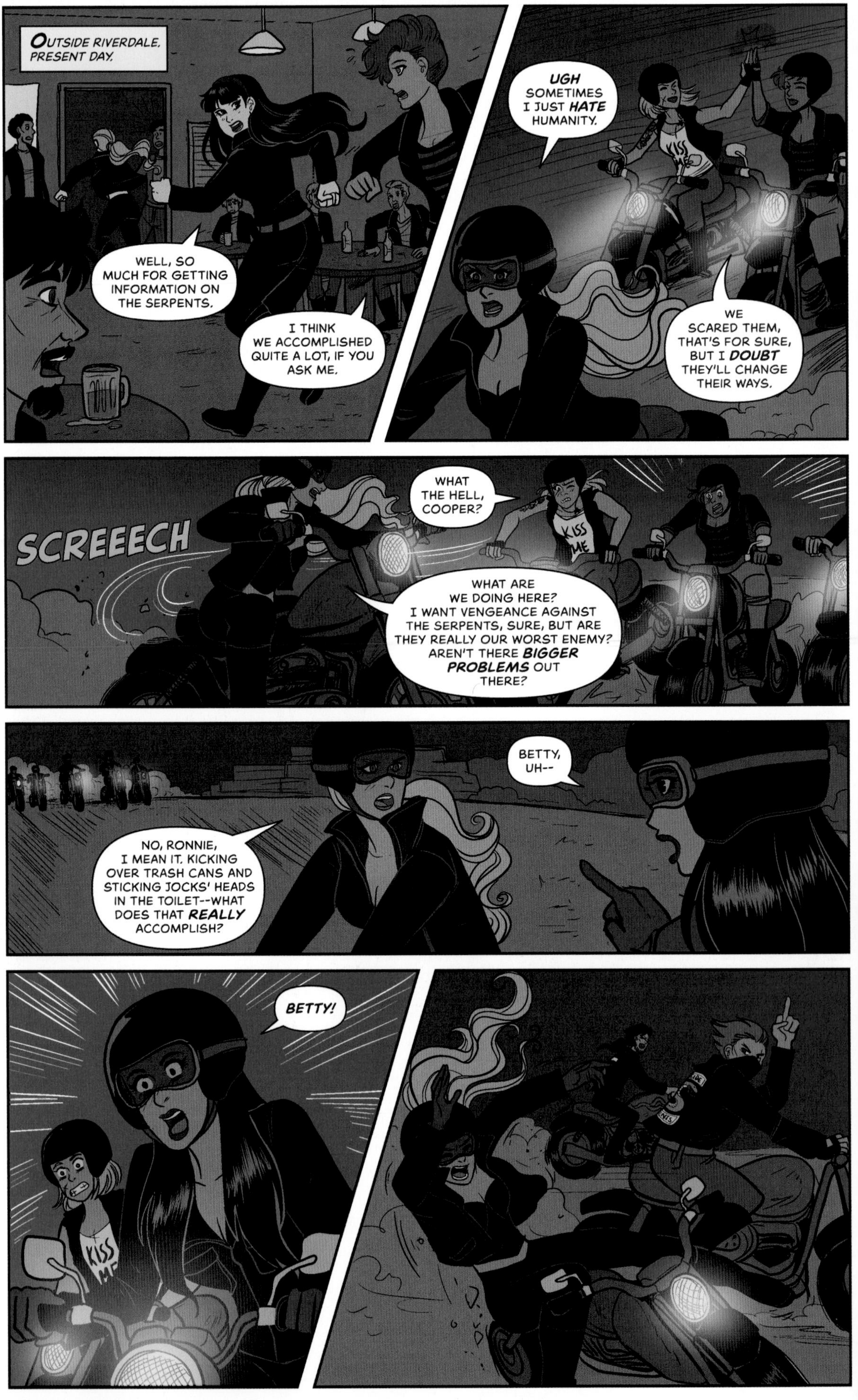
OUTSIDE RIVERDALE, PRESENT DAY.
WELL, SO MUCH FOR GETTING INFORMATION ON THE SERPENTS.
I THINK WE ACCOMPLISHED QUITE A LOT, IF YOU ASK ME.
UGH SOMETIMES I JUST HATE HUMANITY.
WE SCARED THEM, THAT'S FOR SURE, BUT I DOUBT THEY'LL CHANGE THEIR WAYS.
SCREEECH
WHAT THE HELL, COOPER?
WHAT ARE WE DOING HERE? I WANT VENGEANCE AGAINST THE SERPENTS, SURE, BUT ARE THEY REALLY OUR WORST ENEMY? AREN'T THERE BIGGER PROBLEMS OUT THERE?
BETTY, UH--
NO, RONNIE, I MEAN IT. KICKING OVER TRASH CANS AND STICKING JOCKS' HEADS IN THE TOILET--WHAT DOES THAT REALLY ACCOMPLISH?
BETTY!

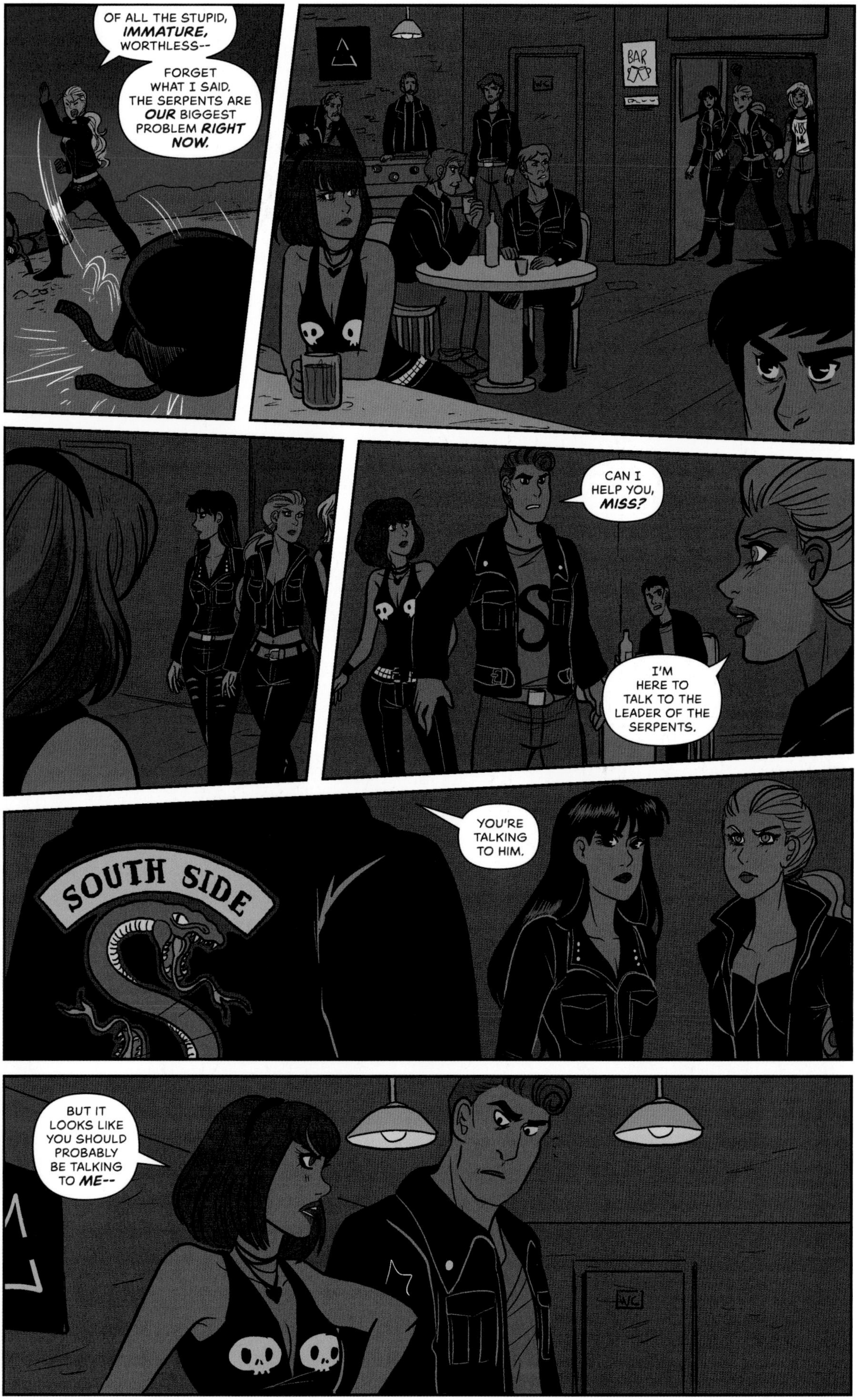
OF ALL THE STUPID, IMMATURE, WORTHLESS--
FORGET WHAT I SAID. THE SERPENTS ARE OUR BIGGEST PROBLEM RIGHT NOW.
BAR
CAN I HELP YOU, MISS?
I'M HERE TO TALK TO THE LEADER OF THE SERPENTS.
YOU'RE TALKING TO HIM.
SOUTH SIDE
BUT IT LOOKS LIKE YOU SHOULD PROBABLY BE TALKING TO ME--

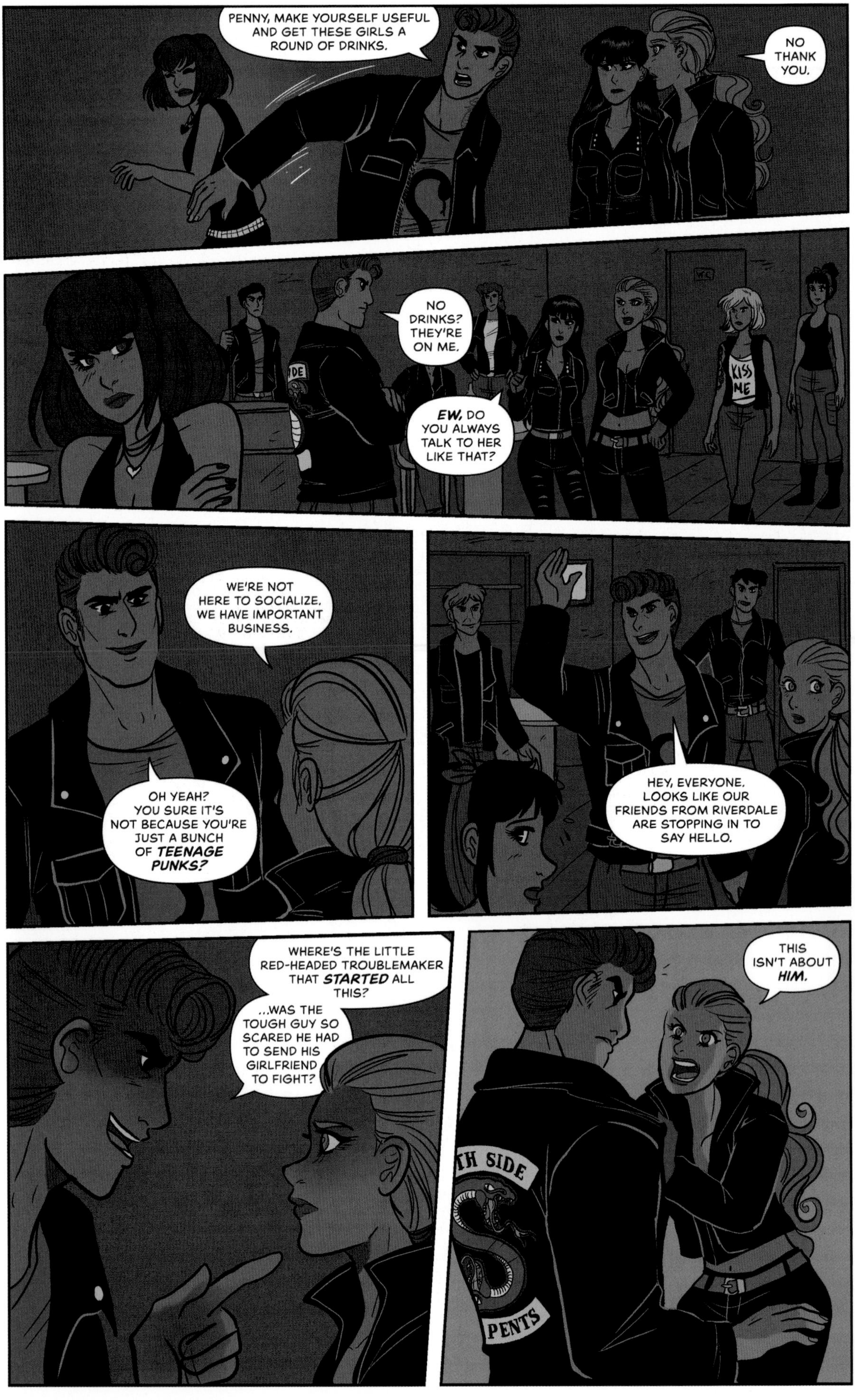
PENNY, MAKE YOURSELF USEFUL AND GET THESE GIRLS A ROUND OF DRINKS.
NO THANK YOU.
NO DRINKS? THEY'RE ON ME.
EW, DO YOU ALWAYS TALK TO HER LIKE THAT?
WE'RE NOT HERE TO SOCIALIZE. WE HAVE IMPORTANT BUSINESS.
OH YEAH? YOU SURE IT'S NOT BECAUSE YOU'RE JUST A BUNCH OF TEENAGE PUNKS?
HEY, EVERYONE. LOOKS LIKE OUR FRIENDS FROM RIVERDALE ARE STOPPING IN TO SAY HELLO.
WHERE'S THE LITTLE RED-HEADED TROUBLEMAKER THAT STARTED ALL THIS?
...WAS THE TOUGH GUY SO SCARED HE HAD TO SEND HIS GIRLFRIEND TO FIGHT?
THIS ISN'T ABOUT HIM.

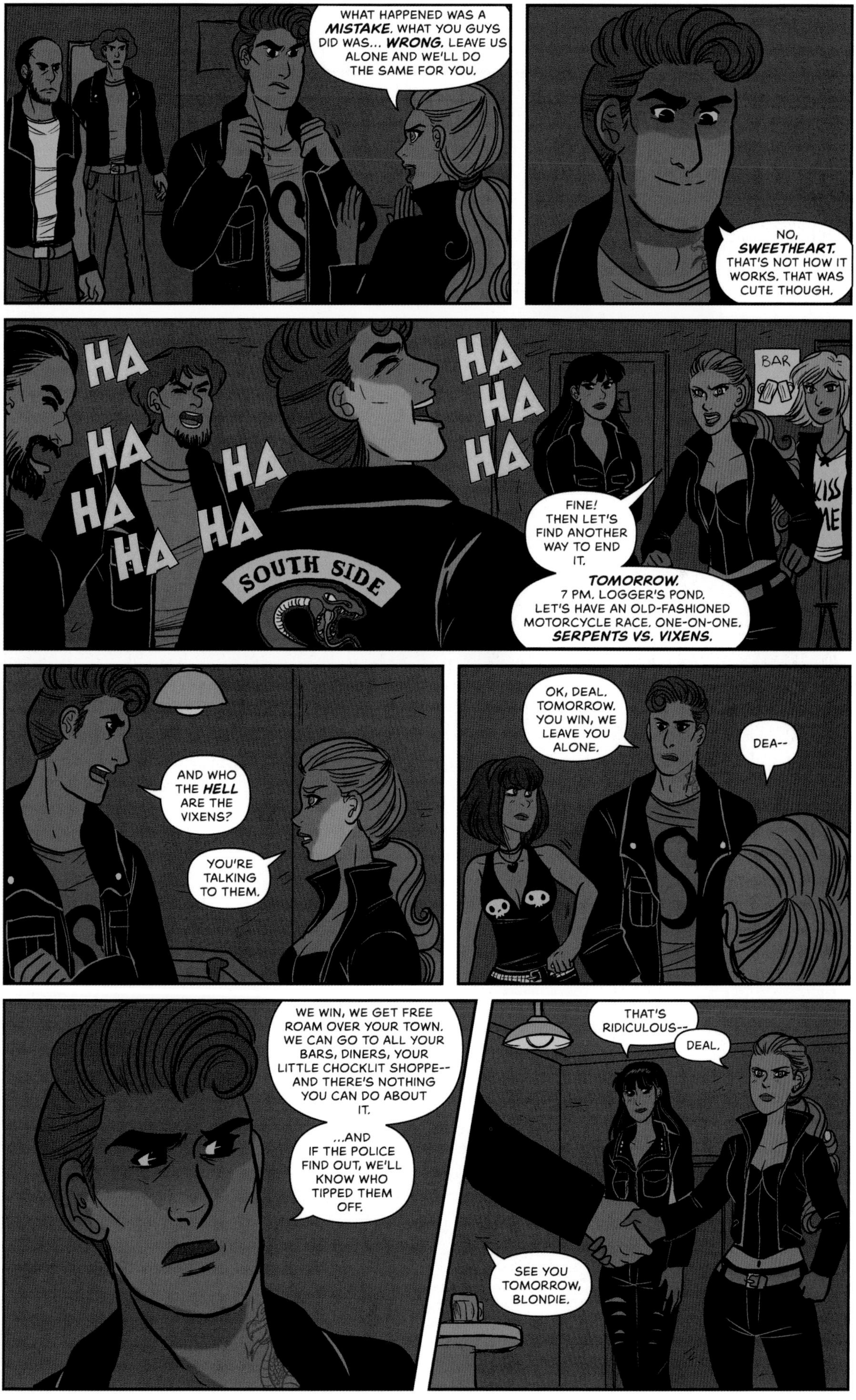
WHAT HAPPENED WAS A MISTAKE. WHAT YOU GUYS DID WAS... WRONG. LEAVE US ALONE AND WE'LL DO THE SAME FOR YOU.
NO, SWEETHEART. THAT'S NOT HOW IT WORKS. THAT WAS CUTE THOUGH.
HA HA HA HA HA HA HA HA HA
SOUTH SIDE
BAR
FINE! THEN LET'S FIND ANOTHER WAY TO END IT.
TOMORROW. 7 PM. LOGGER'S POND. LET'S HAVE AN OLD-FASHIONED MOTORCYCLE RACE. ONE-ON-ONE. SERPENTS VS. VIXENS.
AND WHO THE HELL ARE THE VIXENS?
YOU'RE TALKING TO THEM.
OK, DEAL. TOMORROW. YOU WIN, WE LEAVE YOU ALONE.
DEA--
WE WIN, WE GET FREE ROAM OVER YOUR TOWN. WE CAN GO TO ALL YOUR BARS, DINERS, YOUR LITTLE CHOCKLIT SHOPPE-- AND THERE'S NOTHING YOU CAN DO ABOUT IT.
...AND IF THE POLICE FIND OUT, WE'LL KNOW WHO TIPPED THEM OFF.
THAT'S RIDICULOUS--
DEAL.
SEE YOU TOMORROW, BLONDIE.

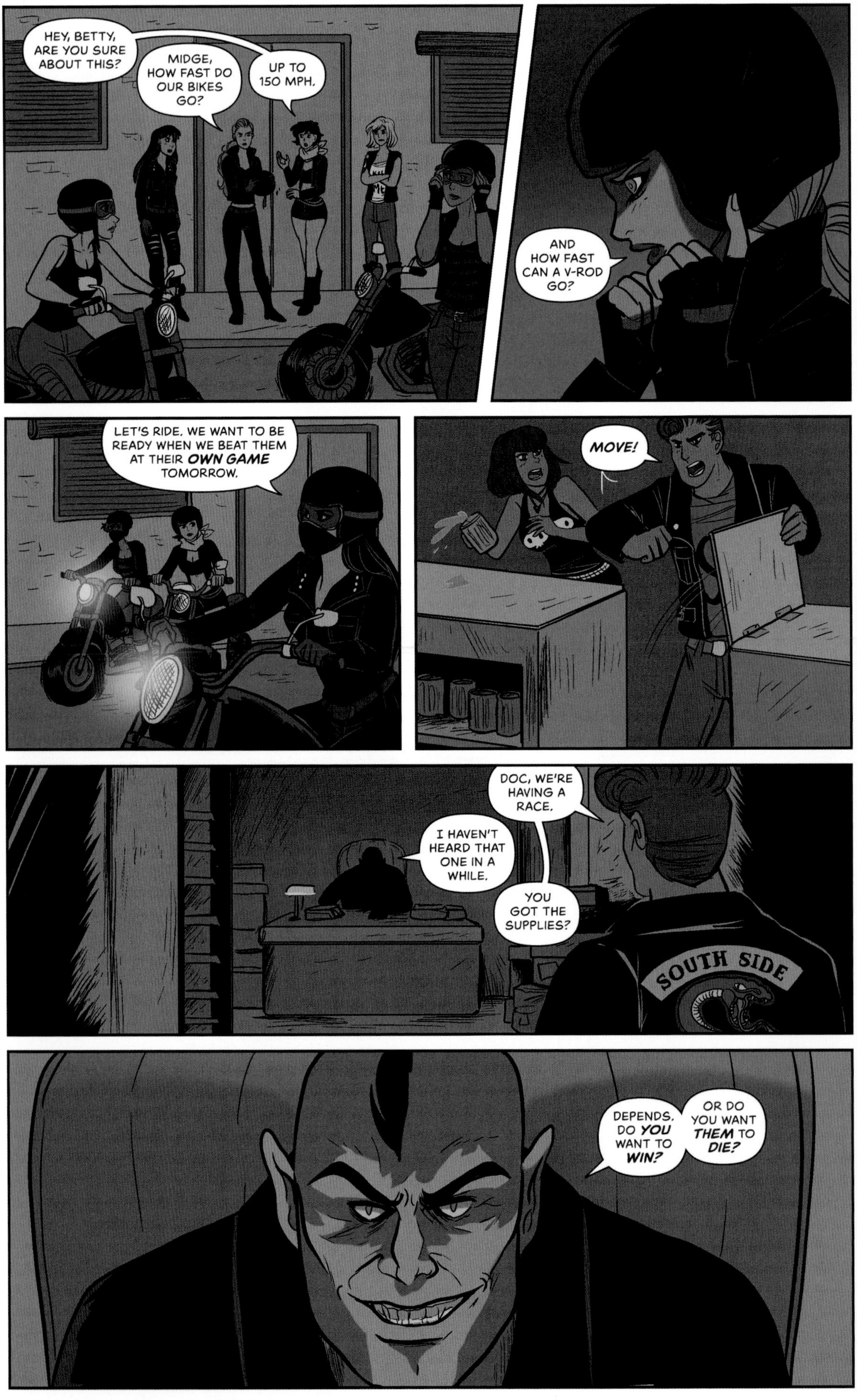
HEY, BETTY, ARE YOU SURE ABOUT THIS?
MIDGE, HOW FAST DO OUR BIKES GO?
UP TO 150 MPH.
AND HOW FAST CAN A V-ROD GO?
LET'S RIDE. WE WANT TO BE READY WHEN WE BEAT THEM AT THEIR OWN GAME TOMORROW.
MOVE!
DOC, WE'RE HAVING A RACE.
I HAVEN'T HEARD THAT ONE IN A WHILE.
YOU GOT THE SUPPLIES?
SOUTH SIDE
DEPENDS. DO YOU WANT TO WIN?
OR DO YOU WANT THEM TO DIE?

to be continued...

Chapter Four

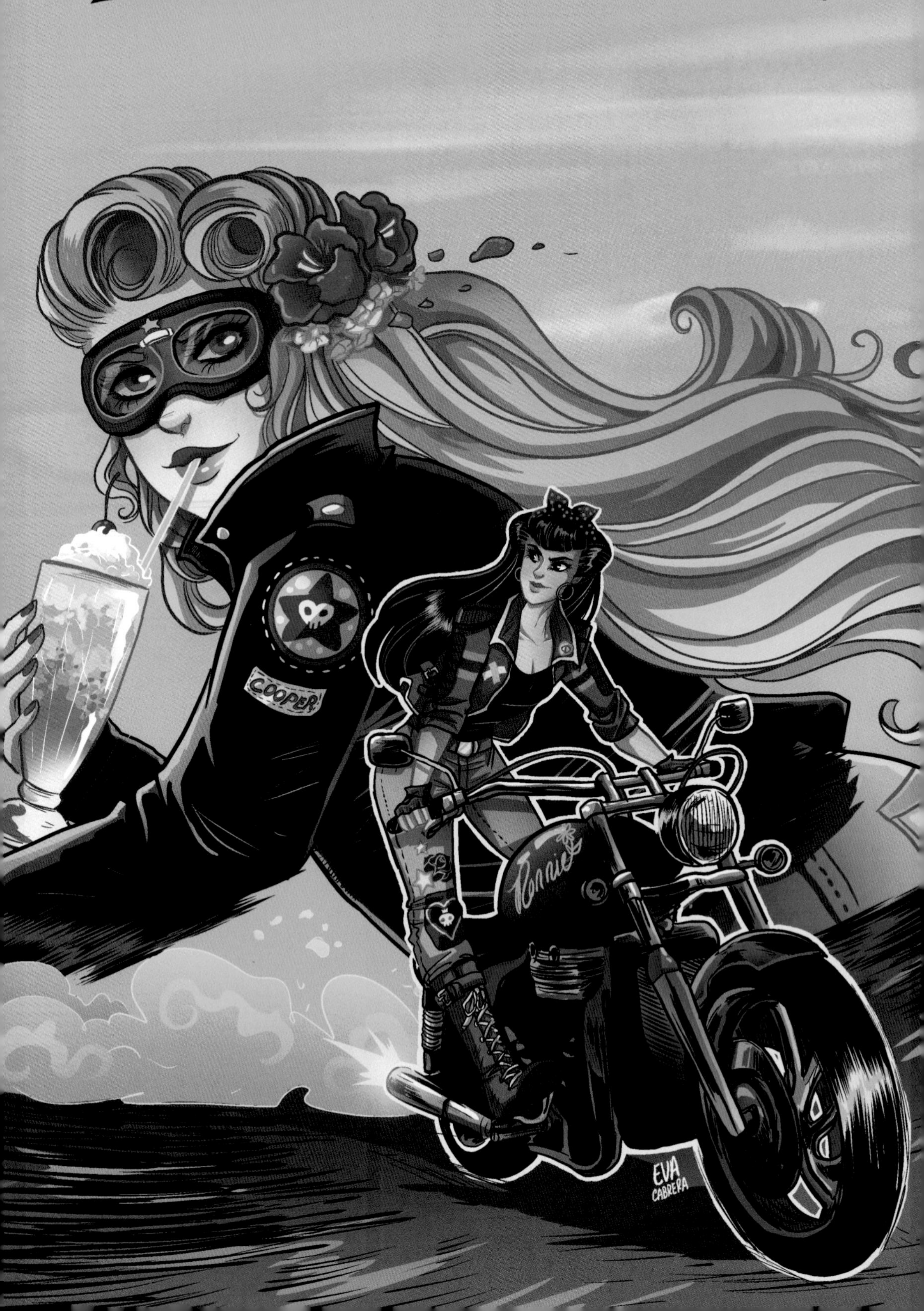
COOPER
EVA CABRERA

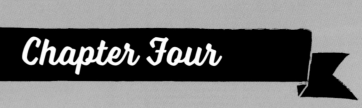

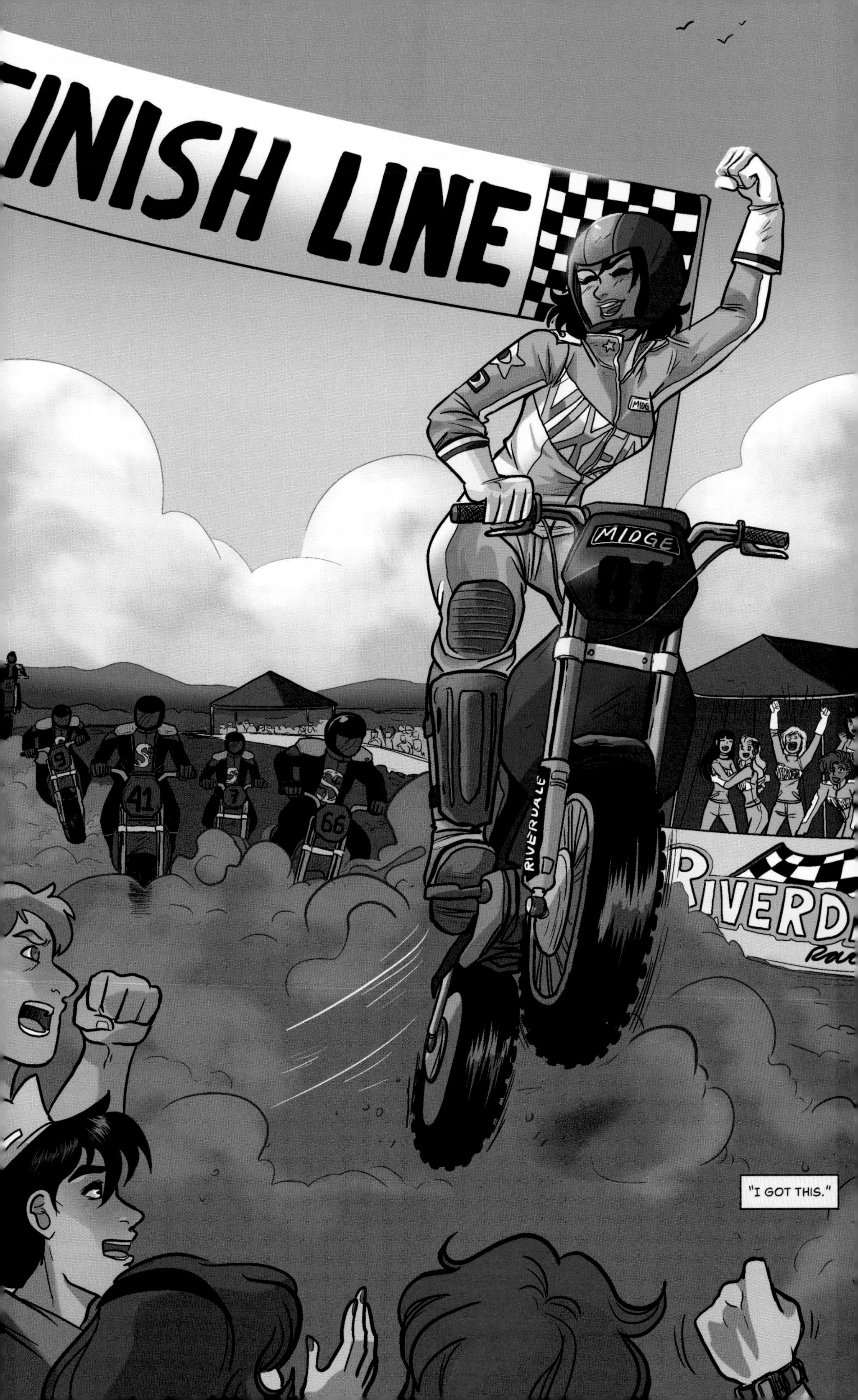
FINISH LINE
MIDGE
RIVERDALE
RIVERD
"I GOT THIS."

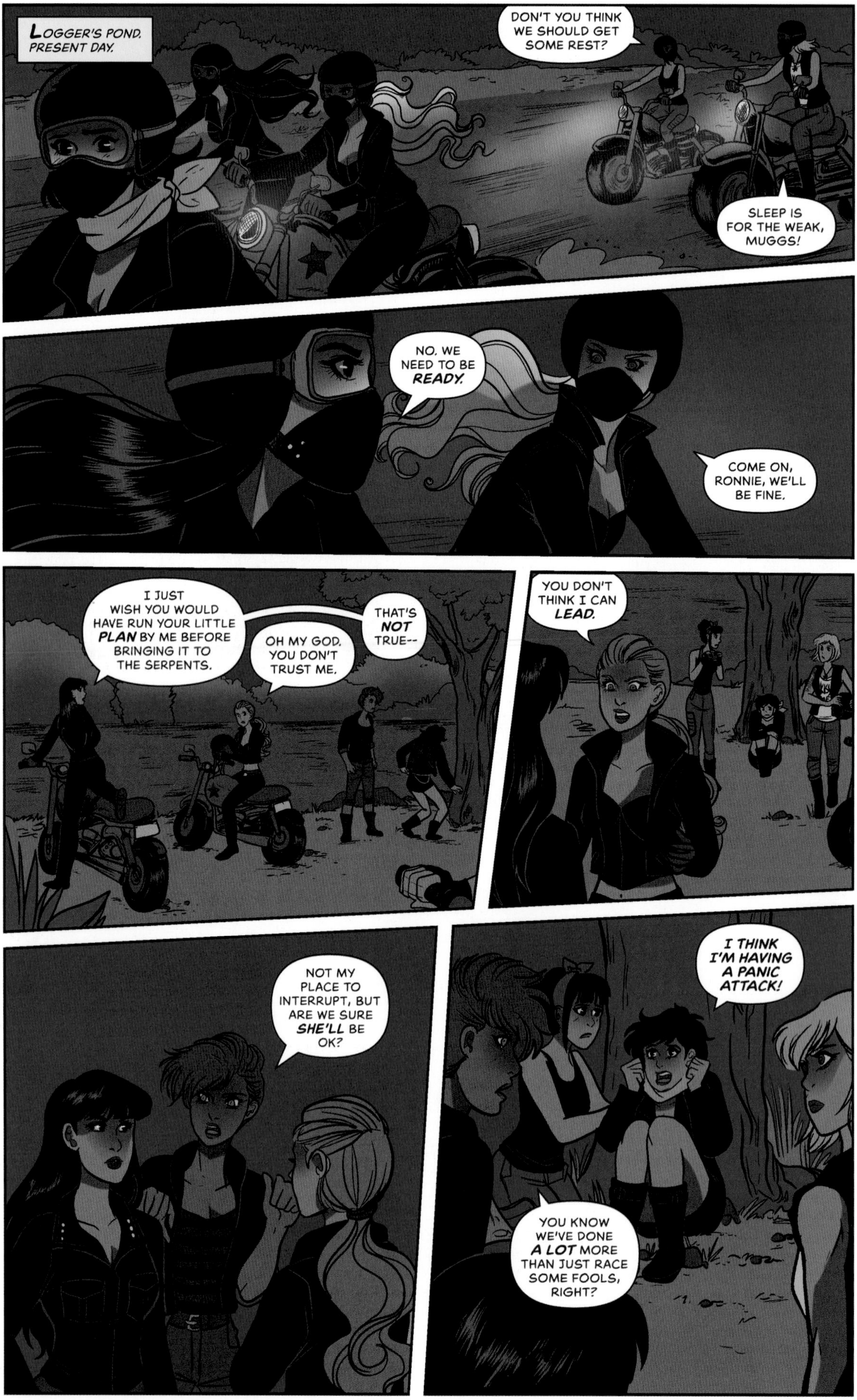
LOGGER'S POND. PRESENT DAY.
DON'T YOU THINK WE SHOULD GET SOME REST?
SLEEP IS FOR THE WEAK, MUGGS!
NO. WE NEED TO BE *READY.*
COME ON, RONNIE, WE'LL BE FINE.
I JUST WISH YOU WOULD HAVE RUN YOUR LITTLE **PLAN** BY ME BEFORE BRINGING IT TO THE SERPENTS.
OH MY GOD. YOU DON'T TRUST ME.
THAT'S ***NOT*** TRUE--
YOU DON'T THINK I CAN ***LEAD.***
NOT MY PLACE TO INTERRUPT, BUT ARE WE SURE ***SHE'LL*** BE OK?
I THINK I'M HAVING A PANIC ATTACK!
YOU KNOW WE'VE DONE ***A LOT*** MORE THAN JUST RACE SOME FOOLS, RIGHT?

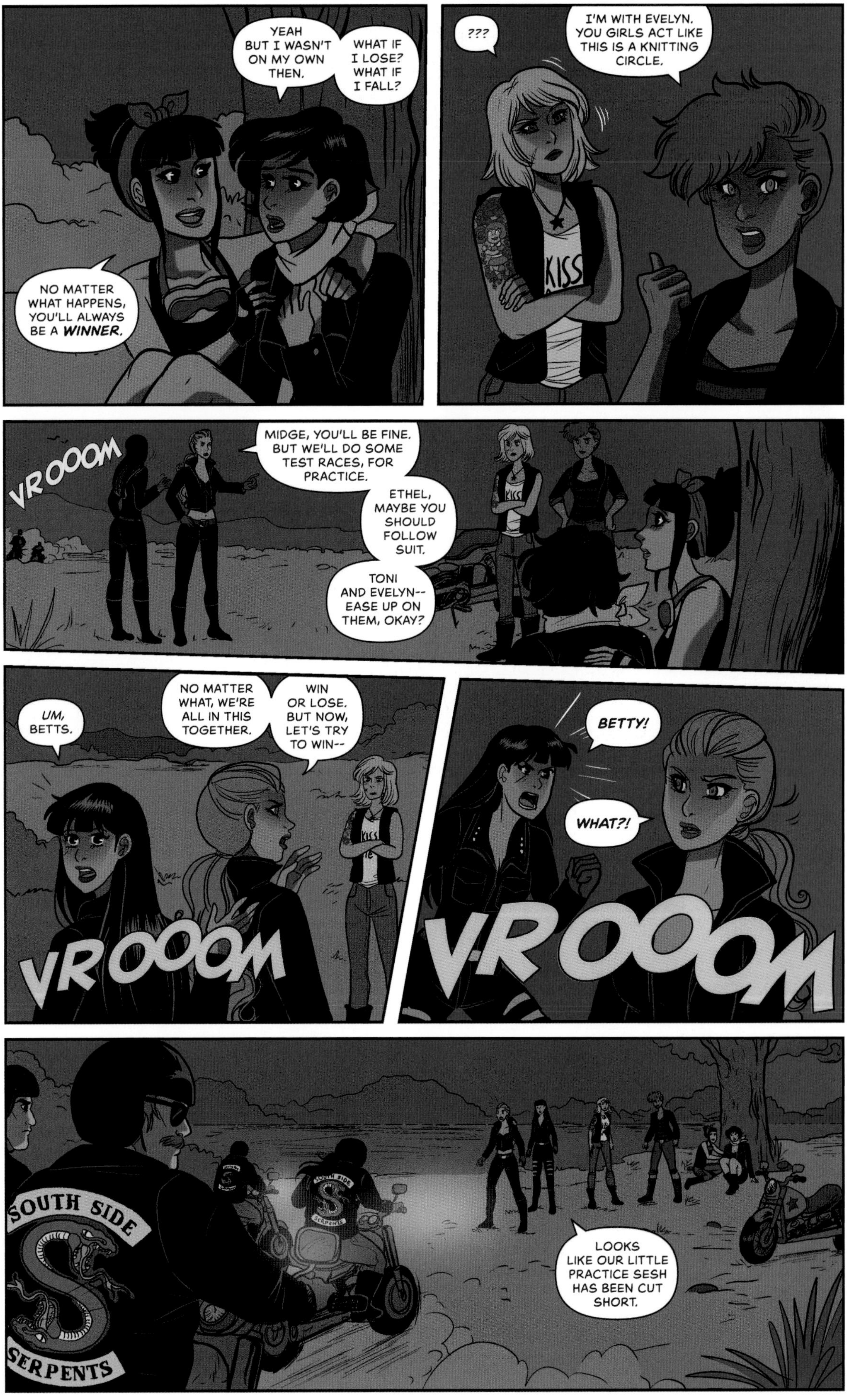
YEAH BUT I WASN'T ON MY OWN THEN.
WHAT IF I LOSE? WHAT IF I FALL?
NO MATTER WHAT HAPPENS, YOU'LL ALWAYS BE A WINNER.
???
I'M WITH EVELYN. YOU GIRLS ACT LIKE THIS IS A KNITTING CIRCLE.
KISS
VROOOM
MIDGE, YOU'LL BE FINE. BUT WE'LL DO SOME TEST RACES, FOR PRACTICE.
ETHEL, MAYBE YOU SHOULD FOLLOW SUIT.
TONI AND EVELYN-- EASE UP ON THEM, OKAY?
UM, BETTS.
NO MATTER WHAT, WE'RE ALL IN THIS TOGETHER.
WIN OR LOSE. BUT NOW, LET'S TRY TO WIN--
VROOOM
BETTY!
WHAT?!
VROOOM
SOUTH SIDE
SERPENTS
LOOKS LIKE OUR LITTLE PRACTICE SESH HAS BEEN CUT SHORT.

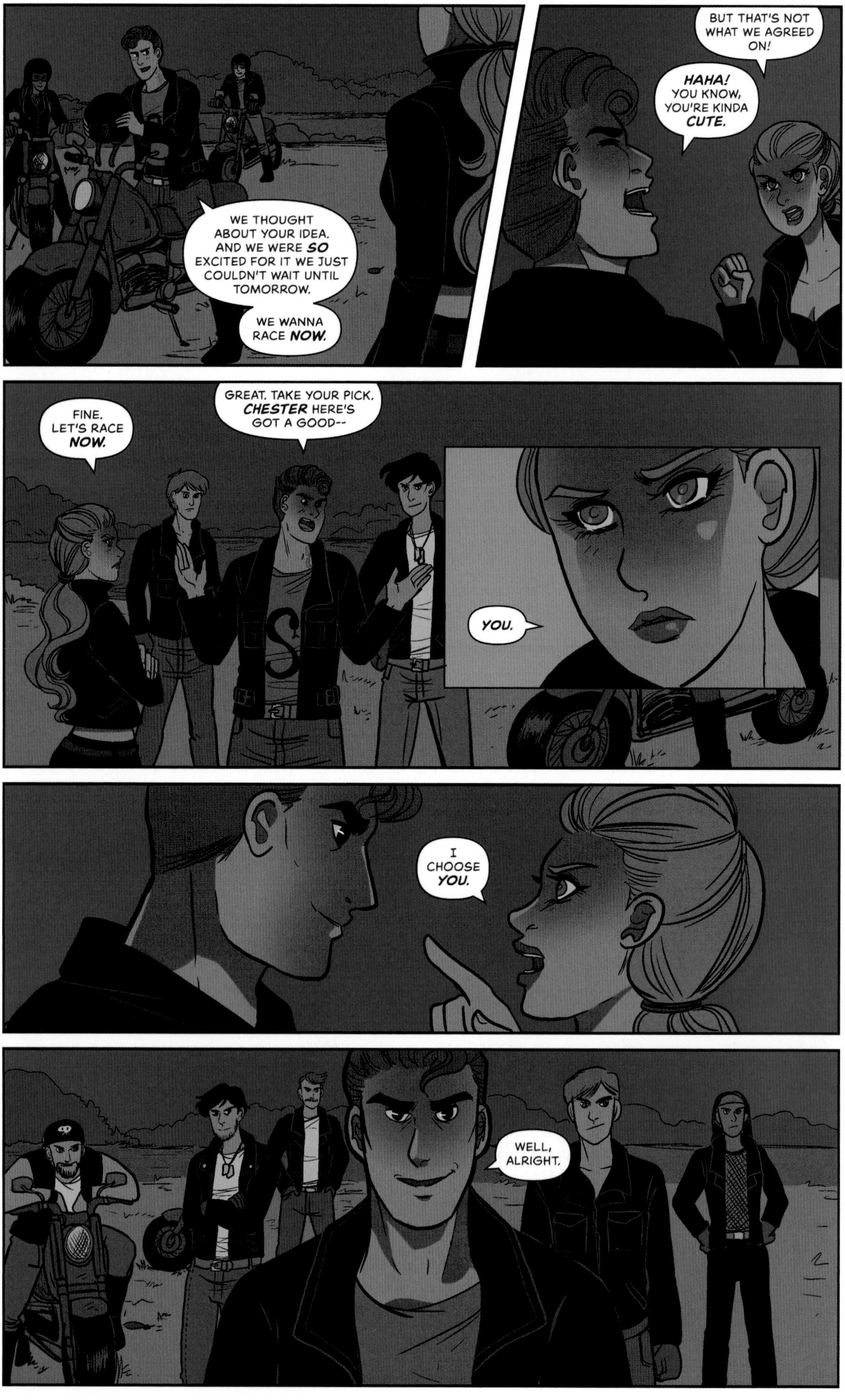
WE THOUGHT ABOUT YOUR IDEA, AND WE WERE SO EXCITED FOR IT WE JUST COULDN'T WAIT UNTIL TOMORROW.
WE WANNA RACE NOW.
BUT THAT'S NOT WHAT WE AGREED ON!
HAHA! YOU KNOW, YOU'RE KINDA CUTE.
FINE, LET'S RACE NOW.
GREAT. TAKE YOUR PICK. CHESTER HERE'S GOT A GOOD--
YOU.
I CHOOSE YOU.
WELL, ALRIGHT.

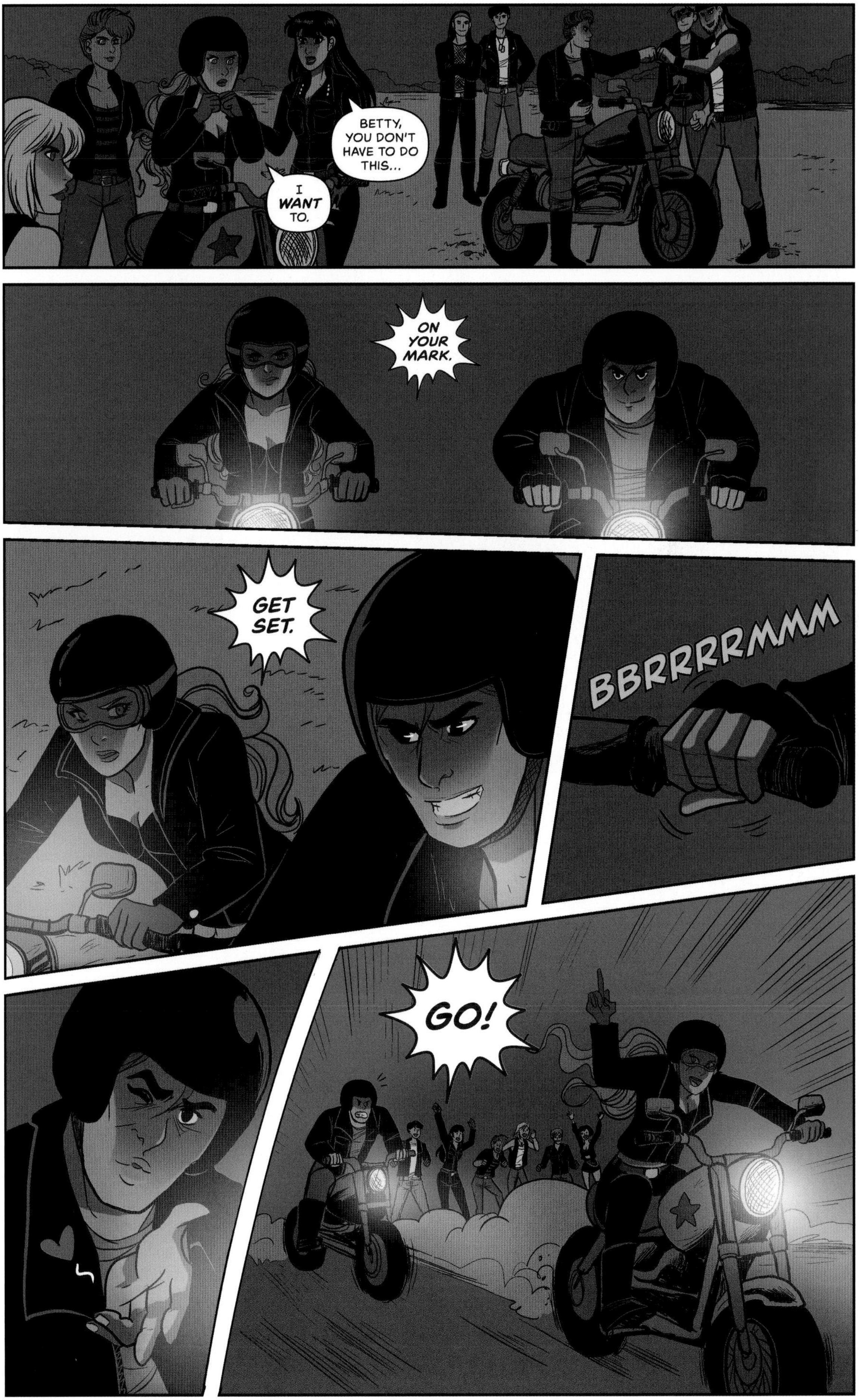
BETTY, YOU DON'T HAVE TO DO THIS...
I WANT TO.
ON YOUR MARK.
GET SET.
BBRRRRMMM
GO!

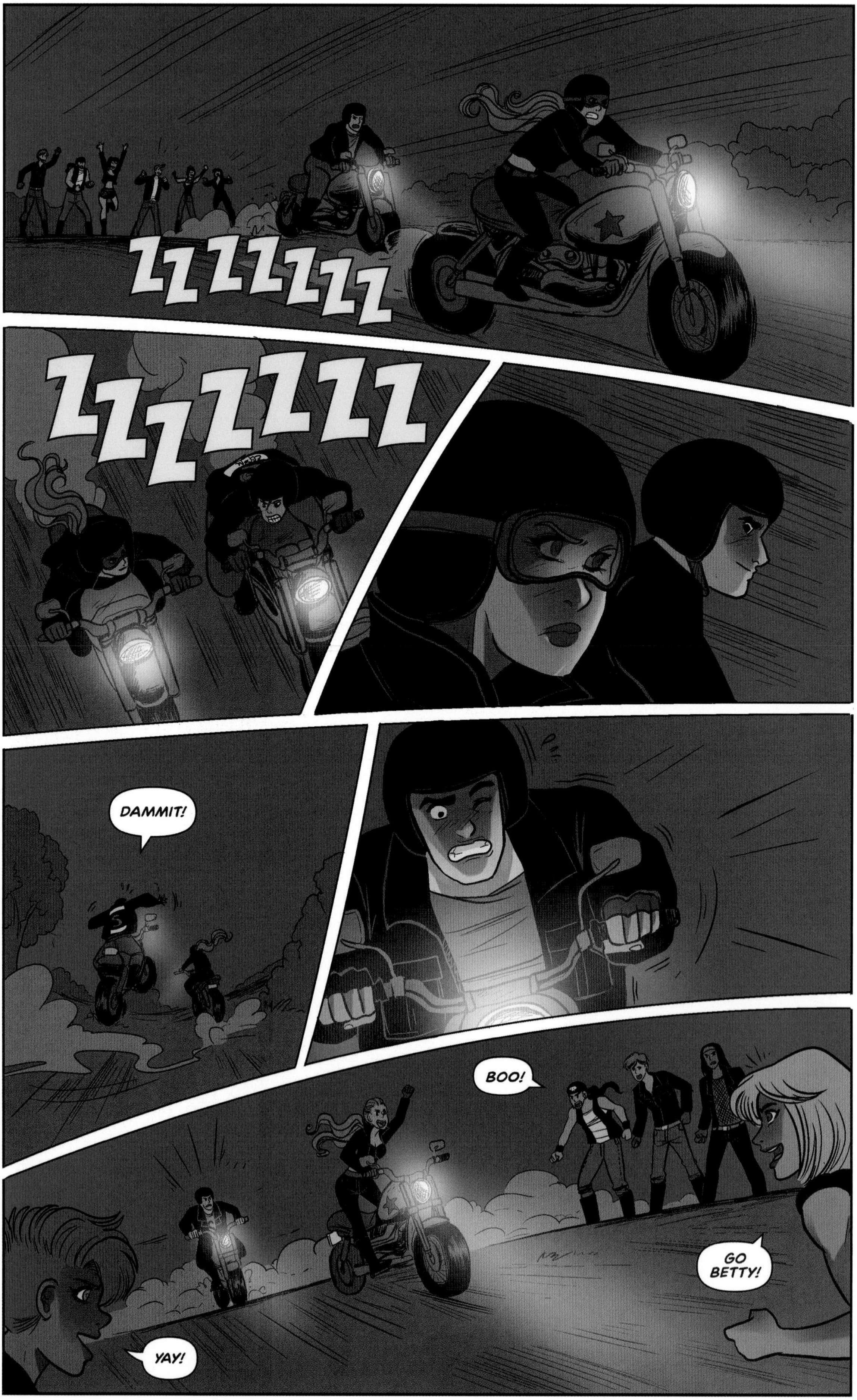
ZZZZZZZZ
ZZZZZZZ
DAMMIT!
BOO!
GO BETTY!
YAY!

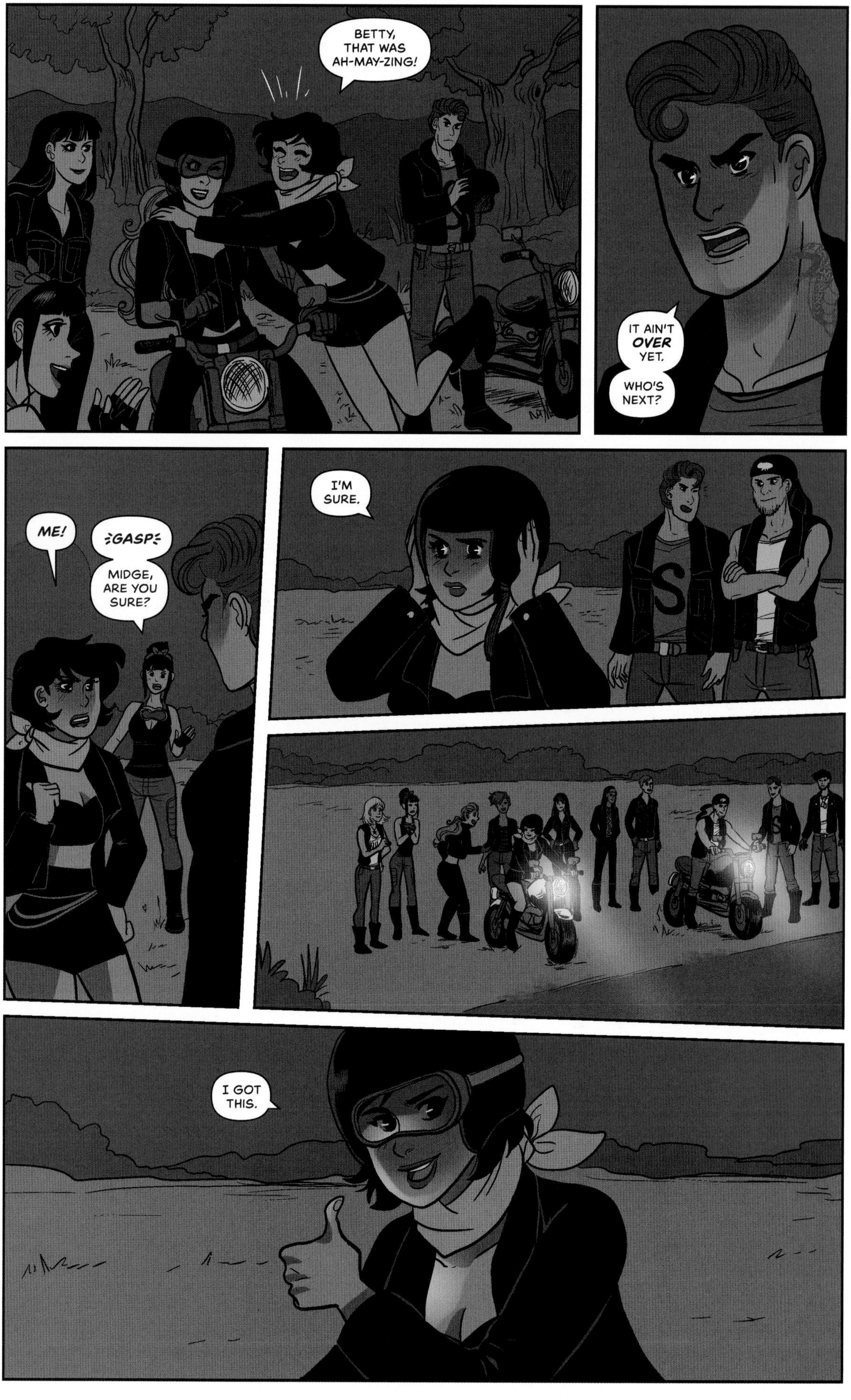
BETTY, THAT WAS AH-MAY-ZING!
IT AIN'T OVER YET.
WHO'S NEXT?
ME!
GASP
MIDGE, ARE YOU SURE?
I'M SURE.
I GOT THIS.

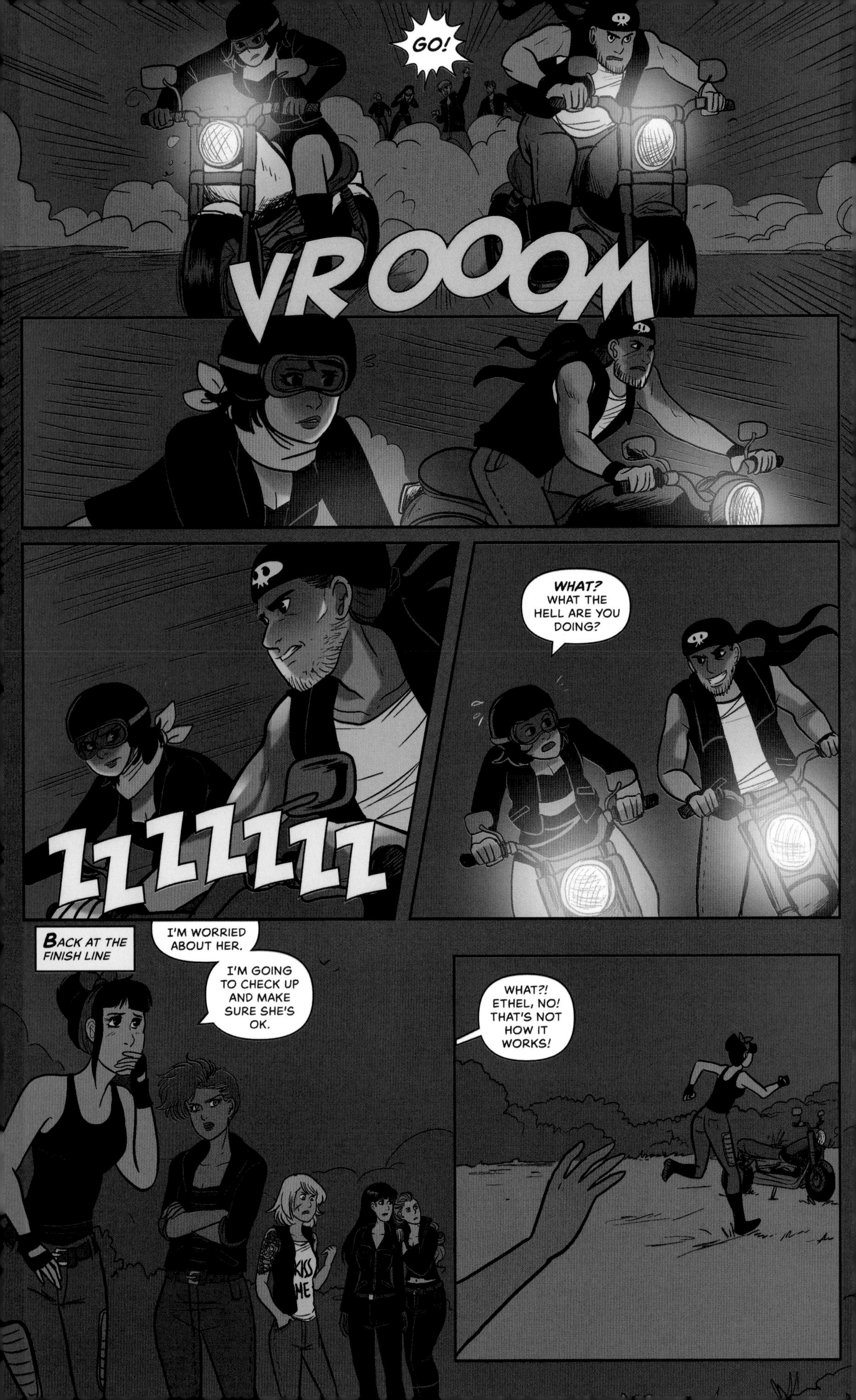
GO!
VROOOM
WHAT? WHAT THE HELL ARE YOU DOING?
ZZZZZZZZ
BACK AT THE FINISH LINE
I'M WORRIED ABOUT HER.
I'M GOING TO CHECK UP AND MAKE SURE SHE'S OK.
WHAT?! ETHEL, NO! THAT'S NOT HOW IT WORKS!

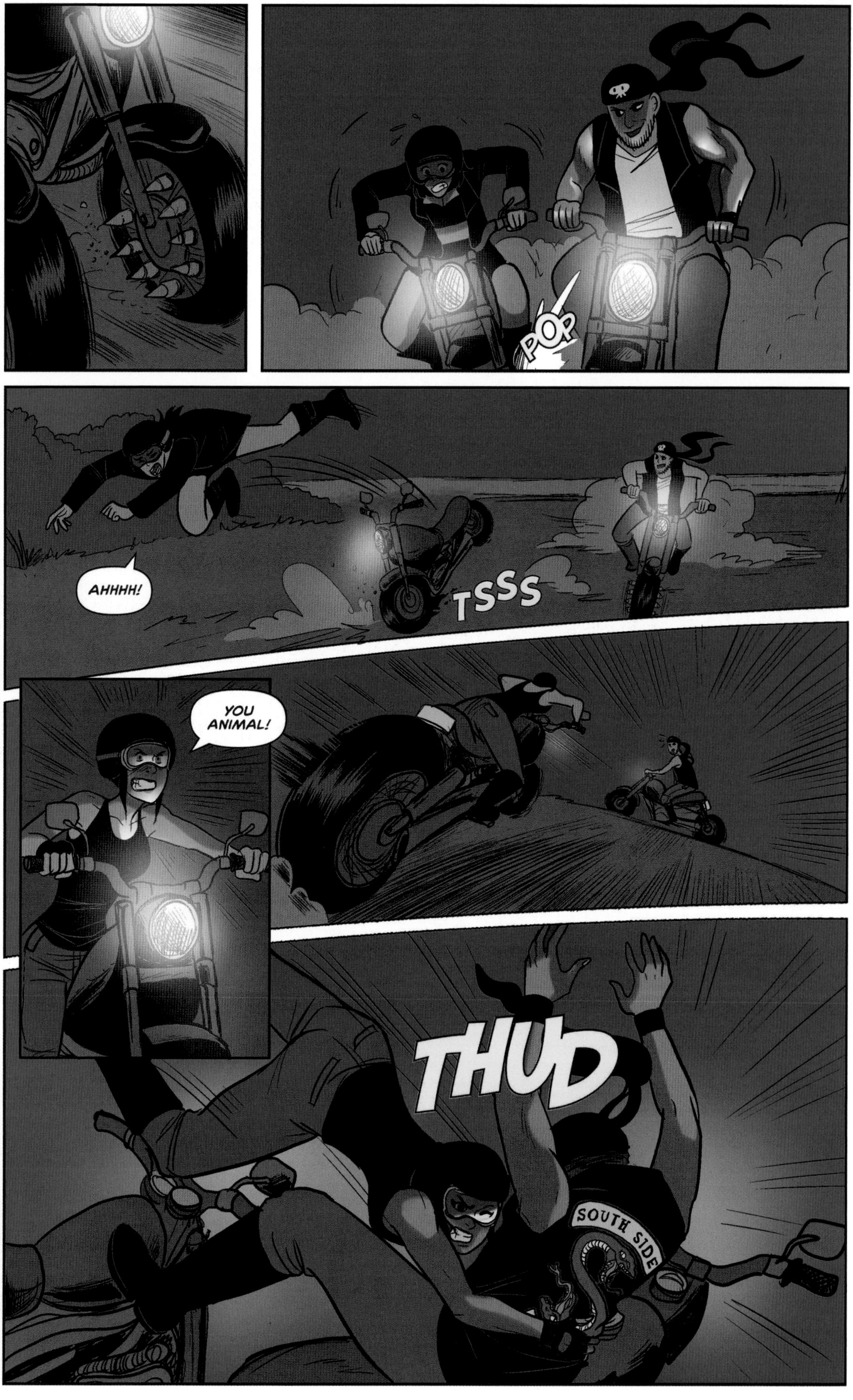
POP
AHHHH!
TSSS
YOU ANIMAL!
THUD
SOUTH SIDE

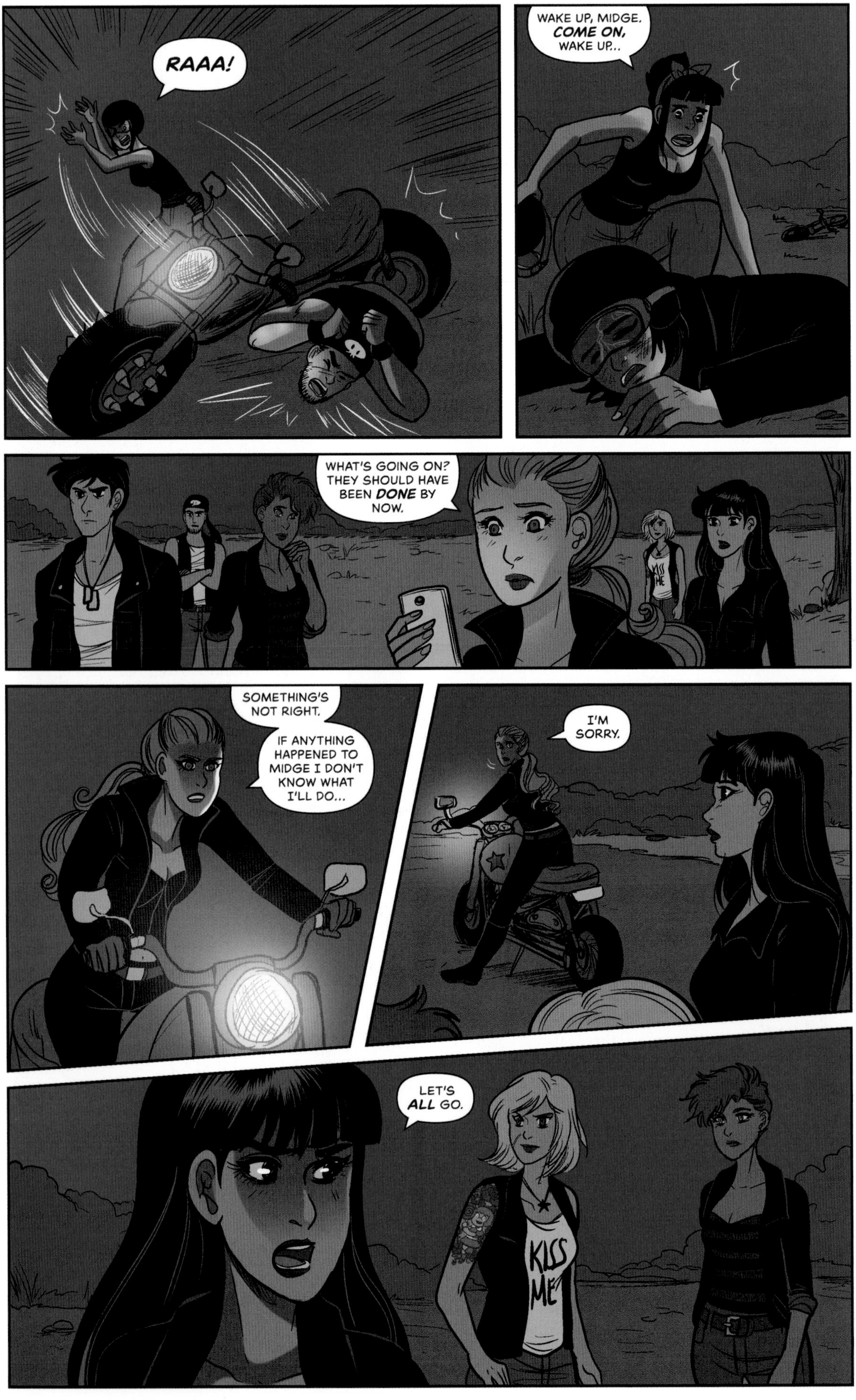
RAAA!
WAKE UP, MIDGE. **COME ON,** WAKE UP...
WHAT'S GOING ON? THEY SHOULD HAVE BEEN **DONE** BY NOW.
KISS ME
SOMETHING'S NOT RIGHT.
IF ANYTHING HAPPENED TO MIDGE I DON'T KNOW WHAT I'LL DO...
I'M SORRY.
LET'S **ALL** GO.
KISS ME

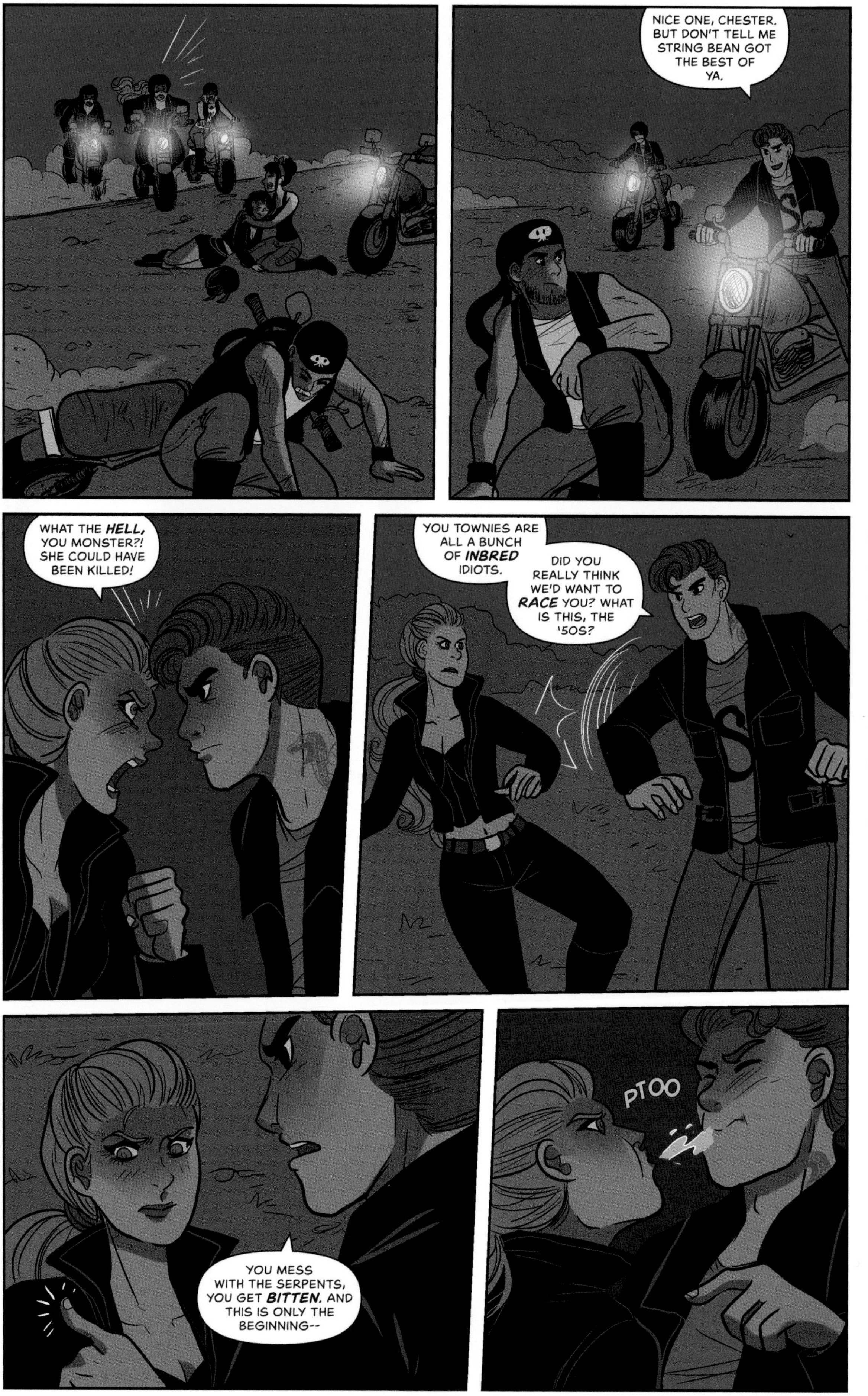
NICE ONE, CHESTER. BUT DON'T TELL ME STRING BEAN GOT THE BEST OF YA.
WHAT THE HELL, YOU MONSTER?! SHE COULD HAVE BEEN KILLED!
YOU TOWNIES ARE ALL A BUNCH OF INBRED IDIOTS.
DID YOU REALLY THINK WE'D WANT TO RACE YOU? WHAT IS THIS, THE '50S?
YOU MESS WITH THE SERPENTS, YOU GET BITTEN. AND THIS IS ONLY THE BEGINNING--
PTOO

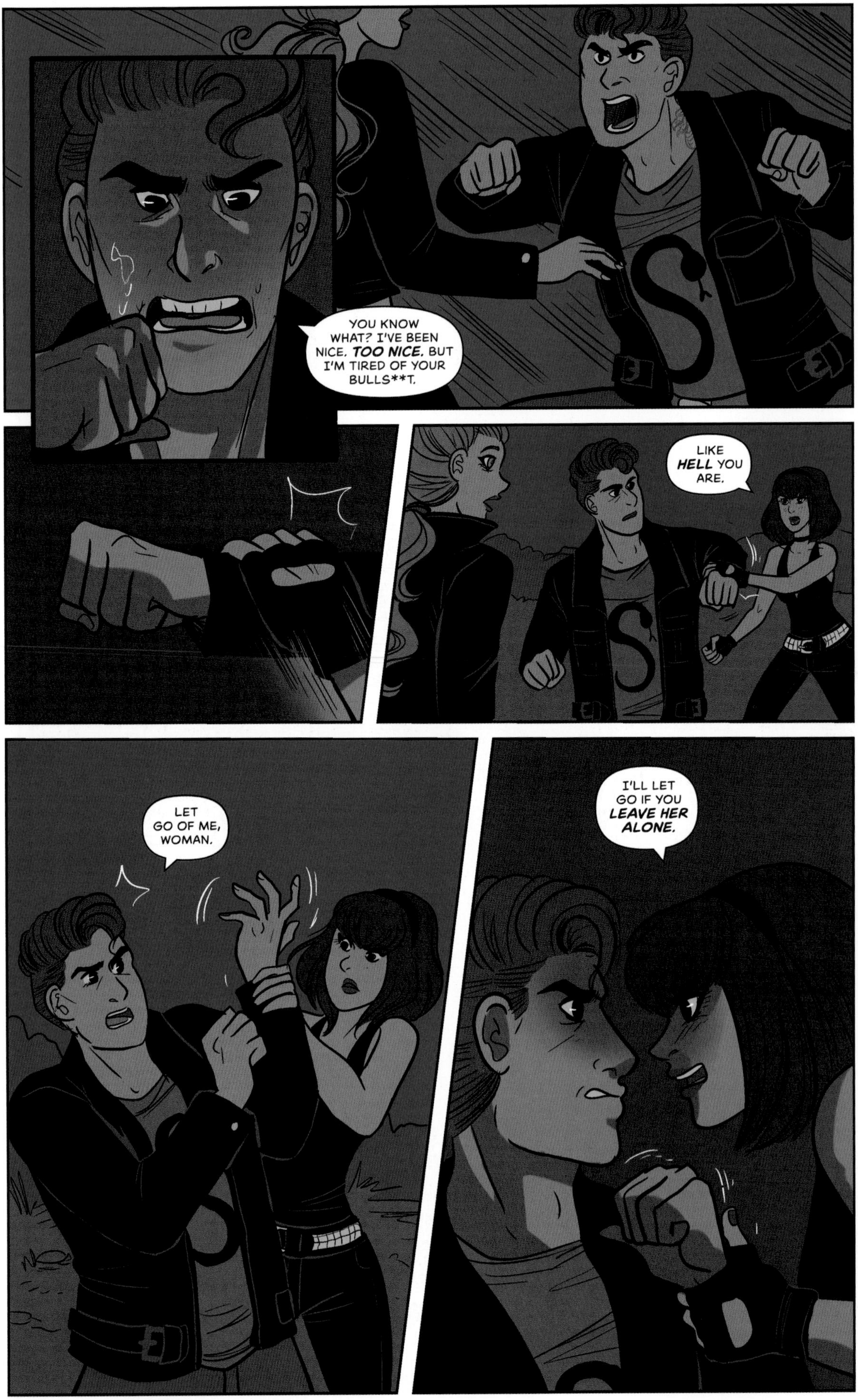

YOU KNOW WHAT? I'VE BEEN NICE. TOO NICE. BUT I'M TIRED OF YOUR BULLS**T.
LIKE HELL YOU ARE.
LET GO OF ME, WOMAN.
I'LL LET GO IF YOU LEAVE HER ALONE.

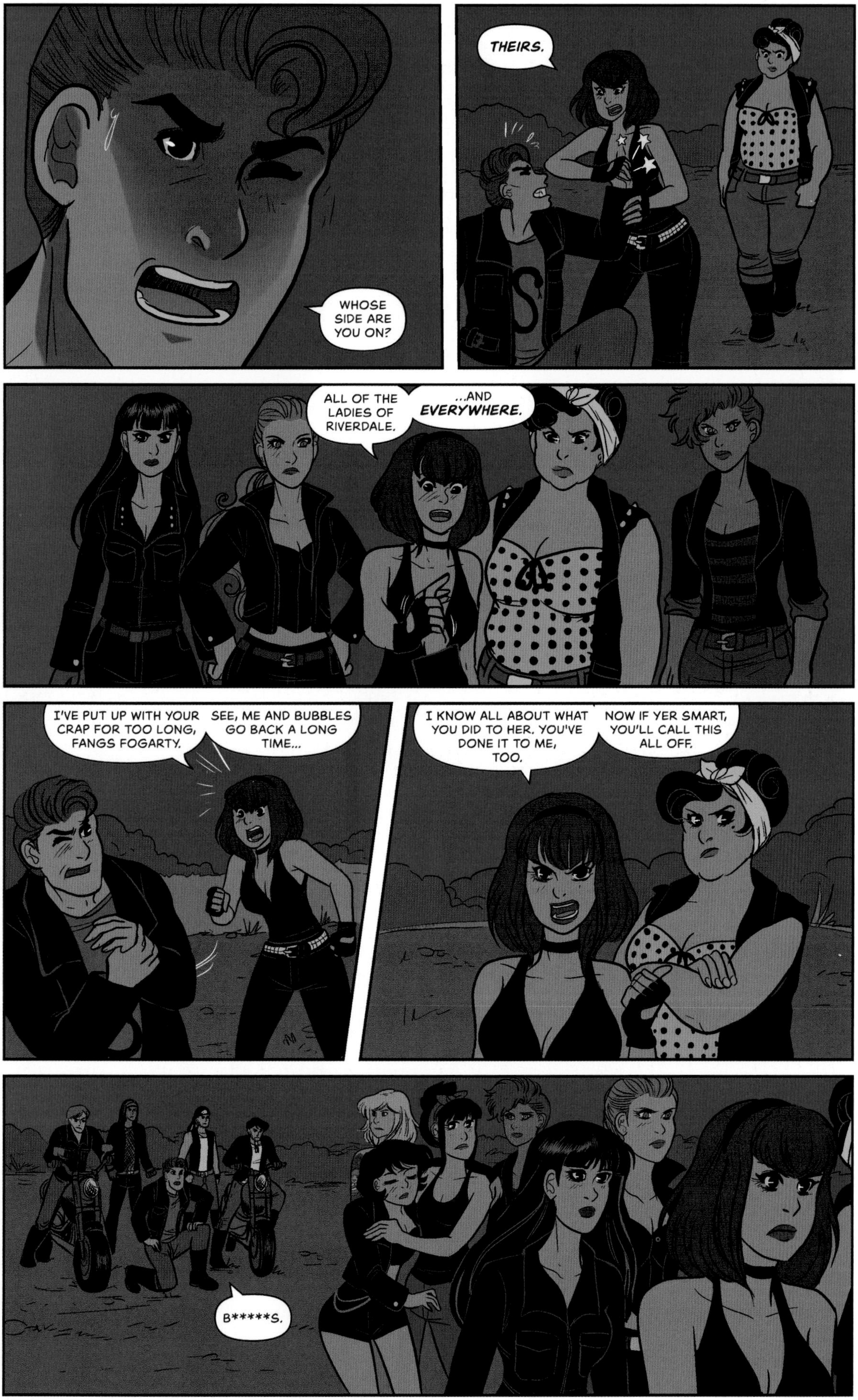
WHOSE SIDE ARE YOU ON?
THEIRS.
ALL OF THE LADIES OF RIVERDALE.
...AND EVERYWHERE.
I'VE PUT UP WITH YOUR CRAP FOR TOO LONG, FANGS FOGARTY.
SEE, ME AND BUBBLES GO BACK A LONG TIME...
I KNOW ALL ABOUT WHAT YOU DID TO HER. YOU'VE DONE IT TO ME, TOO.
NOW IF YER SMART, YOU'LL CALL THIS ALL OFF.
B*****S.

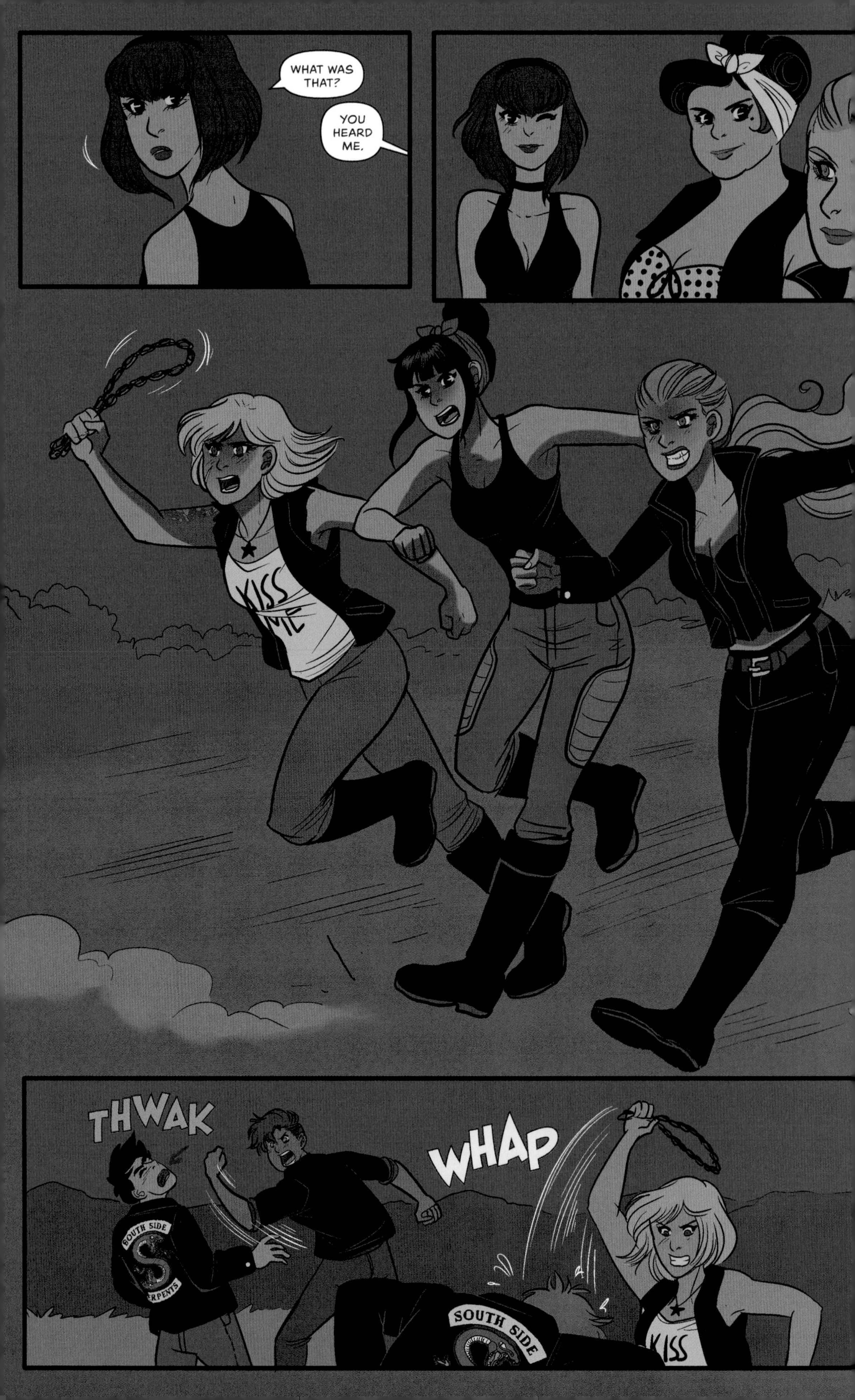
WHAT WAS THAT?
YOU HEARD ME.
KISS ME
THWAK
SOUTH SIDE SERPENTS
WHAP
SOUTH SIDE
KISS

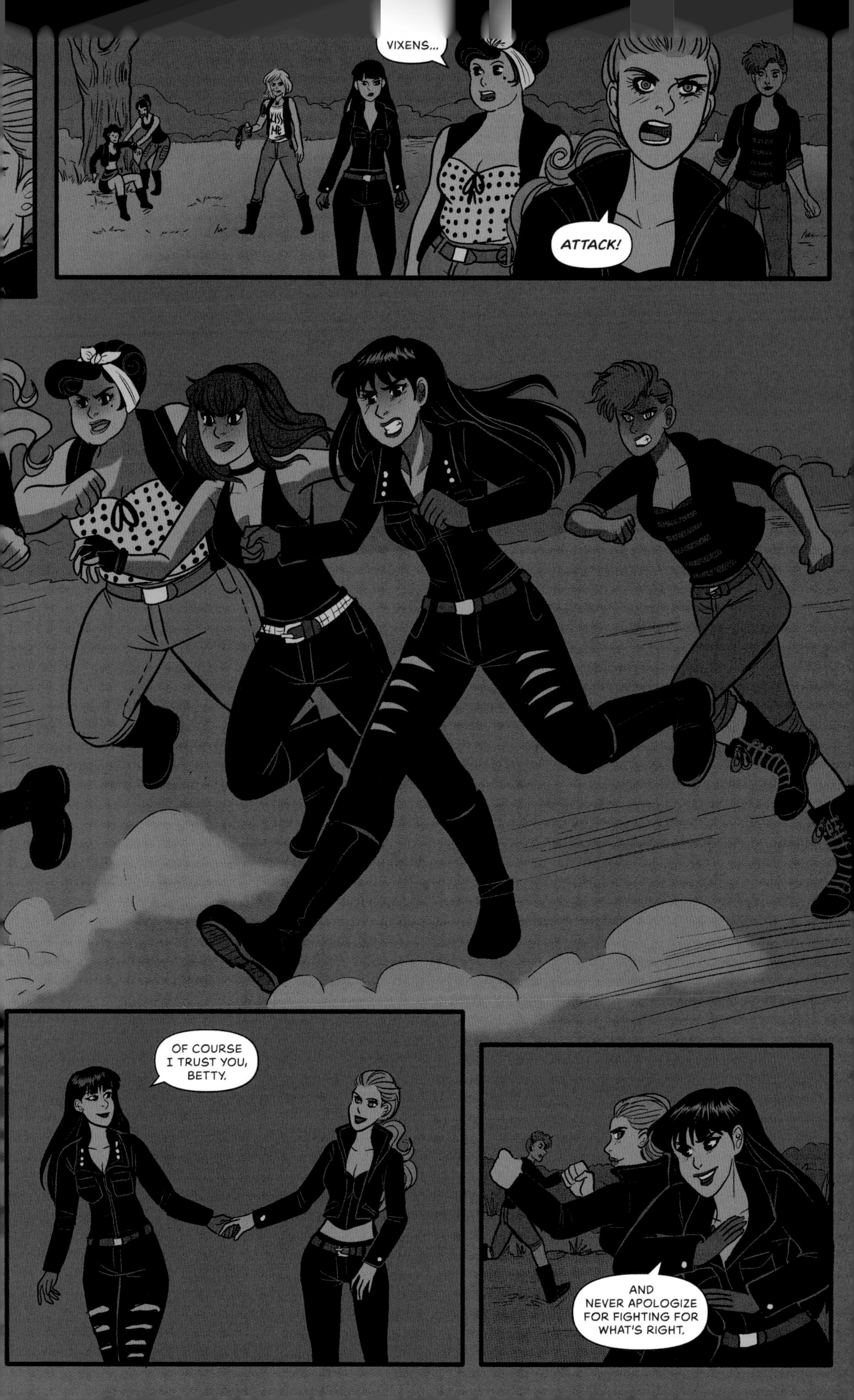
VIXENS...
ATTACK!
OF COURSE I TRUST YOU, BETTY.
AND NEVER APOLOGIZE FOR FIGHTING FOR WHAT'S RIGHT.

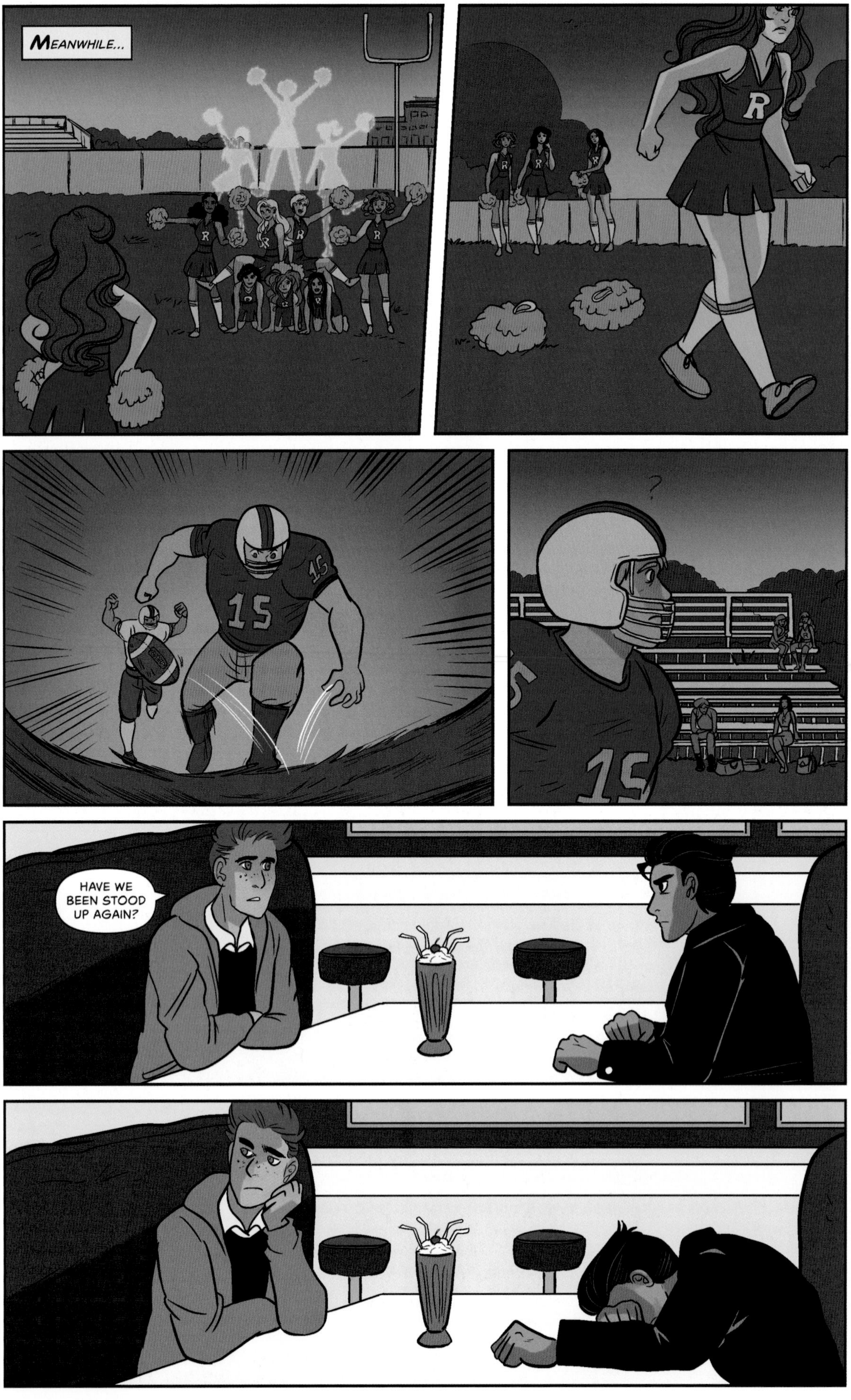
MEANWHILE...
15
15
?
15
15
HAVE WE BEEN STOOD UP AGAIN?

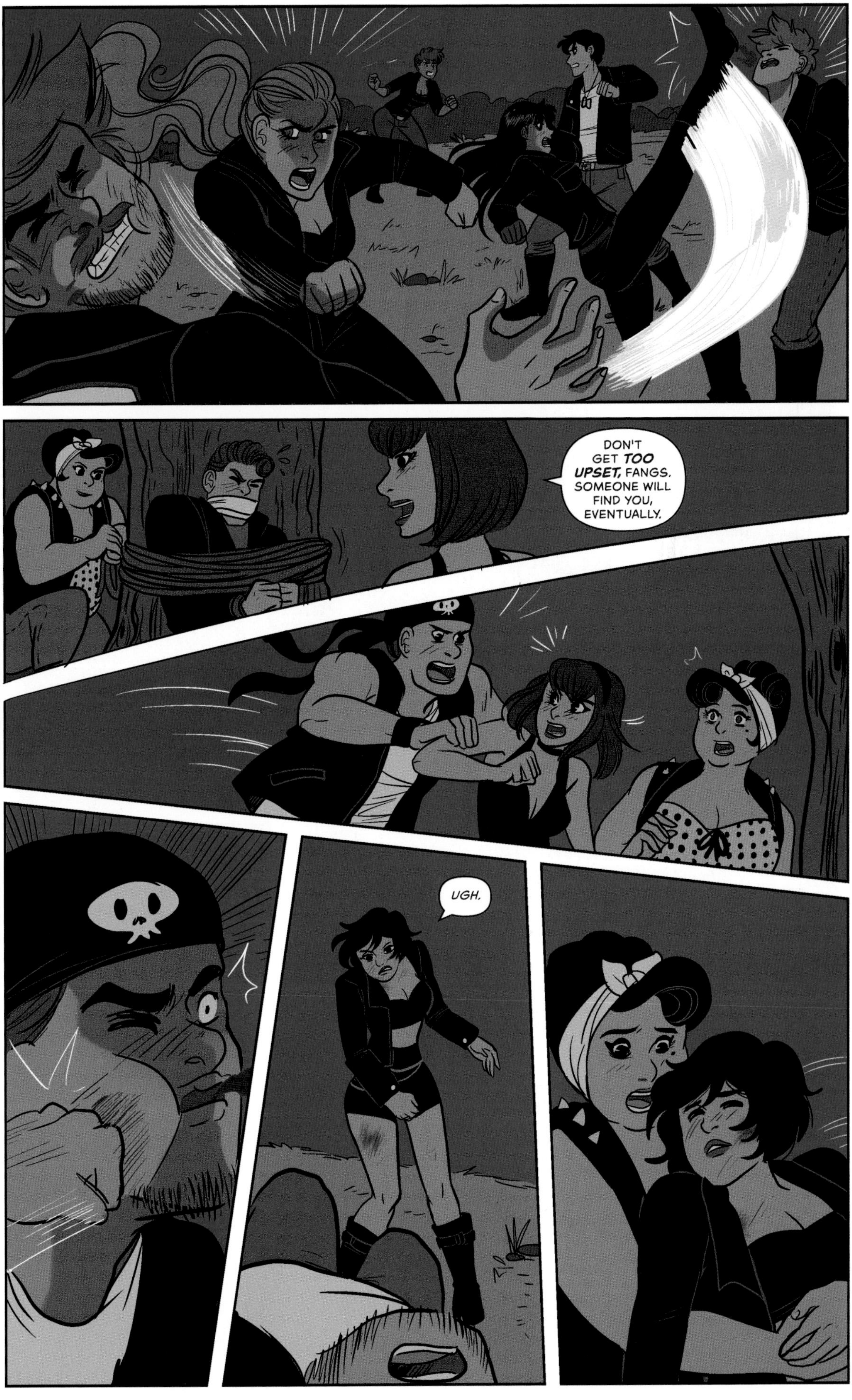
DON'T GET TOO UPSET, FANGS. SOMEONE WILL FIND YOU, EVENTUALLY.
UGH.

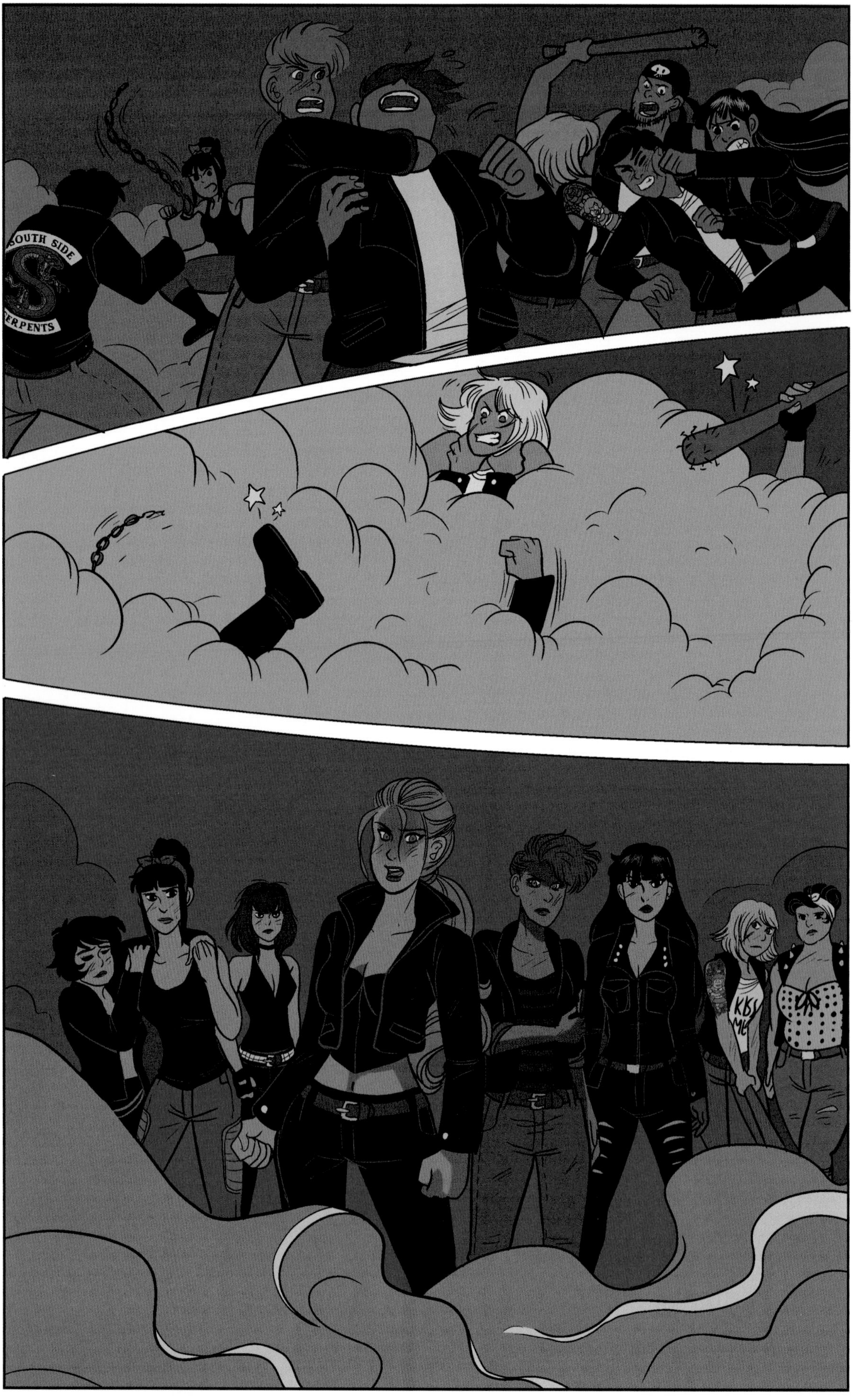
SOUTH SIDE
SERPENTS

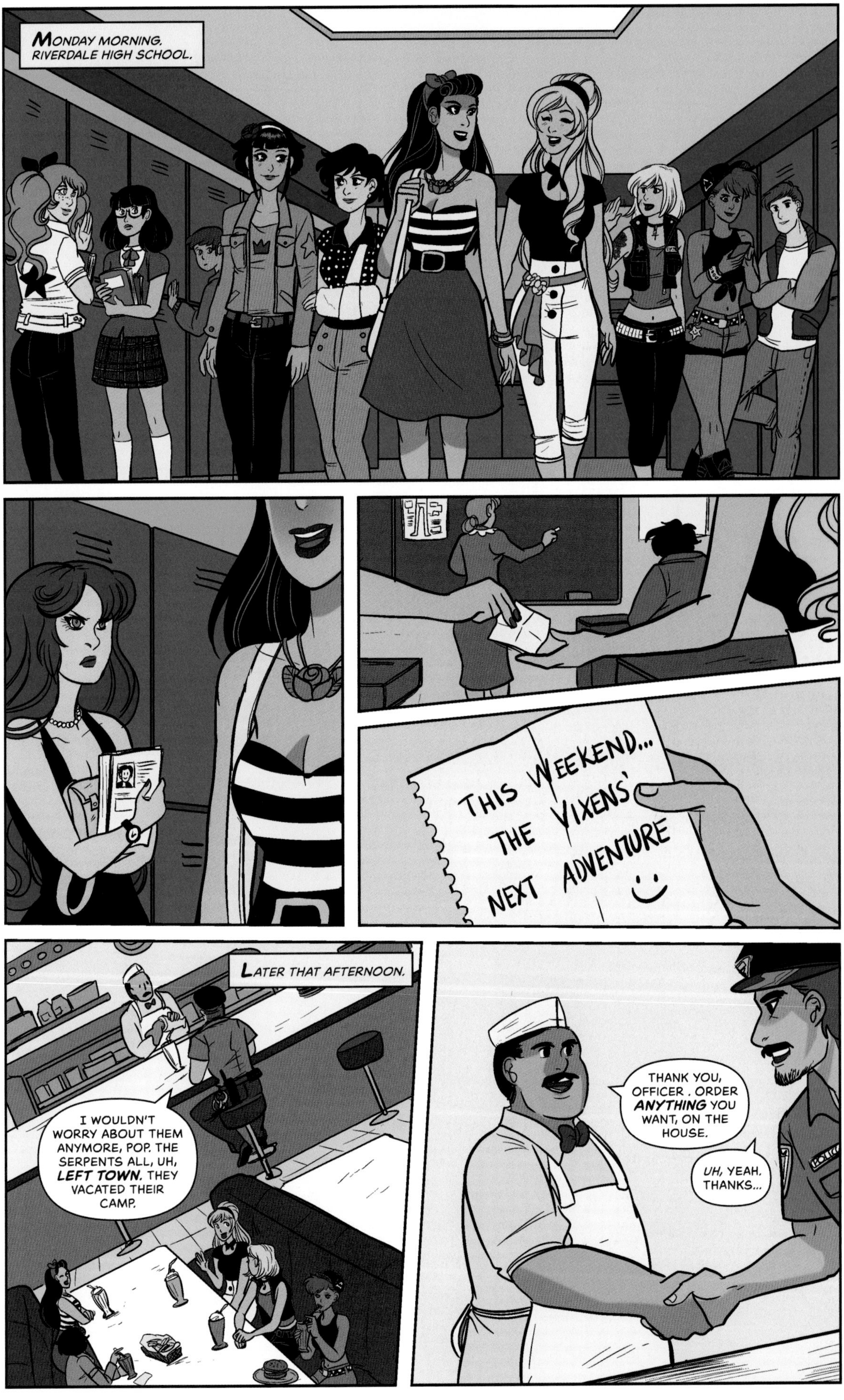
MONDAY MORNING.
RIVERDALE HIGH SCHOOL.
THIS WEEKEND... THE VIXENS' NEXT ADVENTURE
LATER THAT AFTERNOON.
I WOULDN'T WORRY ABOUT THEM ANYMORE, POP. THE SERPENTS ALL, UH, LEFT TOWN. THEY VACATED THEIR CAMP.
THANK YOU, OFFICER . ORDER ANYTHING YOU WANT, ON THE HOUSE.
UH, YEAH. THANKS...

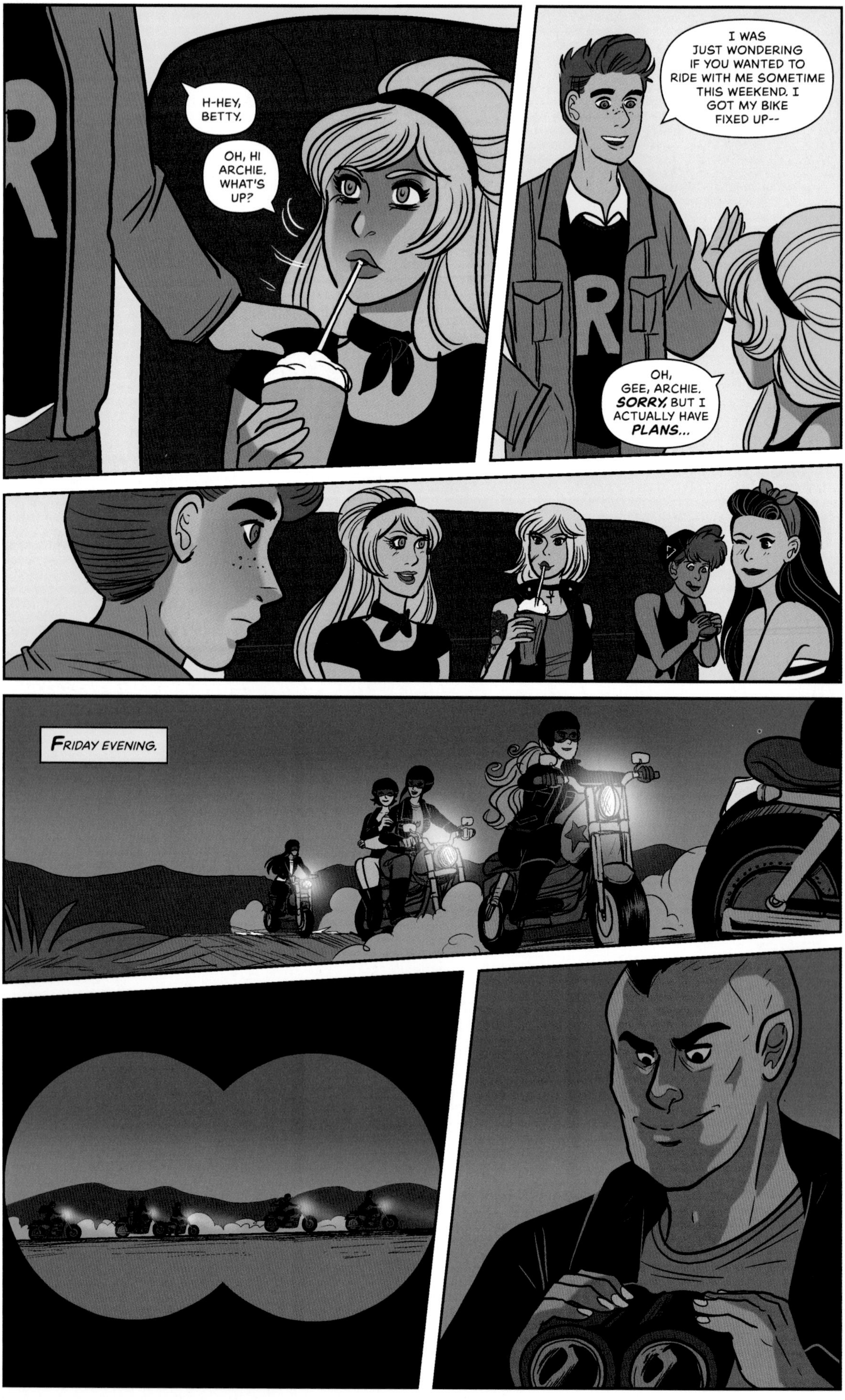
H-HEY, BETTY.
OH, HI ARCHIE. WHAT'S UP?
I WAS JUST WONDERING IF YOU WANTED TO RIDE WITH ME SOMETIME THIS WEEKEND. I GOT MY BIKE FIXED UP--
OH, GEE, ARCHIE. SORRY, BUT I ACTUALLY HAVE PLANS...
FRIDAY EVENING.

to be continued...

Chapter Five

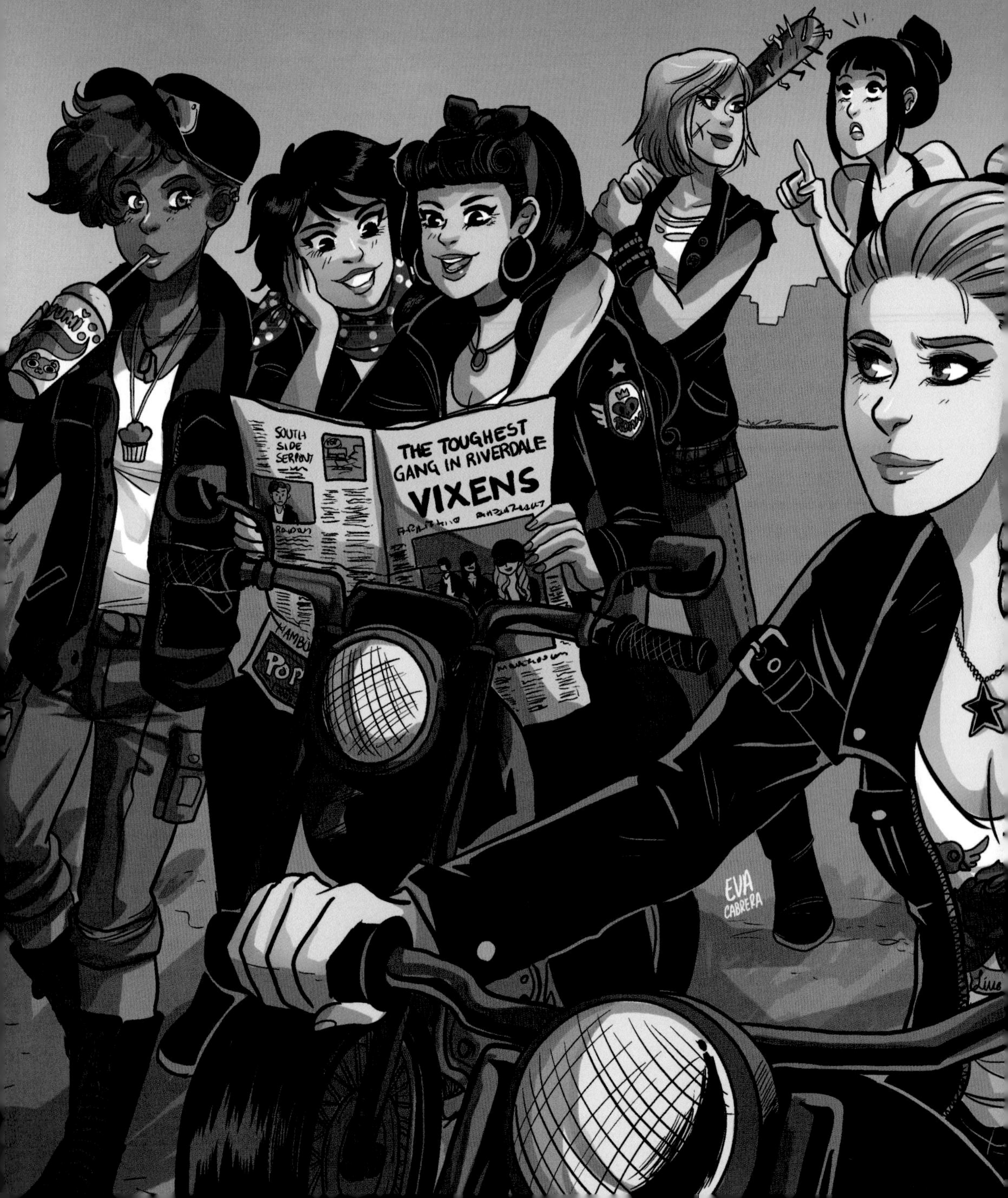

SOUTH SIDE SERPENT
THE TOUGHEST GANG IN RIVERDALE
VIXENS
POP
EVA CABRERA

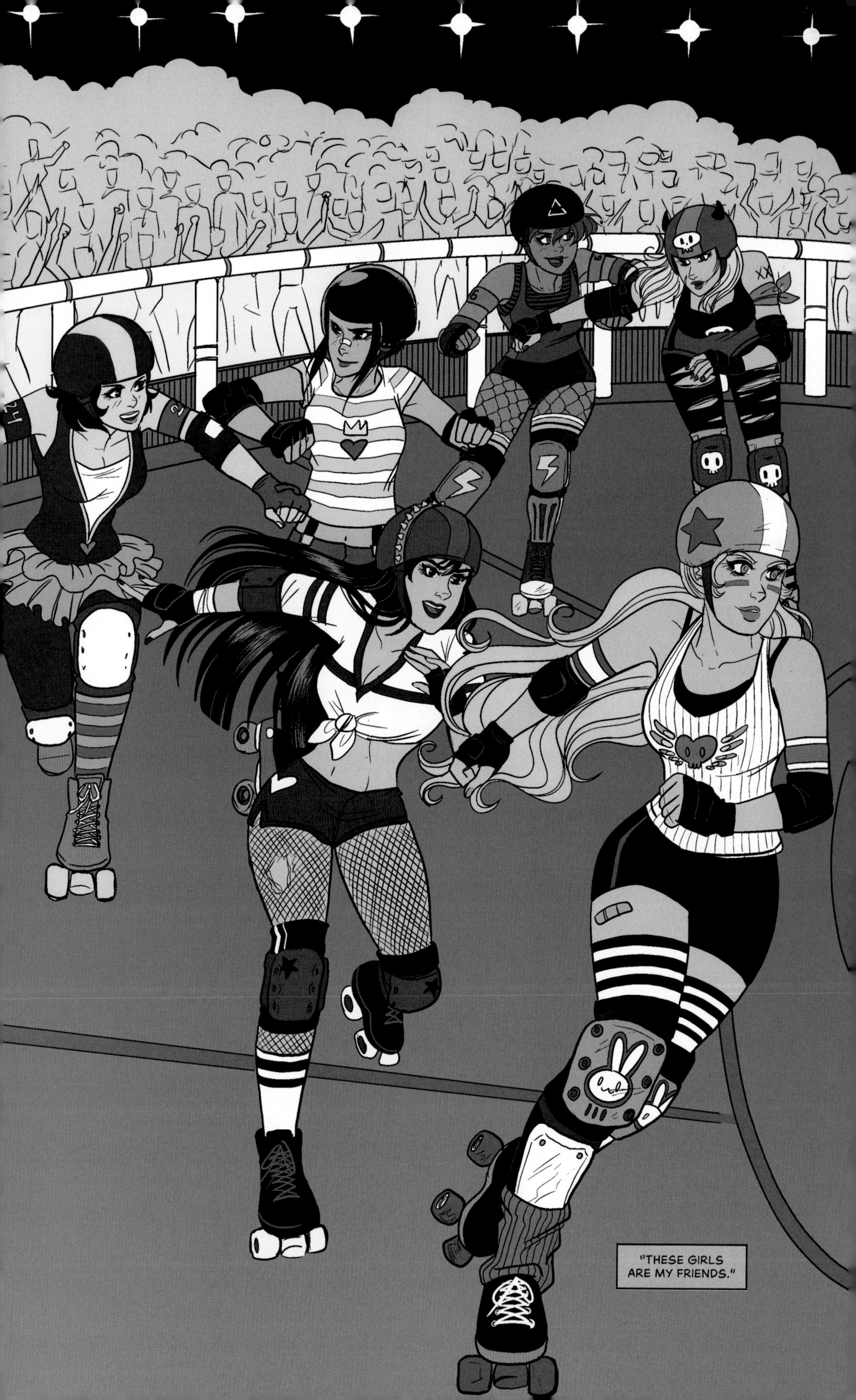
"THESE GIRLS
ARE MY FRIENDS."

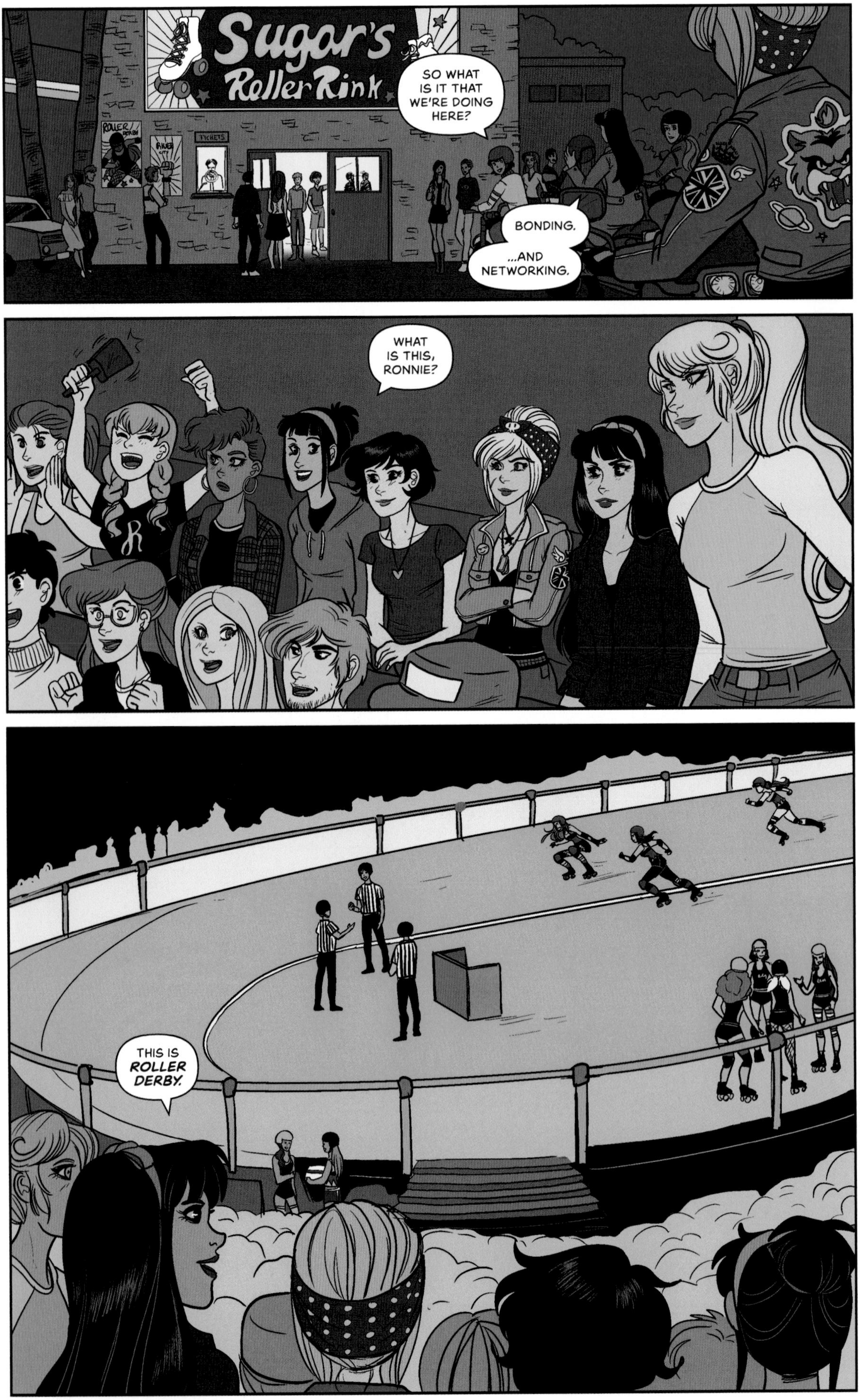
Sugar's Roller Rink
SO WHAT IS IT THAT WE'RE DOING HERE?
BONDING.
...AND NETWORKING.
WHAT IS THIS, RONNIE?
THIS IS ROLLER DERBY.

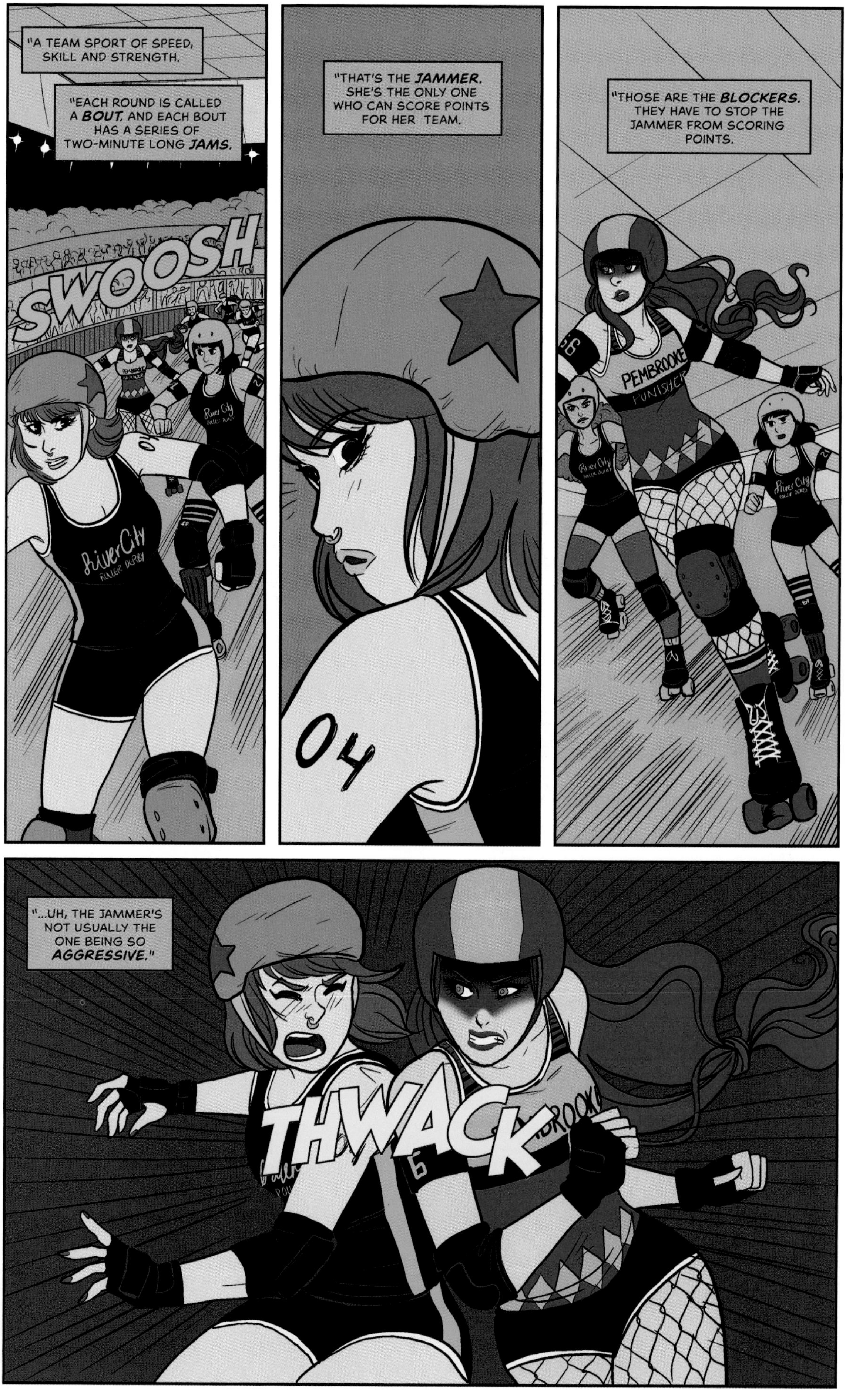
"A TEAM SPORT OF SPEED, SKILL AND STRENGTH.
"EACH ROUND IS CALLED A BOUT, AND EACH BOUT HAS A SERIES OF TWO-MINUTE LONG JAMS.
SWOOSH
"THAT'S THE JAMMER. SHE'S THE ONLY ONE WHO CAN SCORE POINTS FOR HER TEAM.
04
"THOSE ARE THE BLOCKERS. THEY HAVE TO STOP THE JAMMER FROM SCORING POINTS.
PEMBROOKE
PUNISHER
River City
ROLLER DERBY
"...UH, THE JAMMER'S NOT USUALLY THE ONE BEING SO AGGRESSIVE."
THWACK

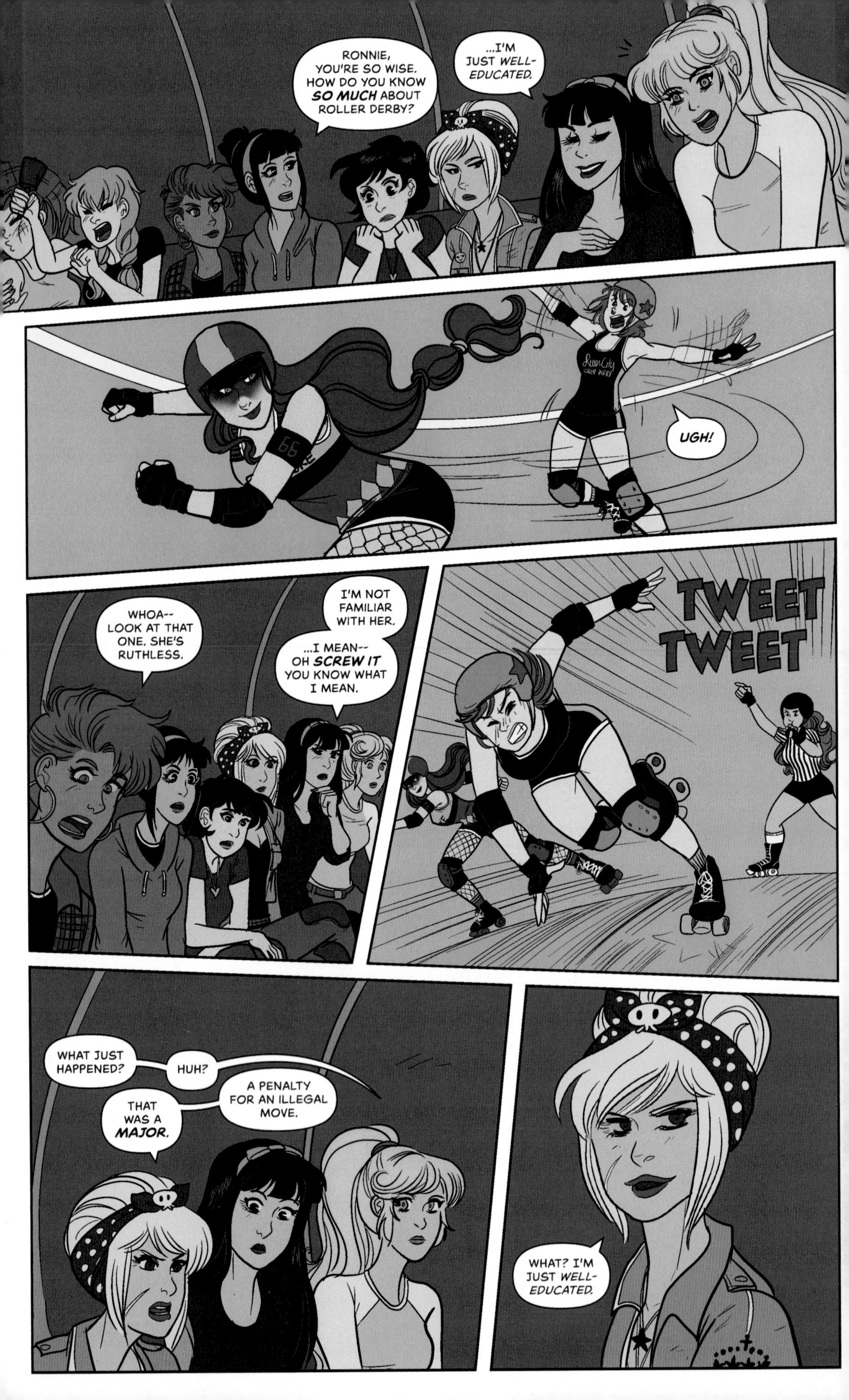
RONNIE, YOU'RE SO WISE. HOW DO YOU KNOW SO MUCH ABOUT ROLLER DERBY?
...I'M JUST WELL-EDUCATED.
UGH!
WHOA-- LOOK AT THAT ONE. SHE'S RUTHLESS.
I'M NOT FAMILIAR WITH HER.
...I MEAN-- OH SCREW IT YOU KNOW WHAT I MEAN.
TWEET TWEET
WHAT JUST HAPPENED?
HUH?
THAT WAS A MAJOR.
A PENALTY FOR AN ILLEGAL MOVE.
WHAT? I'M JUST WELL-EDUCATED.

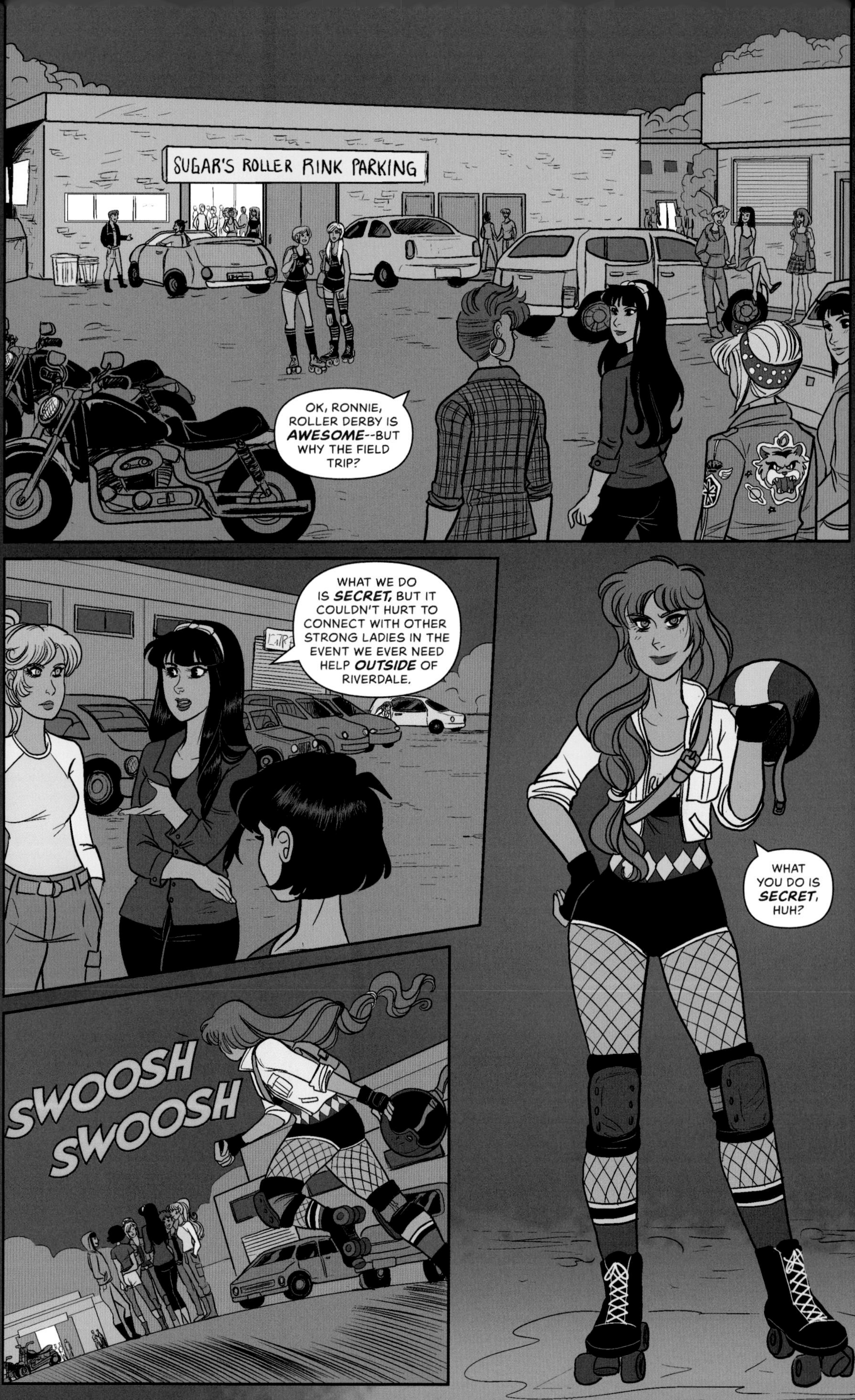

SUGAR'S ROLLER RINK PARKING
OK, RONNIE, ROLLER DERBY IS AWESOME--BUT WHY THE FIELD TRIP?
WHAT WE DO IS SECRET, BUT IT COULDN'T HURT TO CONNECT WITH OTHER STRONG LADIES IN THE EVENT WE EVER NEED HELP OUTSIDE OF RIVERDALE.
WHAT YOU DO IS SECRET, HUH?
SWOOSH
SWOOSH

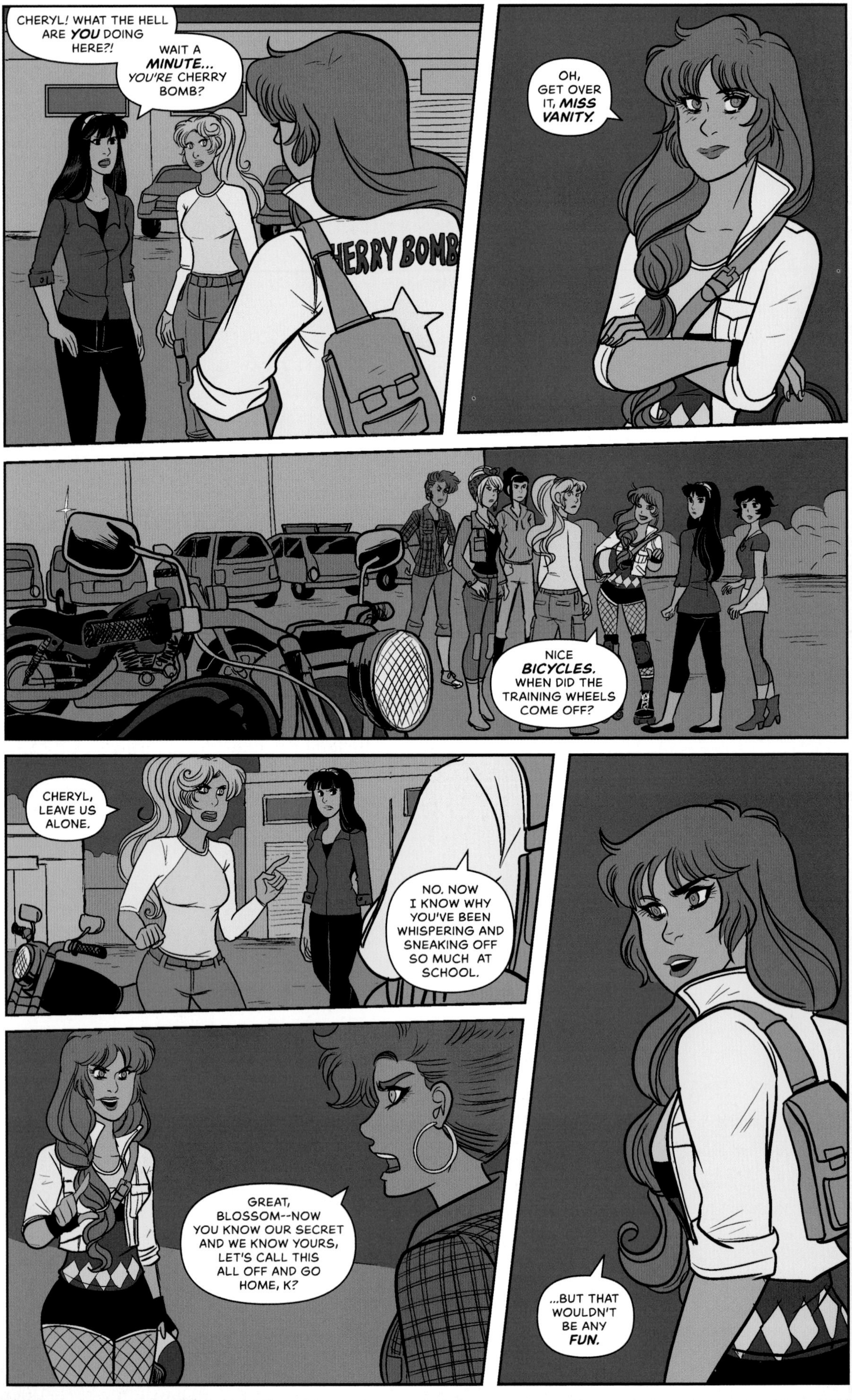

CHERYL! WHAT THE HELL ARE YOU DOING HERE?!
WAIT A MINUTE... YOU'RE CHERRY BOMB?
CHERRY BOMB
OH, GET OVER IT, MISS VANITY.
NICE BICYCLES. WHEN DID THE TRAINING WHEELS COME OFF?
CHERYL, LEAVE US ALONE.
NO. NOW I KNOW WHY YOU'VE BEEN WHISPERING AND SNEAKING OFF SO MUCH AT SCHOOL.
GREAT, BLOSSOM--NOW YOU KNOW OUR SECRET AND WE KNOW YOURS, LET'S CALL THIS ALL OFF AND GO HOME, K?
...BUT THAT WOULDN'T BE ANY FUN.

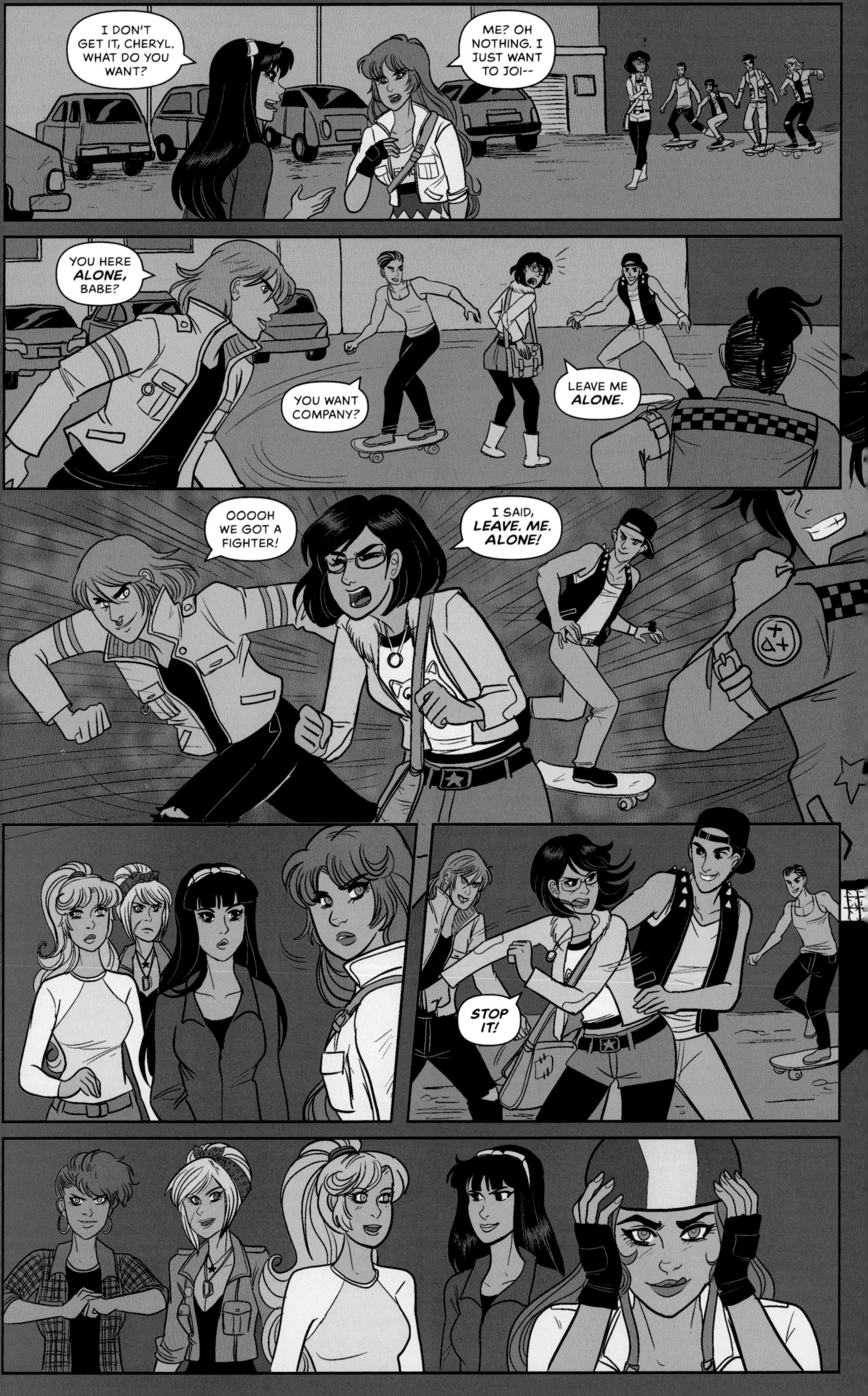
I DON'T GET IT, CHERYL. WHAT DO YOU WANT?
ME? OH NOTHING. I JUST WANT TO JOI--
?
YOU HERE ALONE, BABE?
YOU WANT COMPANY?
LEAVE ME ALONE.
OOOOH WE GOT A FIGHTER!
I SAID, LEAVE. ME. ALONE!
STOP IT!

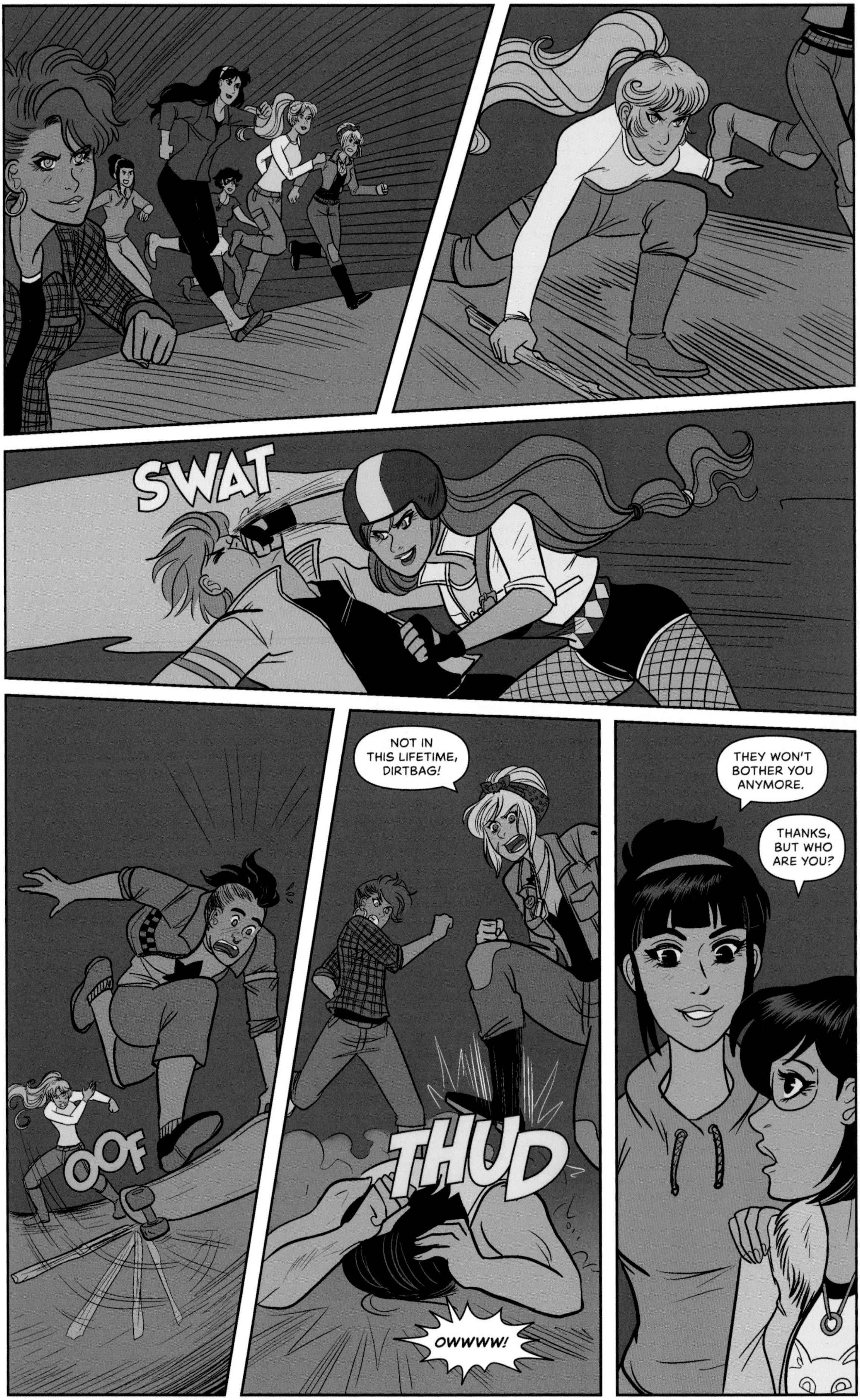
SWAT
OOF
NOT IN THIS LIFETIME, DIRTBAG!
THUD
OWWWW!
THEY WON'T BOTHER YOU ANYMORE.
THANKS, BUT WHO ARE YOU?

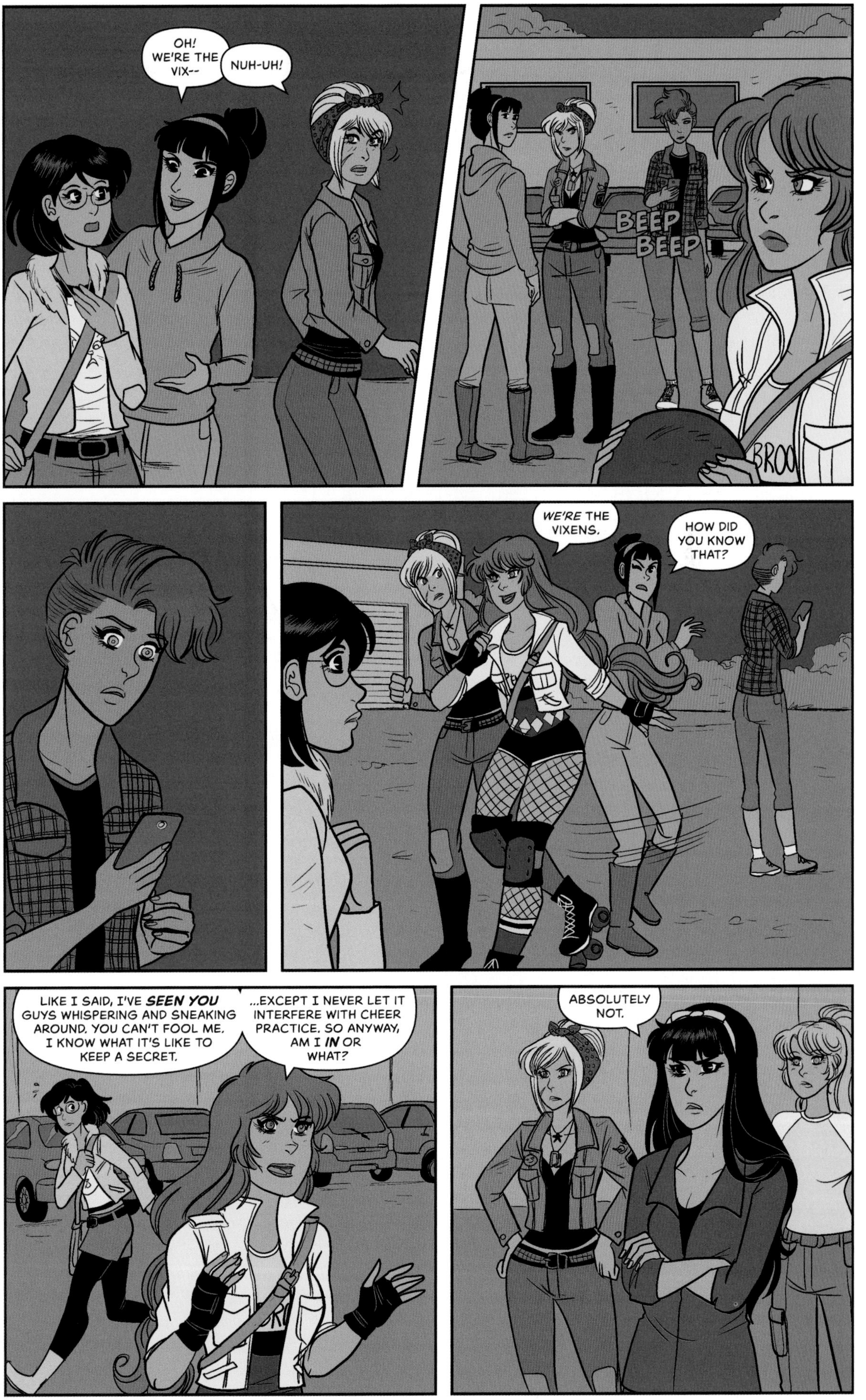
OH! WE'RE THE VIX--
NUH-UH!
BEEP BEEP
BROO
WE'RE THE VIXENS.
HOW DID YOU KNOW THAT?
LIKE I SAID, I'VE SEEN YOU GUYS WHISPERING AND SNEAKING AROUND. YOU CAN'T FOOL ME. I KNOW WHAT IT'S LIKE TO KEEP A SECRET.
...EXCEPT I NEVER LET IT INTERFERE WITH CHEER PRACTICE. SO ANYWAY, AM I IN OR WHAT?
ABSOLUTELY NOT.

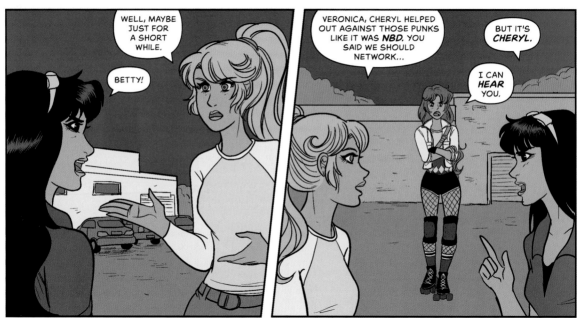

WELL, MAYBE JUST FOR A SHORT WHILE.

BETTY!

VERONICA, CHERYL HELPED OUT AGAINST THOSE PUNKS LIKE IT WAS *NBD*. YOU SAID WE SHOULD NETWORK...

BUT IT'S *CHERYL*.

I CAN *HEAR* YOU.

IF SHE'S IN IT FOR THE GREATER GOOD THEN WHO ARE WE TO STOP HER?

UGH, FINE. GOD I HATE IT WHEN YOU'RE RIGHT.

ALRIGHT, CHERYL. YOU'RE IN.

BUT ONLY ON A *TRIAL* BASIS. YOU SPEAK A WORD OF IT TO ANYONE, YOU BESMIRCH OUR NAME IN ANY WAY, AND YOU'RE OUT.

GOT IT, BOSS. SEE YOU BIRDS MONDAY MORNING.

I'M GOING TO REGRET THIS, AREN'T I?

???

VROOOM

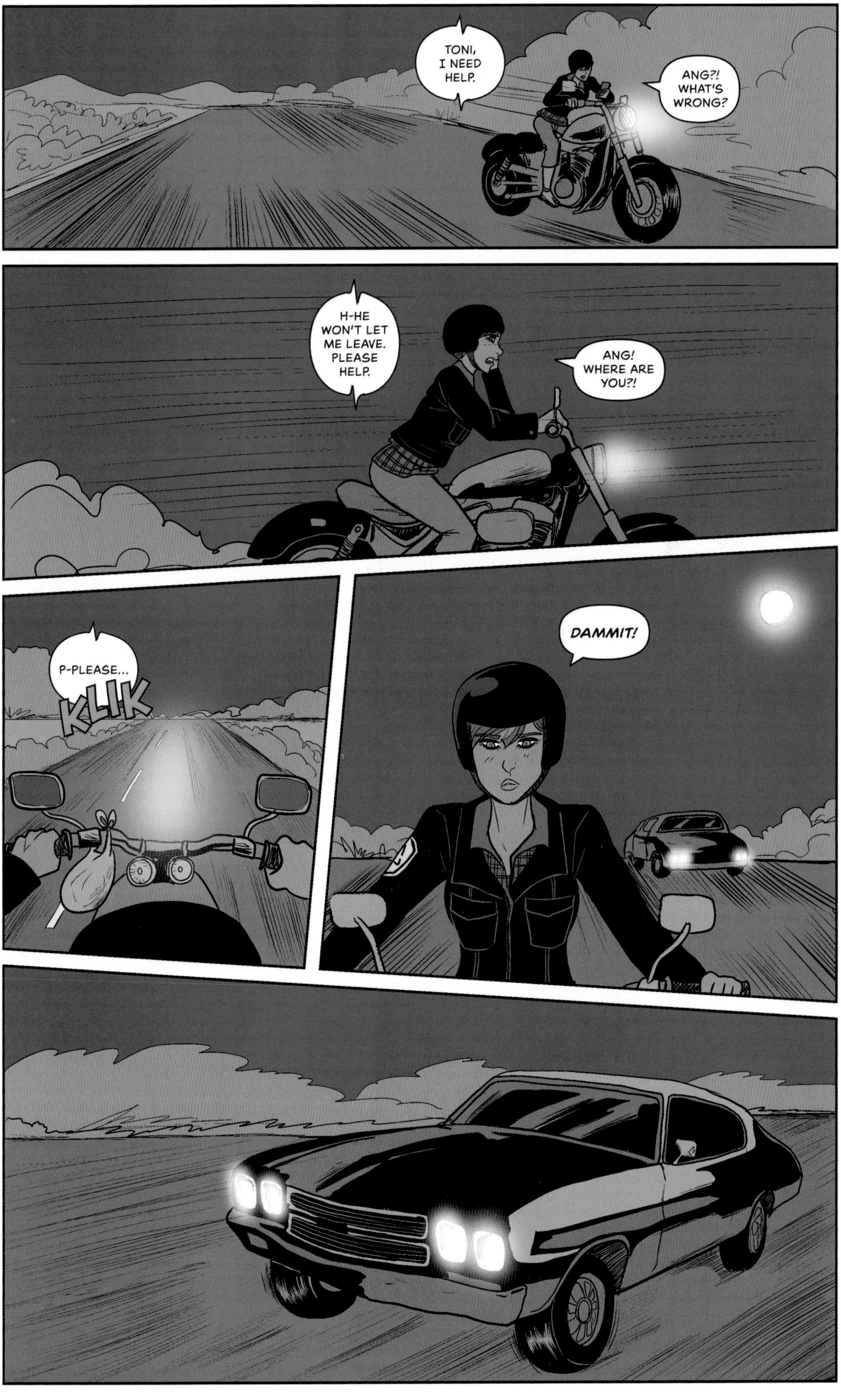
TONI, I NEED HELP.
ANG?! WHAT'S WRONG?
H-HE WON'T LET ME LEAVE. PLEASE HELP.
ANG! WHERE ARE YOU?!
P-PLEASE...
KLIK
DAMMIT!

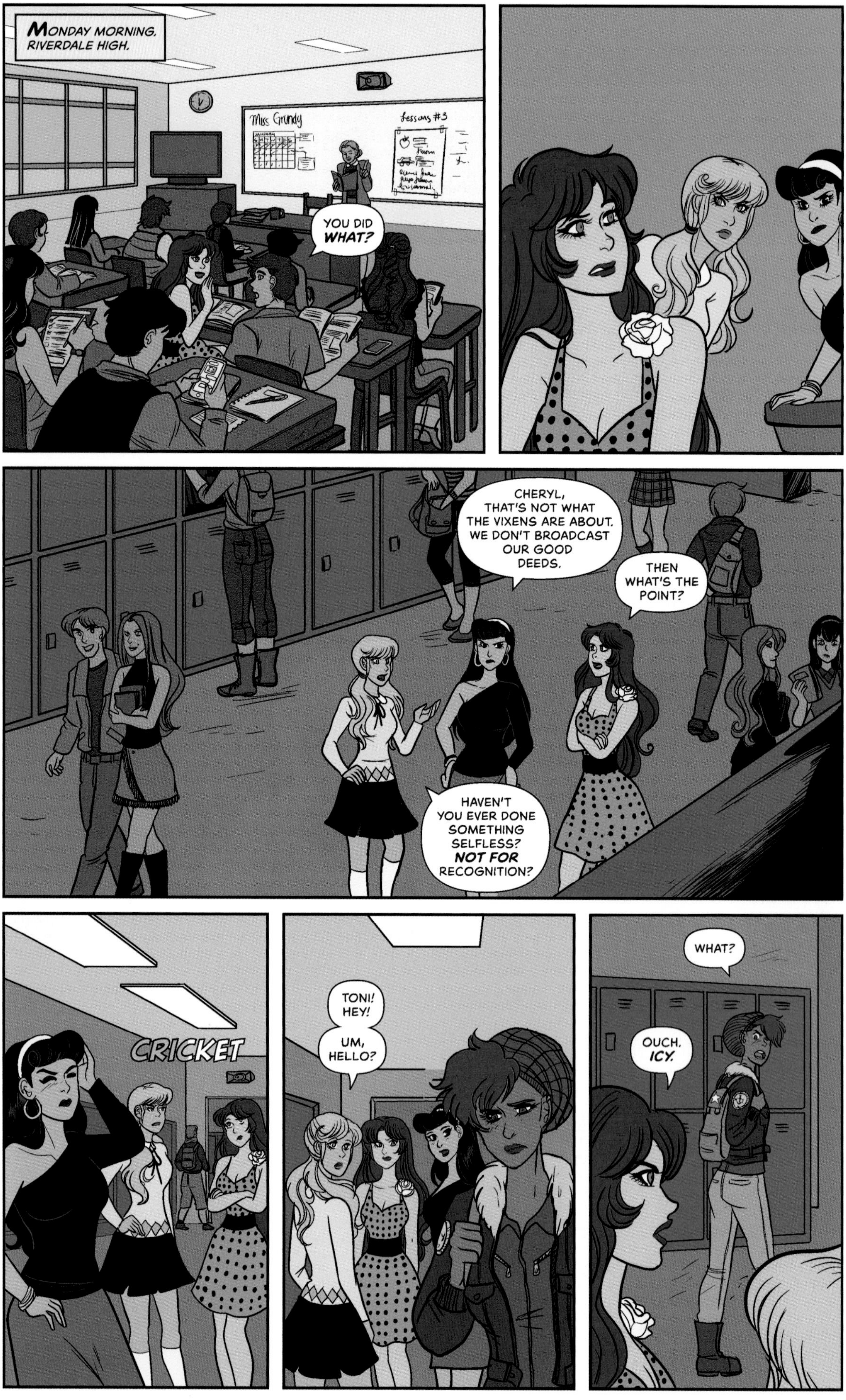
MONDAY MORNING, RIVERDALE HIGH.
YOU DID WHAT?
CHERYL, THAT'S NOT WHAT THE VIXENS ARE ABOUT. WE DON'T BROADCAST OUR GOOD DEEDS.
THEN WHAT'S THE POINT?
HAVEN'T YOU EVER DONE SOMETHING SELFLESS? NOT FOR RECOGNITION?
CRICKET
TONI! HEY!
UM, HELLO?
WHAT?
OUCH. ICY.

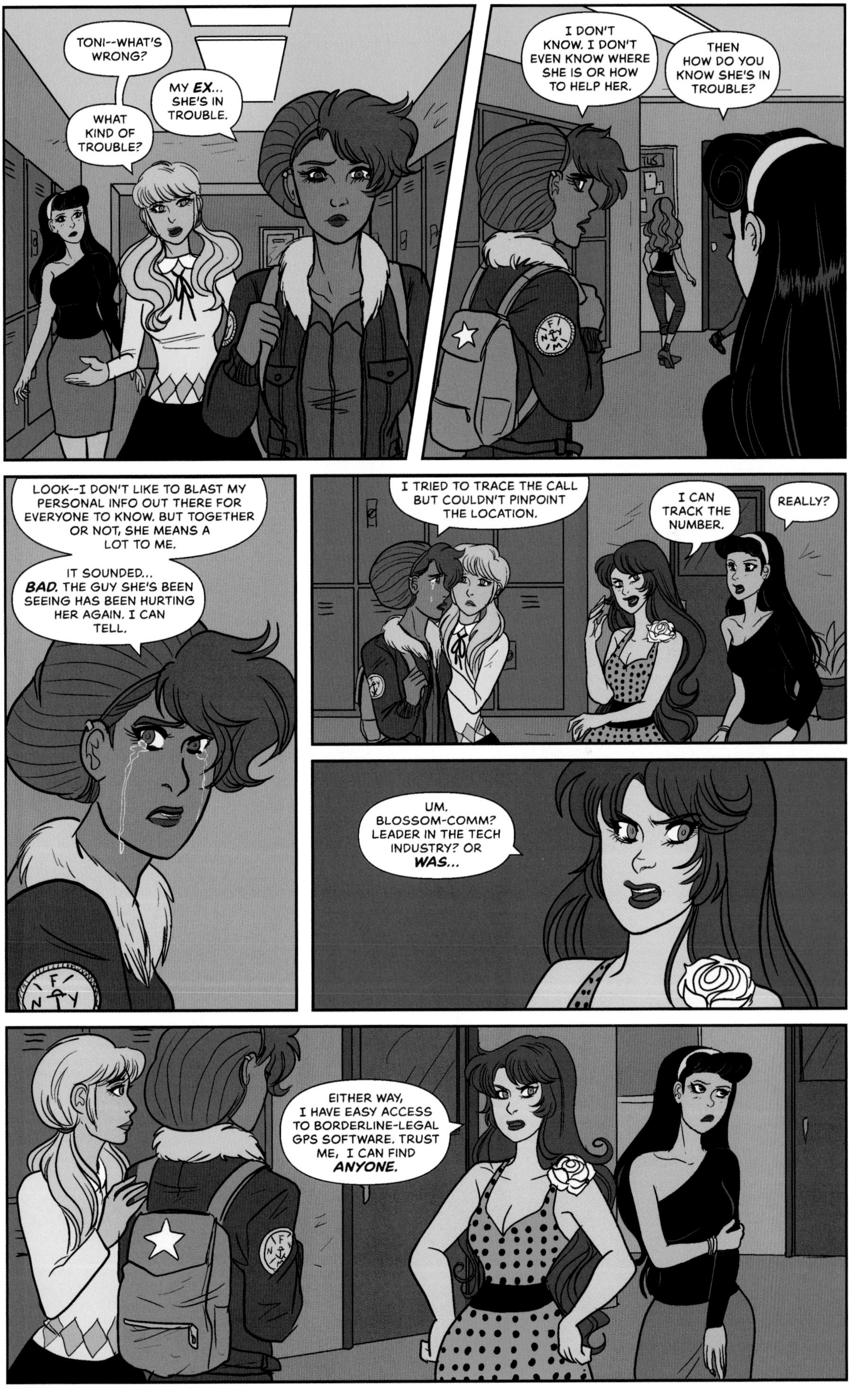
TONI--WHAT'S WRONG?
MY EX... SHE'S IN TROUBLE.
WHAT KIND OF TROUBLE?
I DON'T KNOW. I DON'T EVEN KNOW WHERE SHE IS OR HOW TO HELP HER.
THEN HOW DO YOU KNOW SHE'S IN TROUBLE?
LOOK--I DON'T LIKE TO BLAST MY PERSONAL INFO OUT THERE FOR EVERYONE TO KNOW. BUT TOGETHER OR NOT, SHE MEANS A LOT TO ME.
IT SOUNDED... BAD. THE GUY SHE'S BEEN SEEING HAS BEEN HURTING HER AGAIN. I CAN TELL.
I TRIED TO TRACE THE CALL BUT COULDN'T PINPOINT THE LOCATION.
I CAN TRACK THE NUMBER.
REALLY?
UM. BLOSSOM-COMM? LEADER IN THE TECH INDUSTRY? OR WAS...
EITHER WAY, I HAVE EASY ACCESS TO BORDERLINE-LEGAL GPS SOFTWARE. TRUST ME, I CAN FIND ANYONE.

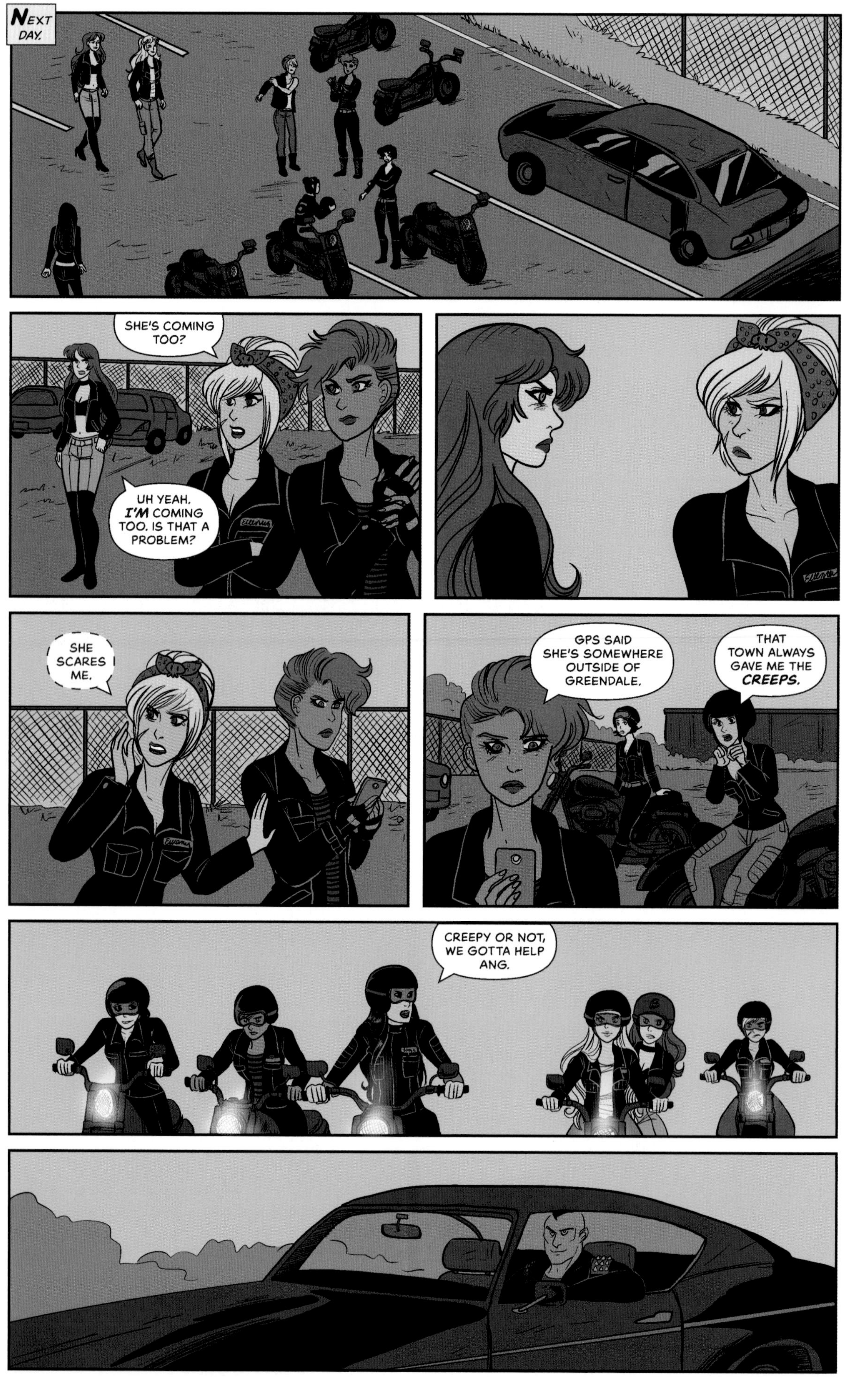
NEXT DAY.
SHE'S COMING TOO?
UH YEAH. I'M COMING TOO. IS THAT A PROBLEM?
SHE SCARES ME.
GPS SAID SHE'S SOMEWHERE OUTSIDE OF GREENDALE.
THAT TOWN ALWAYS GAVE ME THE CREEPS.
CREEPY OR NOT, WE GOTTA HELP ANG.

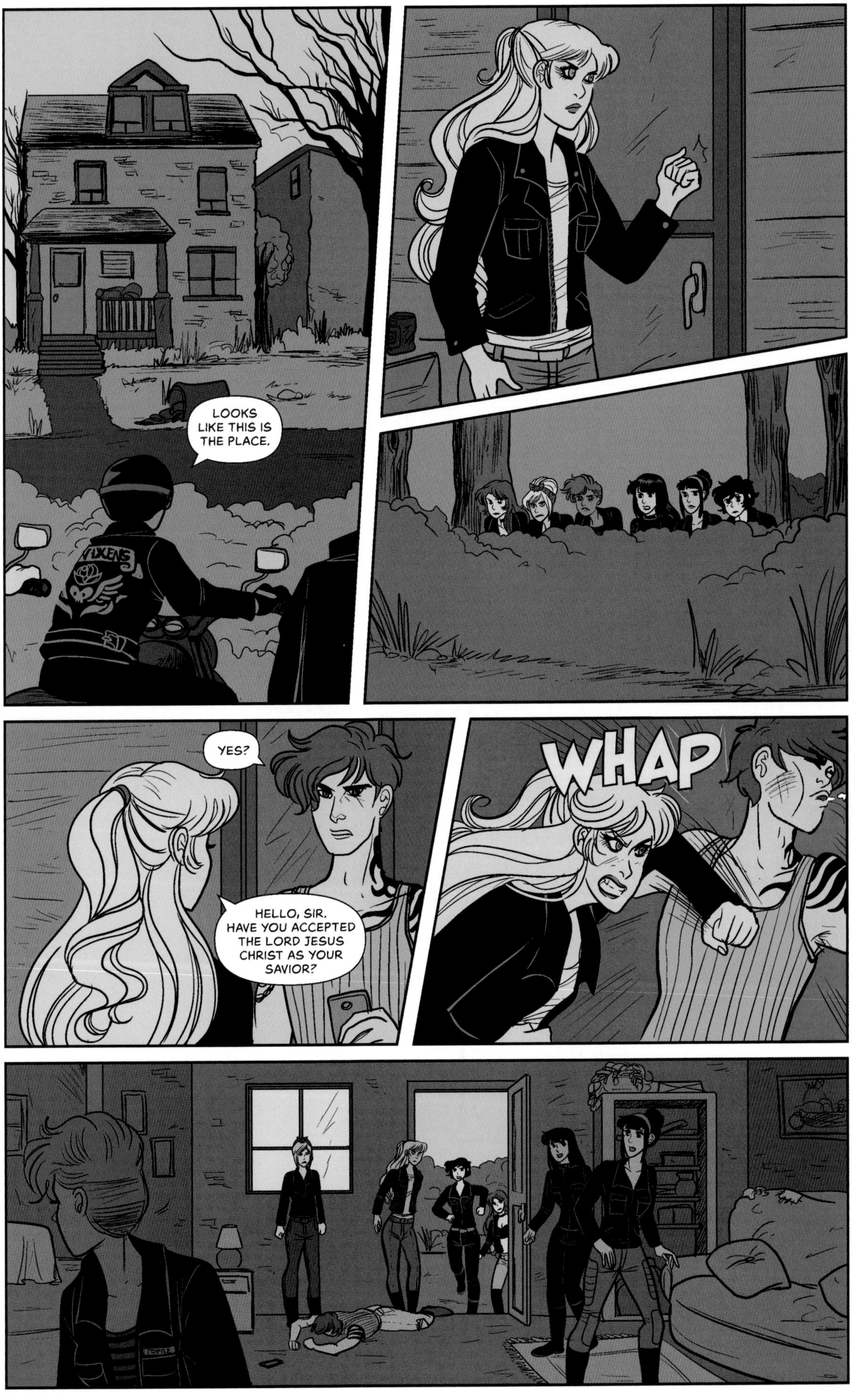
LOOKS LIKE THIS IS THE PLACE.
VIXENS
YES?
HELLO, SIR. HAVE YOU ACCEPTED THE LORD JESUS CHRIST AS YOUR SAVIOR?
WHAP

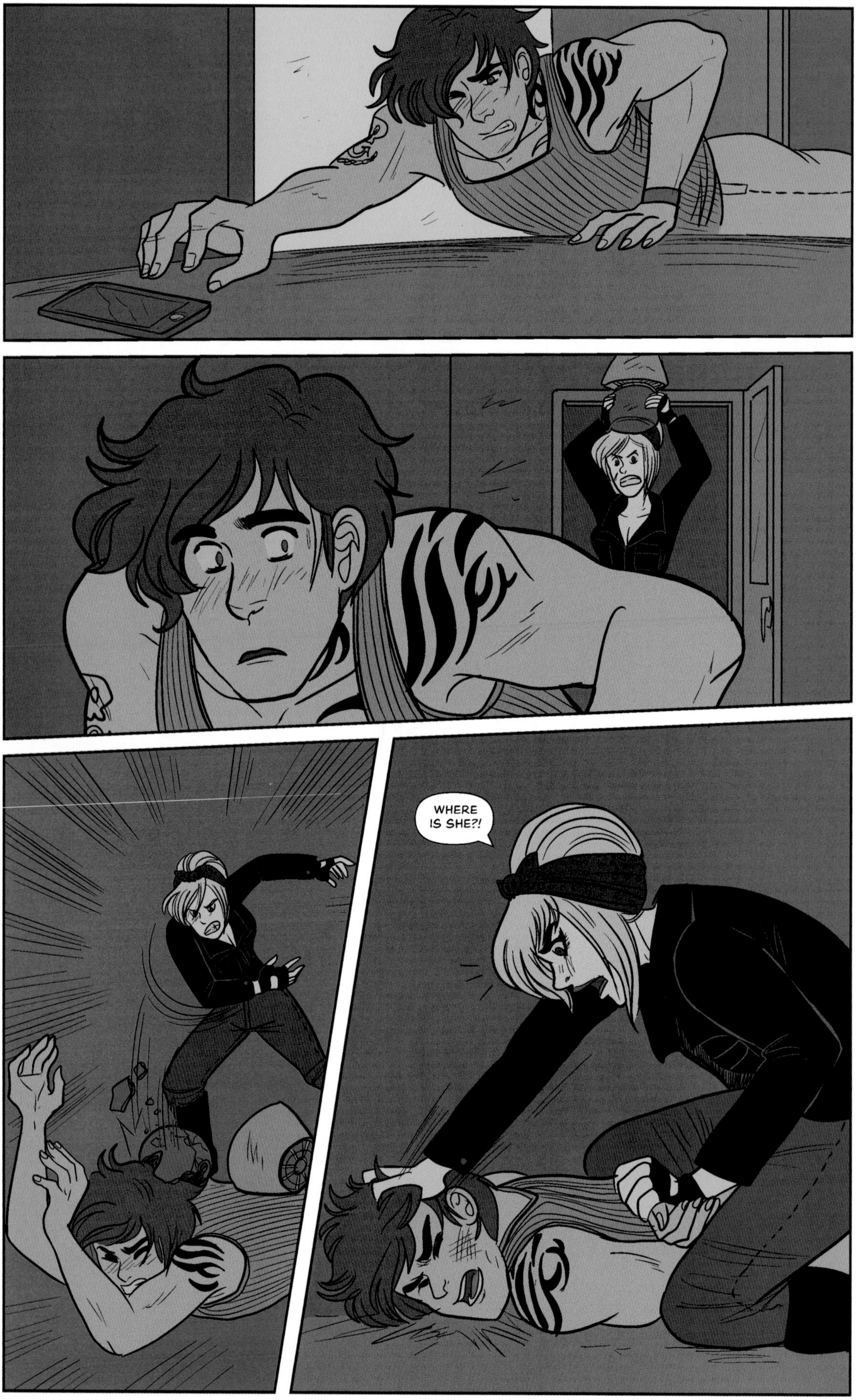
WHERE IS SHE?!

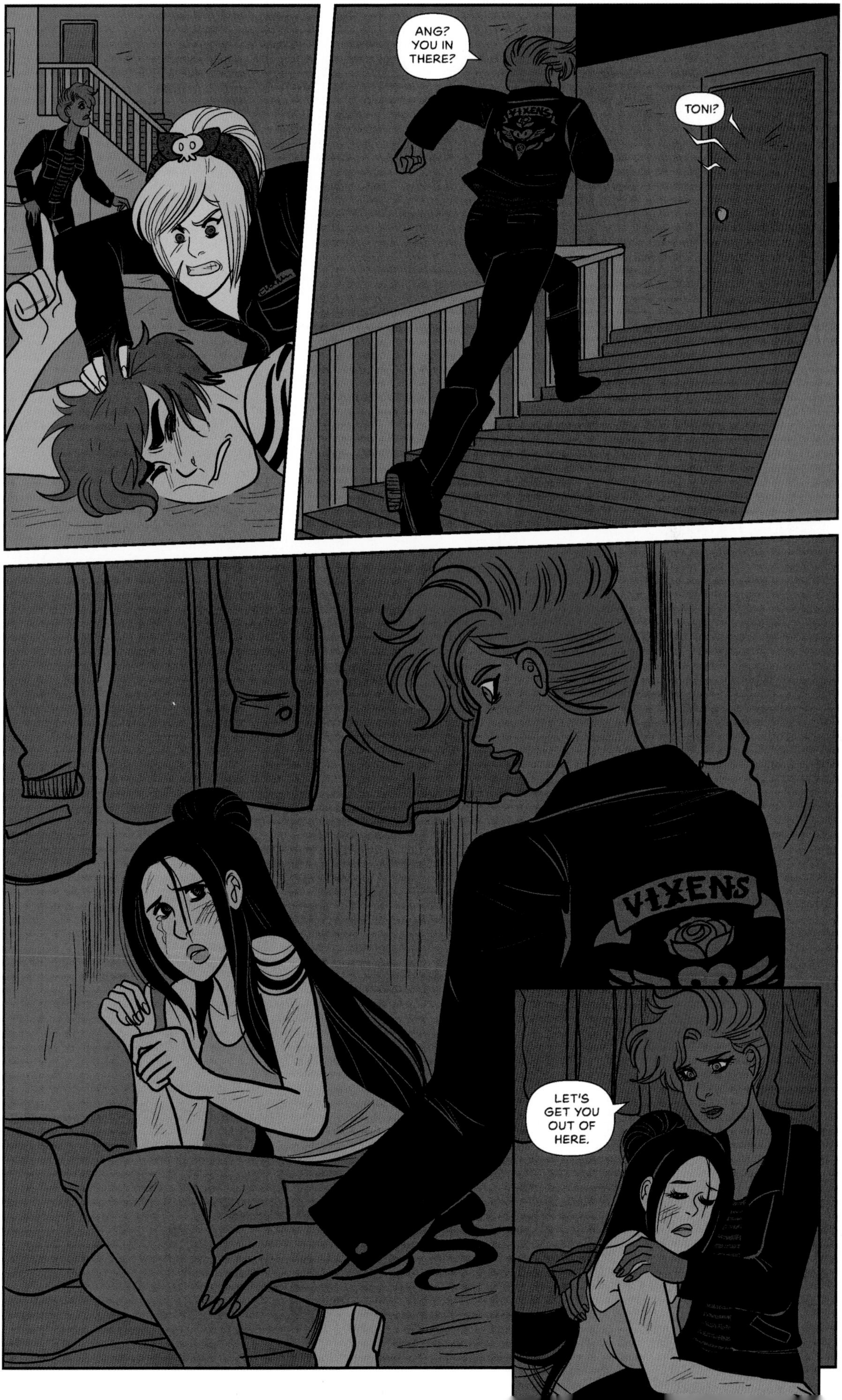
ANG? YOU IN THERE?
TONI?
LET'S GET YOU OUT OF HERE.

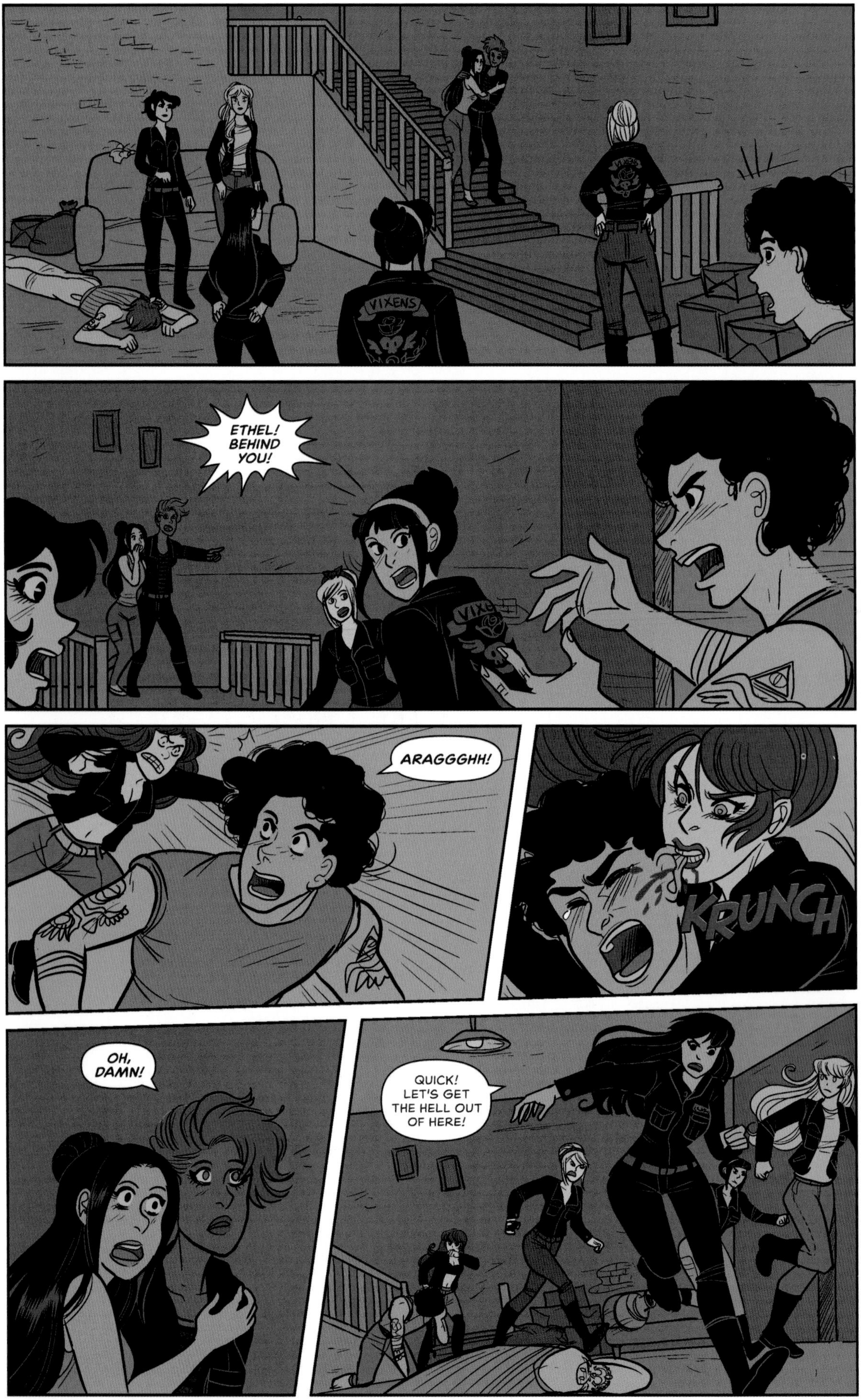
VIXENS
ETHEL! BEHIND YOU!
VIXENS
ARAGGGHH!
KRUNCH
OH, DAMN!
QUICK! LET'S GET THE HELL OUT OF HERE!

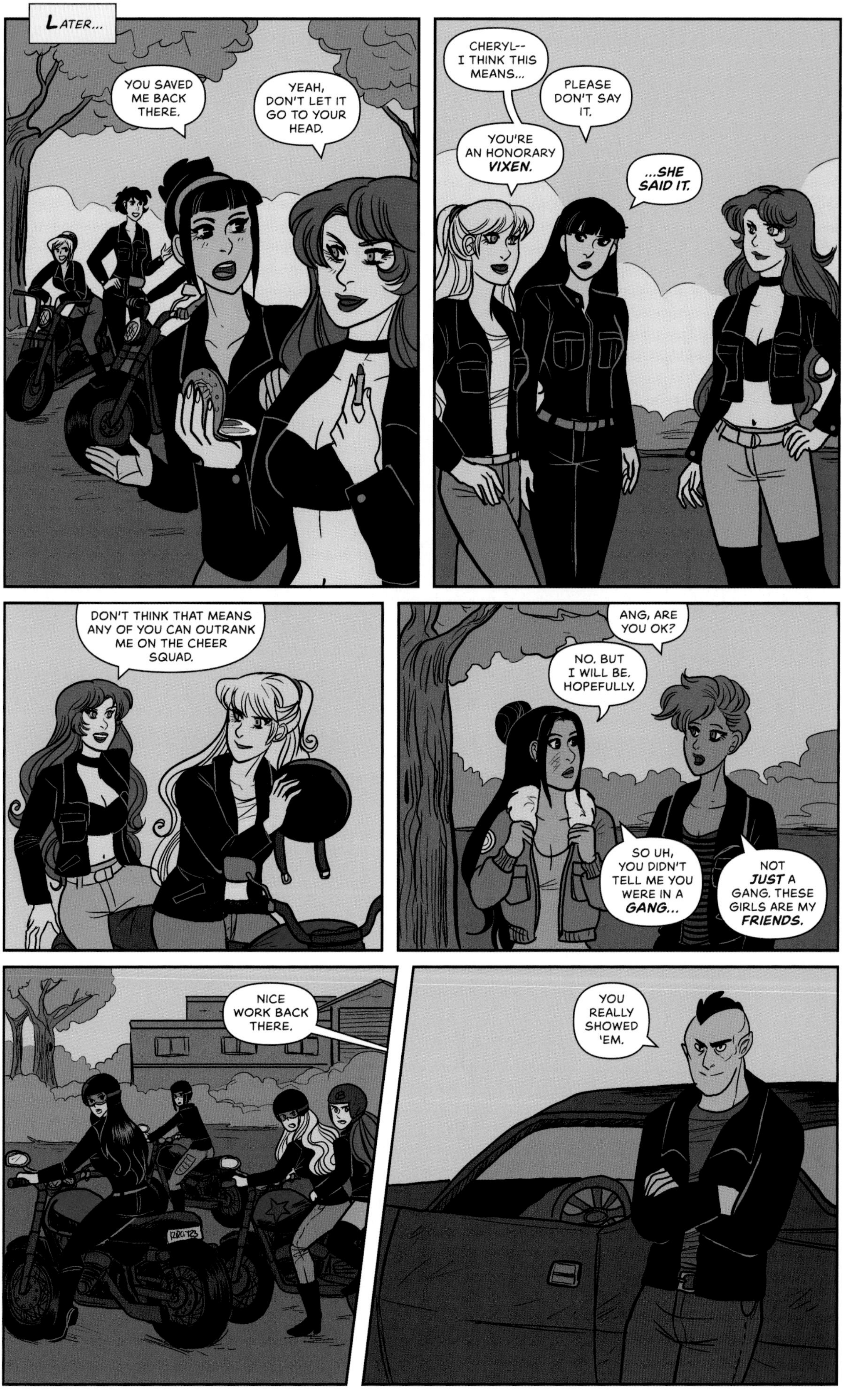
LATER...
YOU SAVED ME BACK THERE.
YEAH, DON'T LET IT GO TO YOUR HEAD.
CHERYL-- I THINK THIS MEANS...
PLEASE DON'T SAY IT.
YOU'RE AN HONORARY VIXEN.
...SHE SAID IT.
DON'T THINK THAT MEANS ANY OF YOU CAN OUTRANK ME ON THE CHEER SQUAD.
ANG, ARE YOU OK?
NO. BUT I WILL BE. HOPEFULLY.
SO UH, YOU DIDN'T TELL ME YOU WERE IN A GANG...
NOT JUST A GANG. THESE GIRLS ARE MY FRIENDS.
NICE WORK BACK THERE.
YOU REALLY SHOWED 'EM.

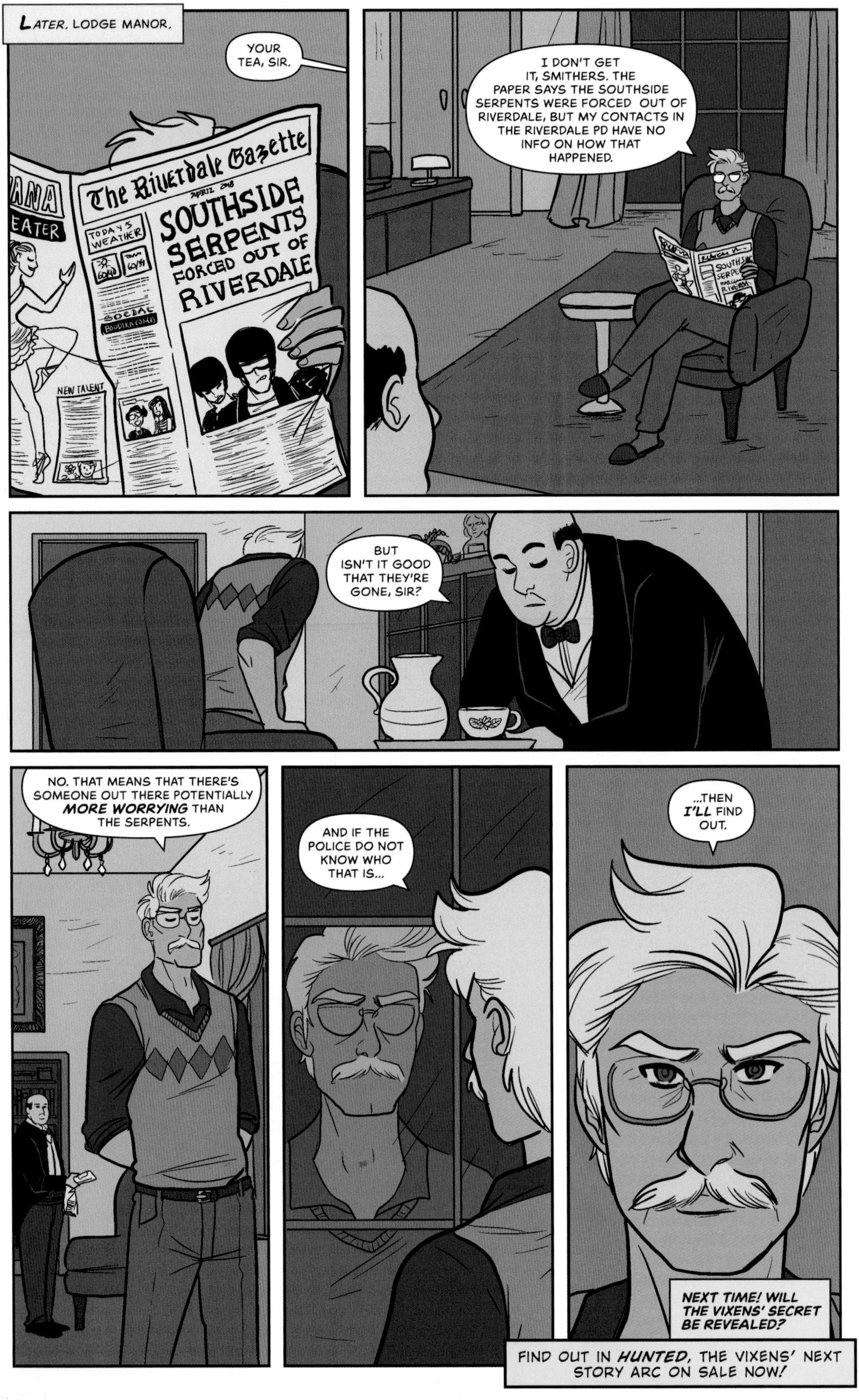
LATER. LODGE MANOR.
YOUR TEA, SIR.
The Riverdale Gazette
APRIL 2018
SOUTHSIDE SERPENTS FORCED OUT OF RIVERDALE
TODAY'S WEATHER
SOCIAL
NEW TALENT
I DON'T GET IT, SMITHERS. THE PAPER SAYS THE SOUTHSIDE SERPENTS WERE FORCED OUT OF RIVERDALE, BUT MY CONTACTS IN THE RIVERDALE PD HAVE NO INFO ON HOW THAT HAPPENED.
BUT ISN'T IT GOOD THAT THEY'RE GONE, SIR?
NO. THAT MEANS THAT THERE'S SOMEONE OUT THERE POTENTIALLY MORE WORRYING THAN THE SERPENTS.
AND IF THE POLICE DO NOT KNOW WHO THAT IS...
...THEN I'LL FIND OUT.
NEXT TIME! WILL THE VIXENS' SECRET BE REVEALED?
FIND OUT IN HUNTED, THE VIXENS' NEXT STORY ARC ON SALE NOW!

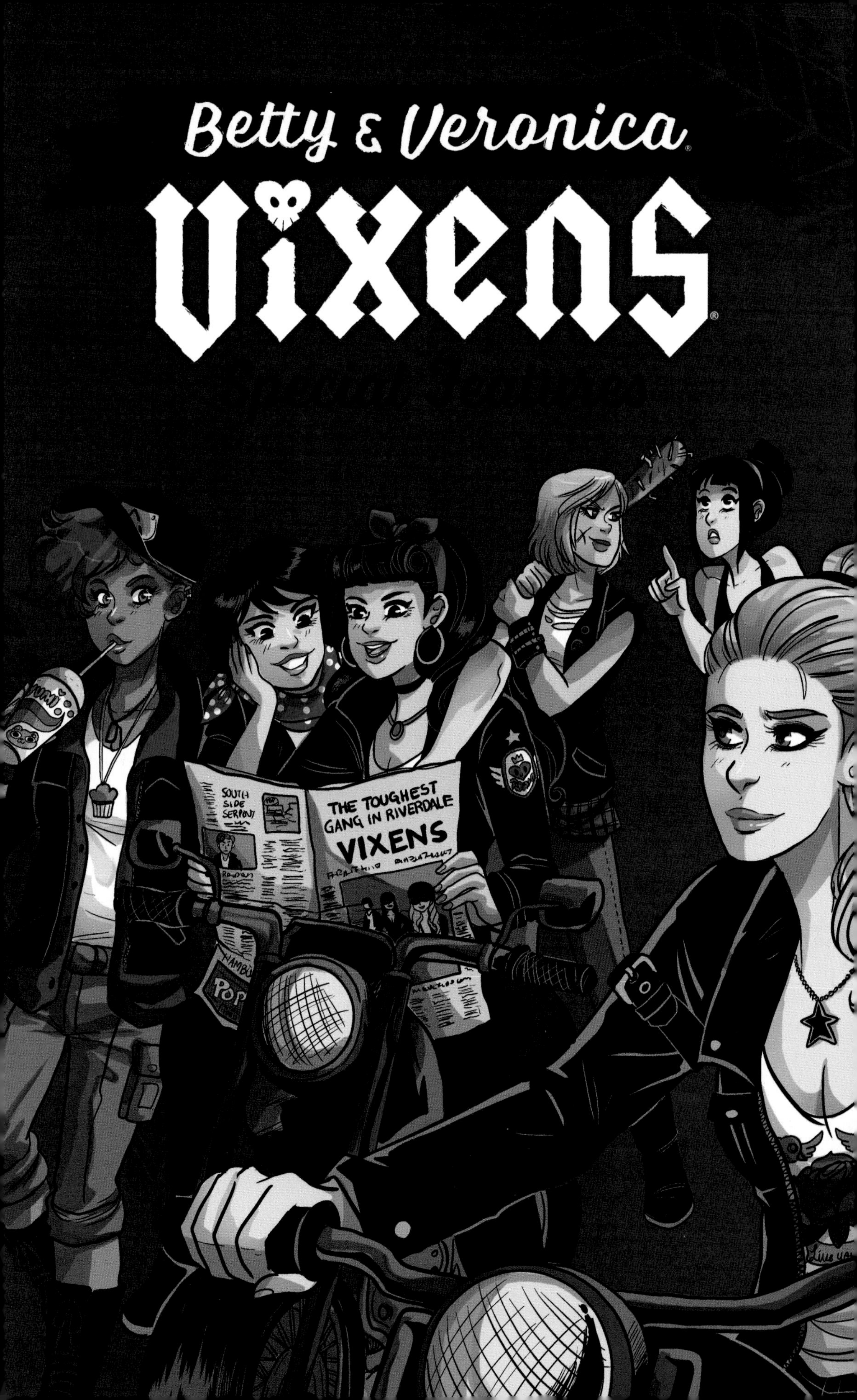
Betty & Veronica
VIXENS
SOUTH SIDE SERPENT
THE TOUGHEST GANG IN RIVERDALE
VIXENS
POP

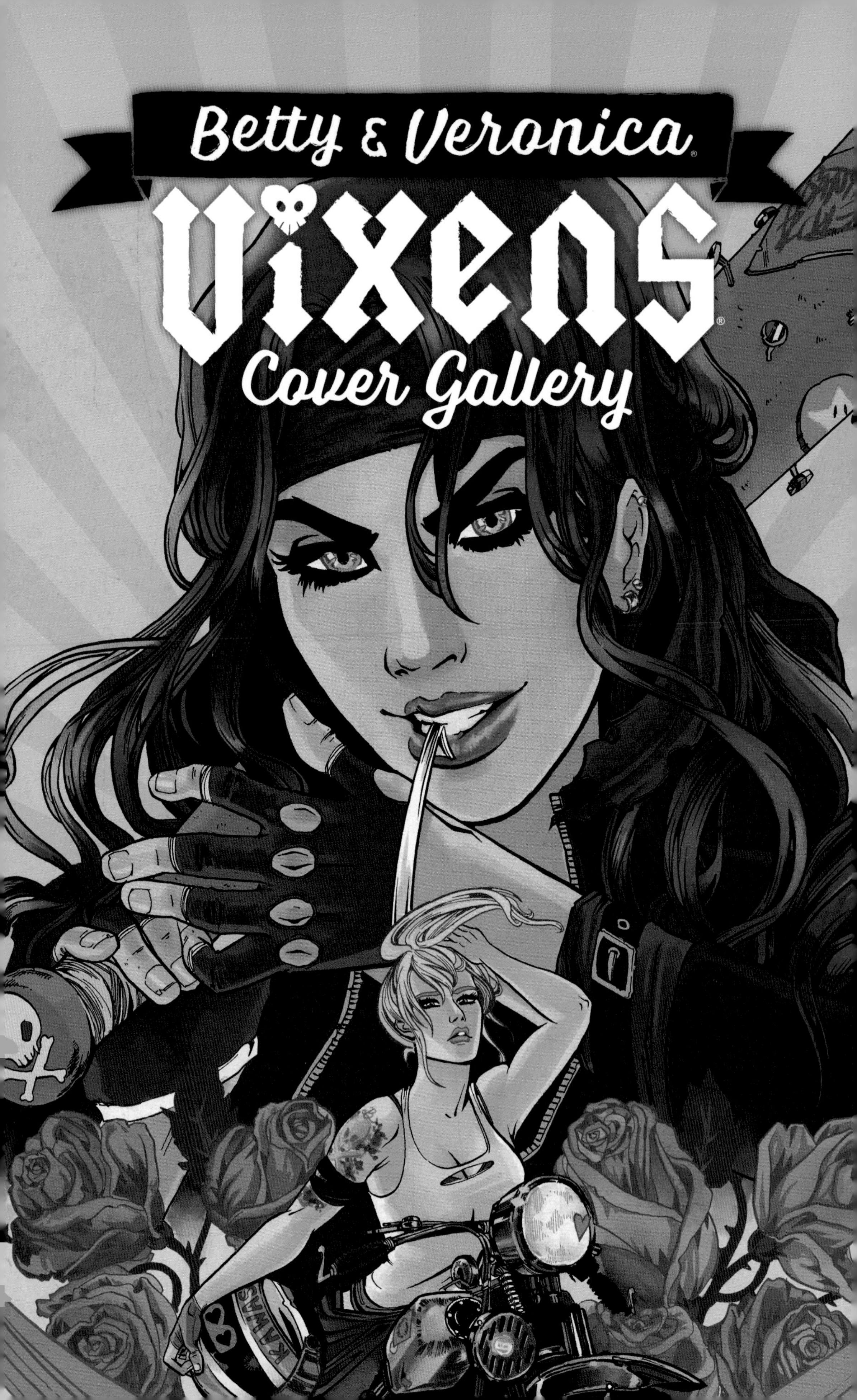
Betty & Veronica
Vixens
Cover Gallery

Issue One

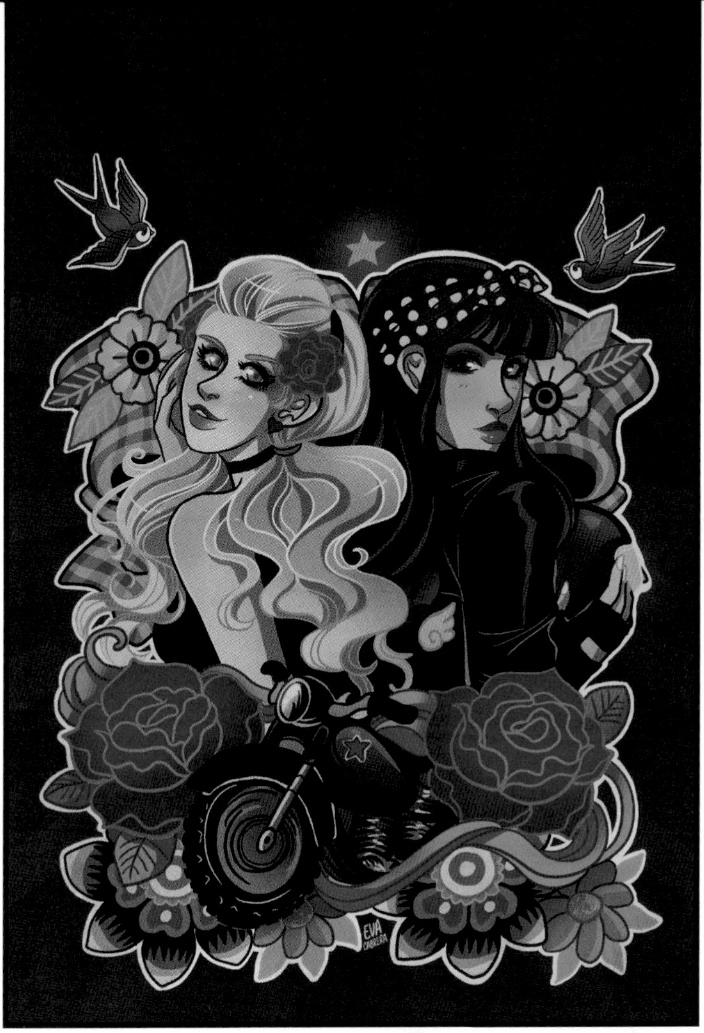

EVA CABRERA

EVA CABRERA

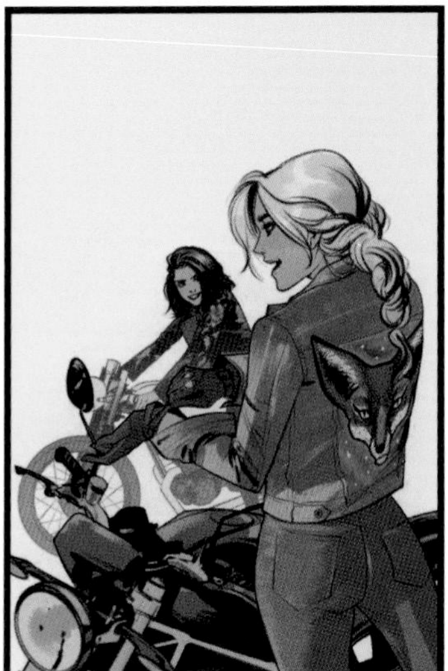

FIONA STAPLES

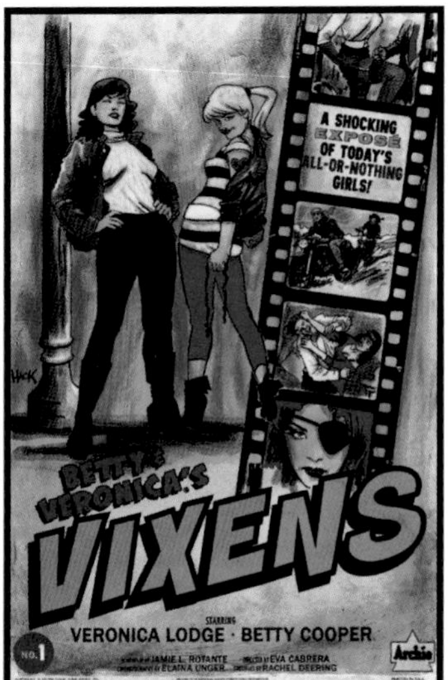

A SHOCKING EXPOSÉ OF TODAY'S ALL-OR-NOTHING GIRLS!
HACK
BETTY & VERONICA'S
VIXENS
STARRING
VERONICA LODGE · BETTY COOPER
NO.1
Archie

ROBERT HACK

Issue Two

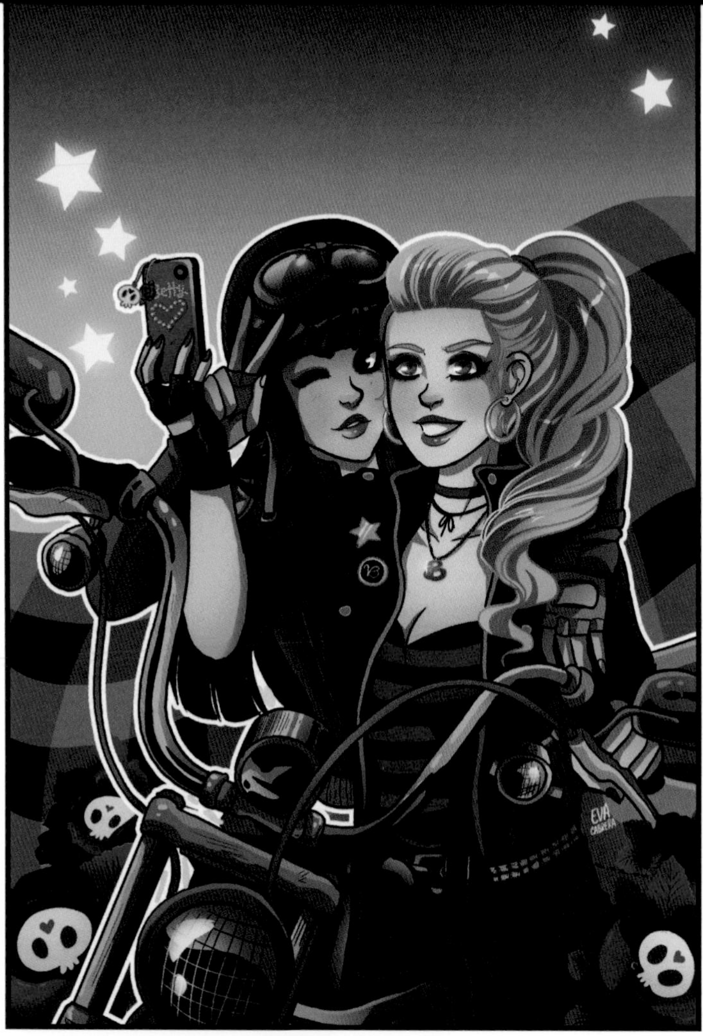

EVA CABRERA

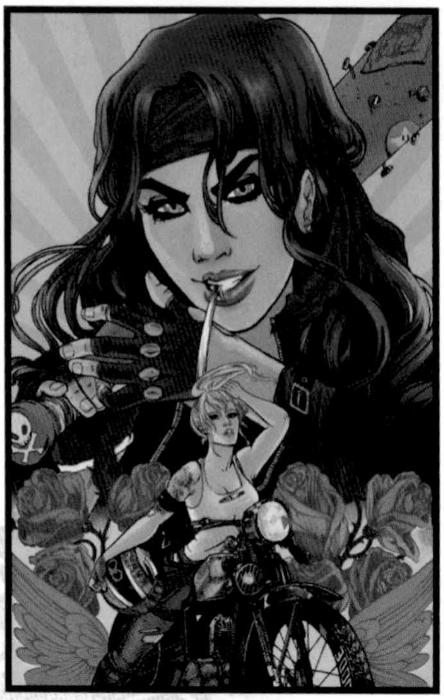

SANYA ANWAR

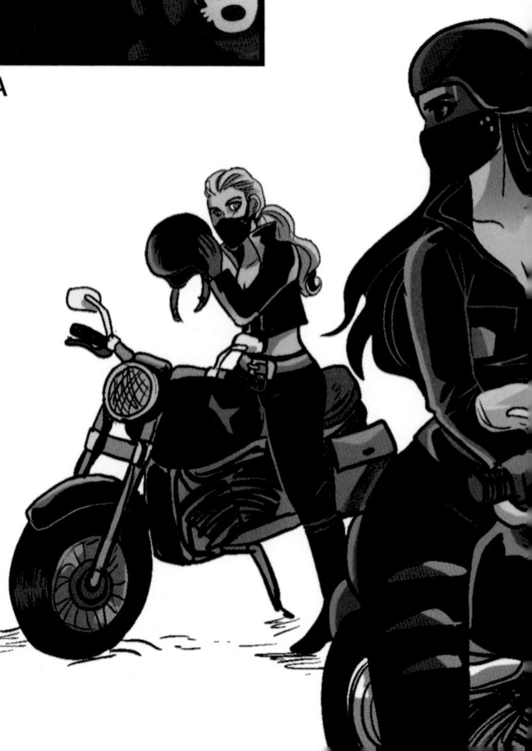

Issue Three

EVA CABRERA

SANDRA LANZ

JEN VAUGHN

Issue Four

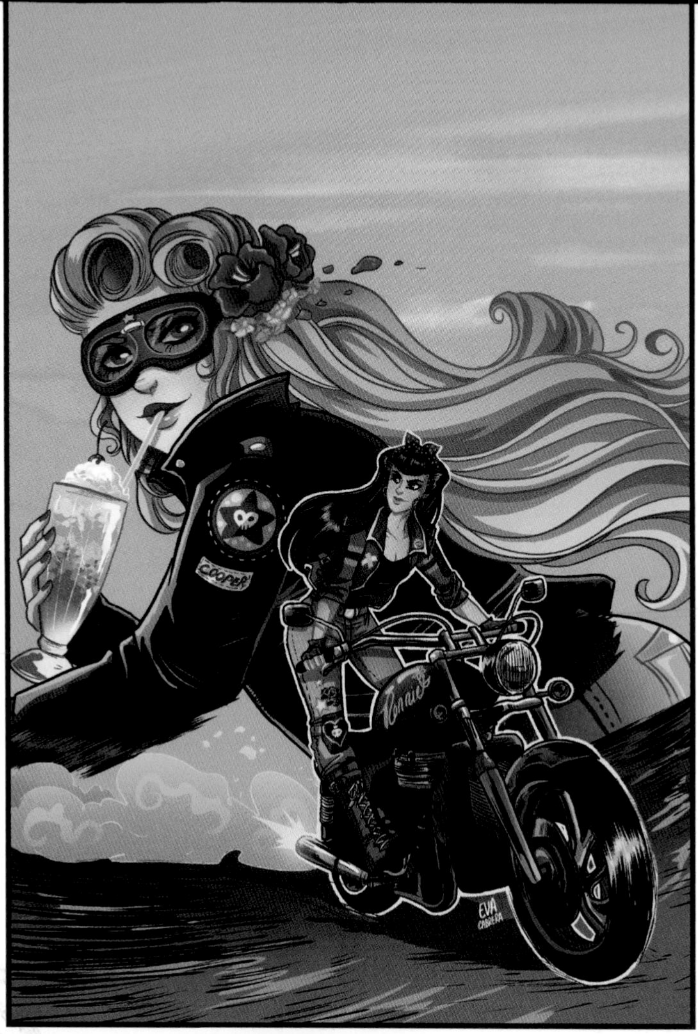

EVA CABRERA

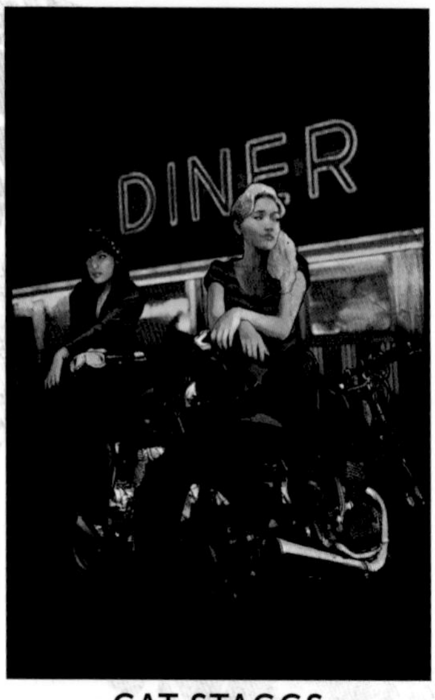
DINER

CAT STAGGS

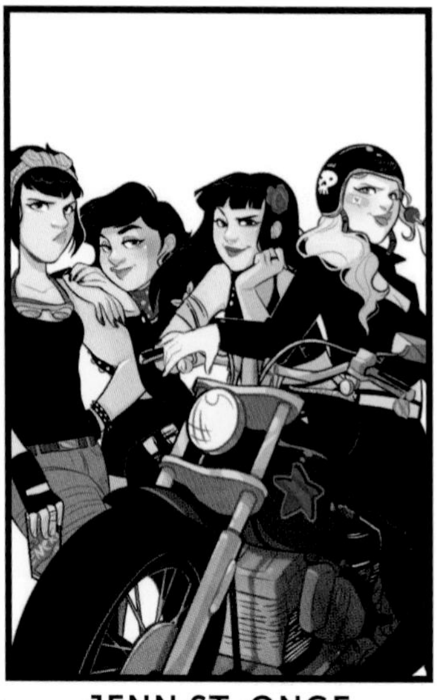

JENN ST. ONGE

Issue Five

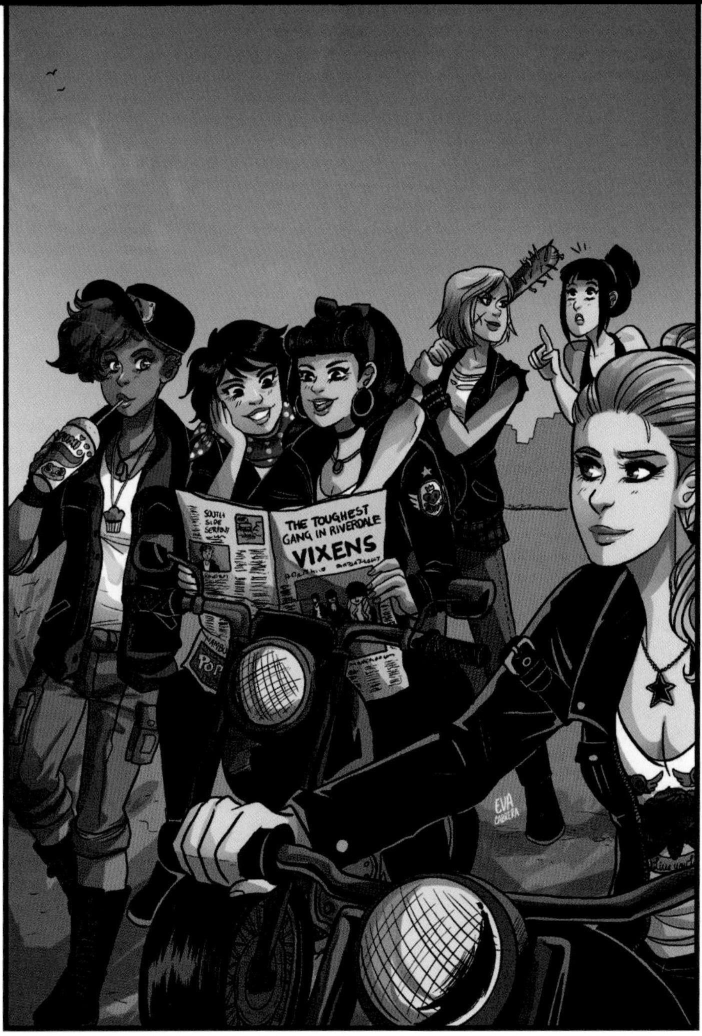
THE TOUGHEST GANG IN RIVERDALE
VIXENS
EVA CABRERA

EVA CABRERA

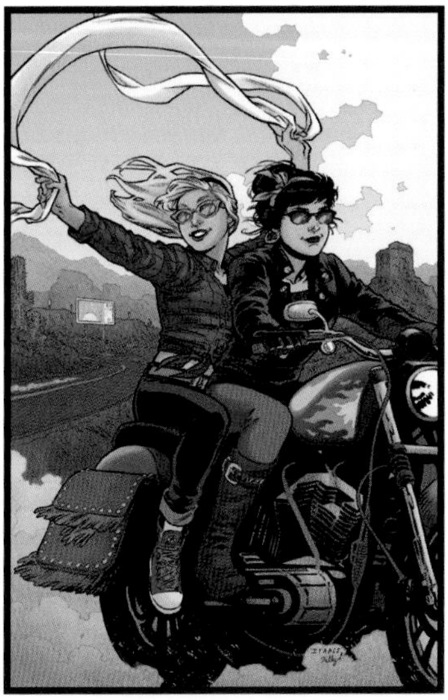

REBEKAH ISAACS
WITH KELLY FITZPATRICK

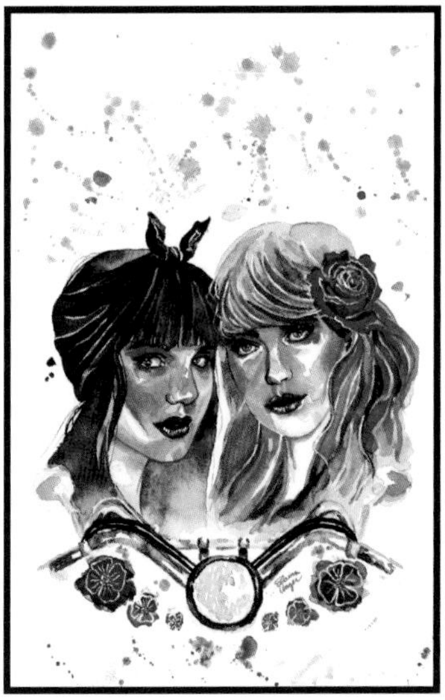

ELAINA UNGER

Betty & Veronica Vixens

When the idea of *Betty & Veronica: Vixens* was first discussed, we knew that it only made sense to feature the Southside Serpents as the Vixens' first formidable group of foes. But if we were going to bring back a few characters from yesteryear, why stop there? The original *Little Archie* series is chock-full of characters that haven't gotten much time in the spotlight in the past few decades. Here's a look at a few classic characters that have made their return (with some updated appearances!):

FANGS FOGARTY

Fangs Fogarty, a snaggle-tooth bully, and his band of misfits were the number one enemy of Little Archie and his pals 'n' gals. An unreasonable thug that intimidated his classmates, Fangs led the Serpents, a group of equally mean bullies, that lived in the southern district of Riverdale.

Now Fangs is the de-facto leader of the just-as-mean biker gang Serpents, who are involved in worse things than just intimidating people.

MAD DOCTOR DOOM

Mad Doctor Doom was a green-skinned mad scientist who terrorized Little Archie and the gang, though they would constantly foil his plans of gaining great wealth and conquering the world.

Mad Doctor Doom—now better known just as "Doc"—is a behind-the-scenes madman, leading the Serpents in their dangerous endeavors.

PENNY PEABODY

Penny Peabody was Fangs Fogarty's girlfriend. Their relationship was exactly like Moose and Midge's: Fangs will hurt any boy who even talks to Penny.

Not too much has changed over time— Fangs is still a jerk but this time Penny's not standing for it. No longer just defined as Fangs' girlfriend, she's got a mind and attitude all her own.

EVELYN EVERNEVER

Evelyn Evernever was a young girl who knew Archie and friends when they were young. A shy girl with an inferiority complex, Evelyn's only real friend was her doll, Minerva. Despite often being picked on, Evelyn always of herself as a "bou'tiful" gal.

In the time since the rest of the group saw Evelyn a lot has gone on in her life— but the details are murky. All we know is that she's been involved in some weird stuff and she's a changed person now. Mysterious and tough, Evelyn exudes confidence and carves her own path.

BUBBLES McBOUNCE

Bubbles McBounce was a tough girl from Little Archie. Being heavier than the other kids, she would often use her weight to her advantage, such as saving the day by holding down an air balloon that risked taking Little Archie and the gang on a magical voyage.

Bubbles McBounce is still a tough girl who won't stand down to anyone. She's proud of who she is and uses her experience and street smarts to guide the Vixens.

AMBROSE PIPPS

A small, shy boy with a large nose and an oversized baseball cap, Li'l Ambrose Pipps was the tagalong of Archie's gang when they were young. Although Ambrose's loyalty was unwavering, Little Archie took pride in bullying and exploiting him, without ever letting him join the "good ol' gang."

Ambrose is now surer of himself and runs a successful business in Riverdale as the town mechanic. He and Bubbles are an item and the two repair cars and motorcycles together.

Betty & Veronica

Vixens

Original Sketches

Check out these amazing sketches and character designs from artist Eva Cabrera for some of your favorite *Betty & Veronica: Vixens* characters.

Betty Cooper

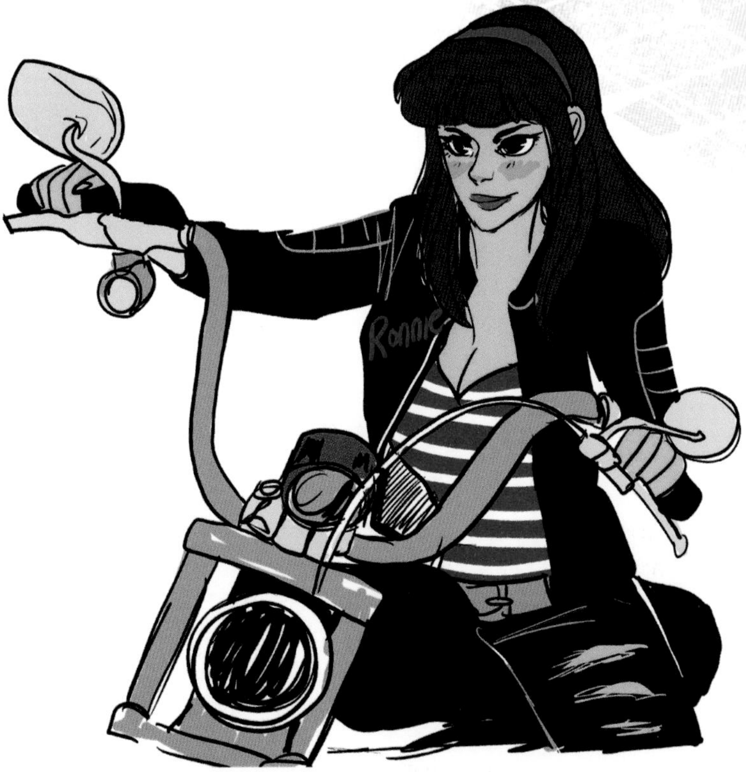
Ronnie

Veronica Lodge

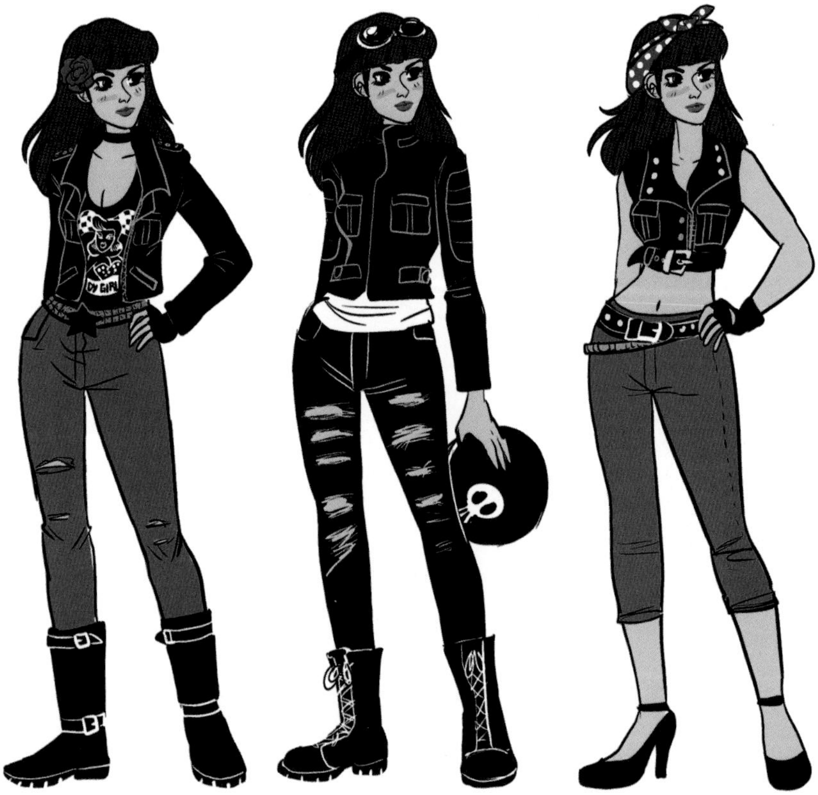

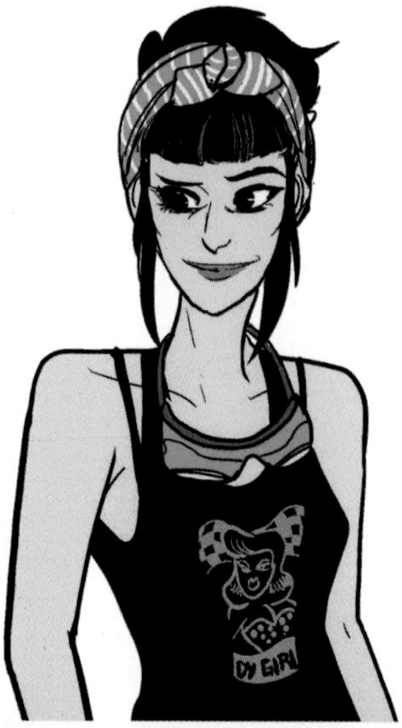

Ethel Muggs

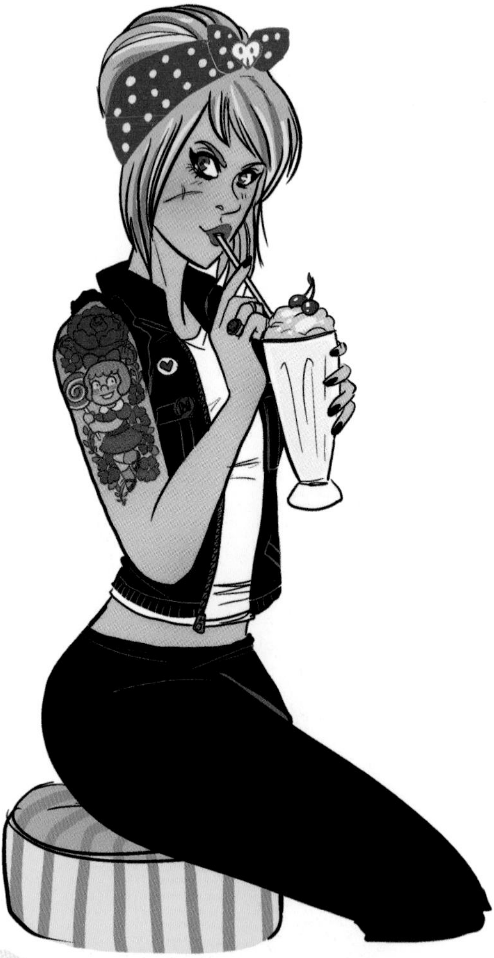

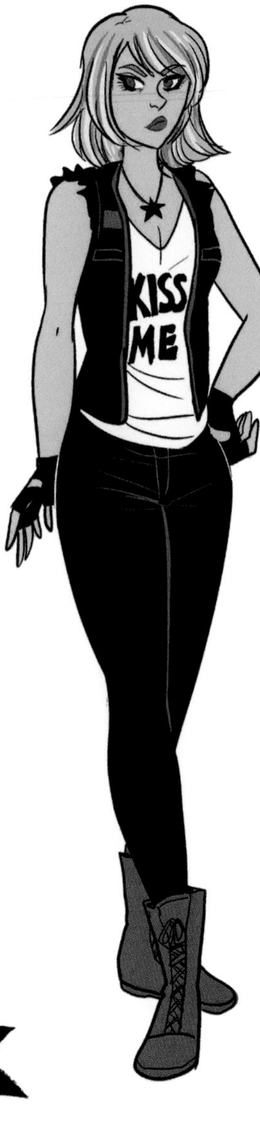
KISS ME

Evelyn Evernever

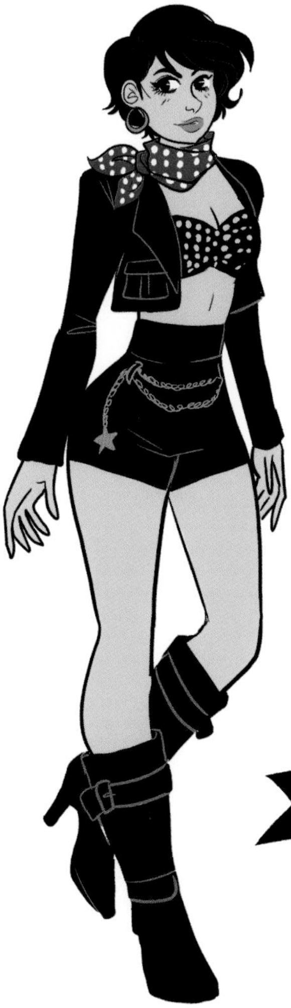

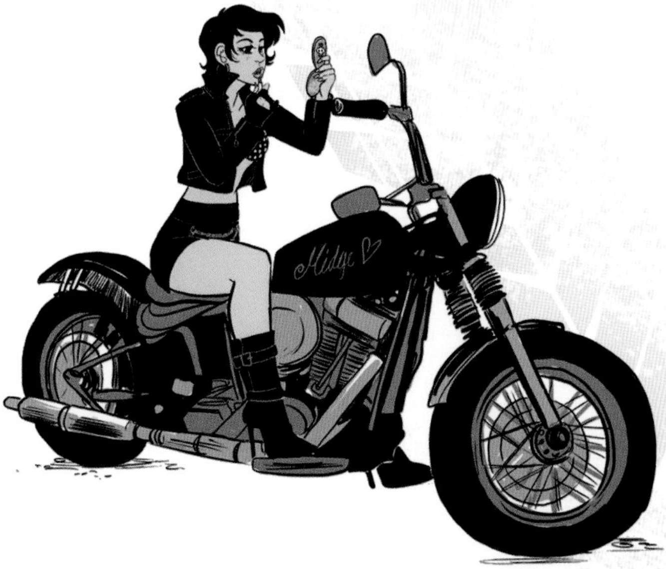
Midge ♡

Midge Klump

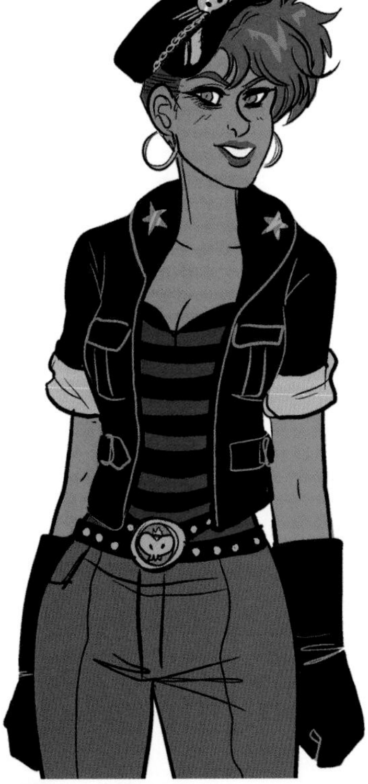

Toni Topaz

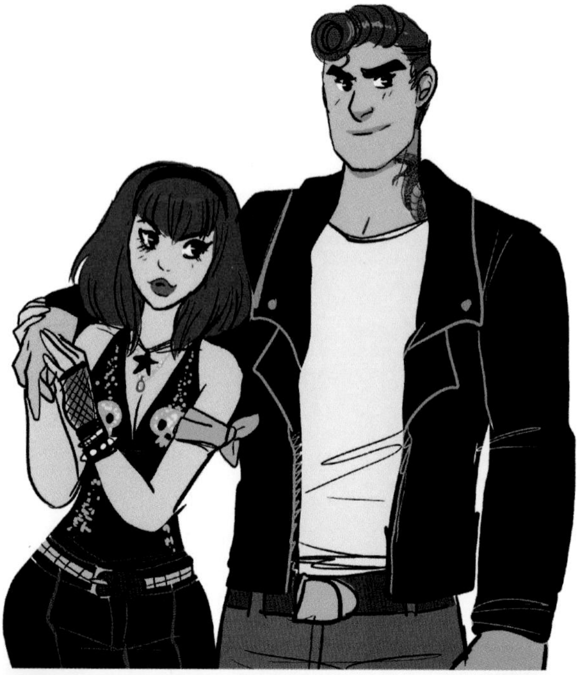

Penny and Fangs

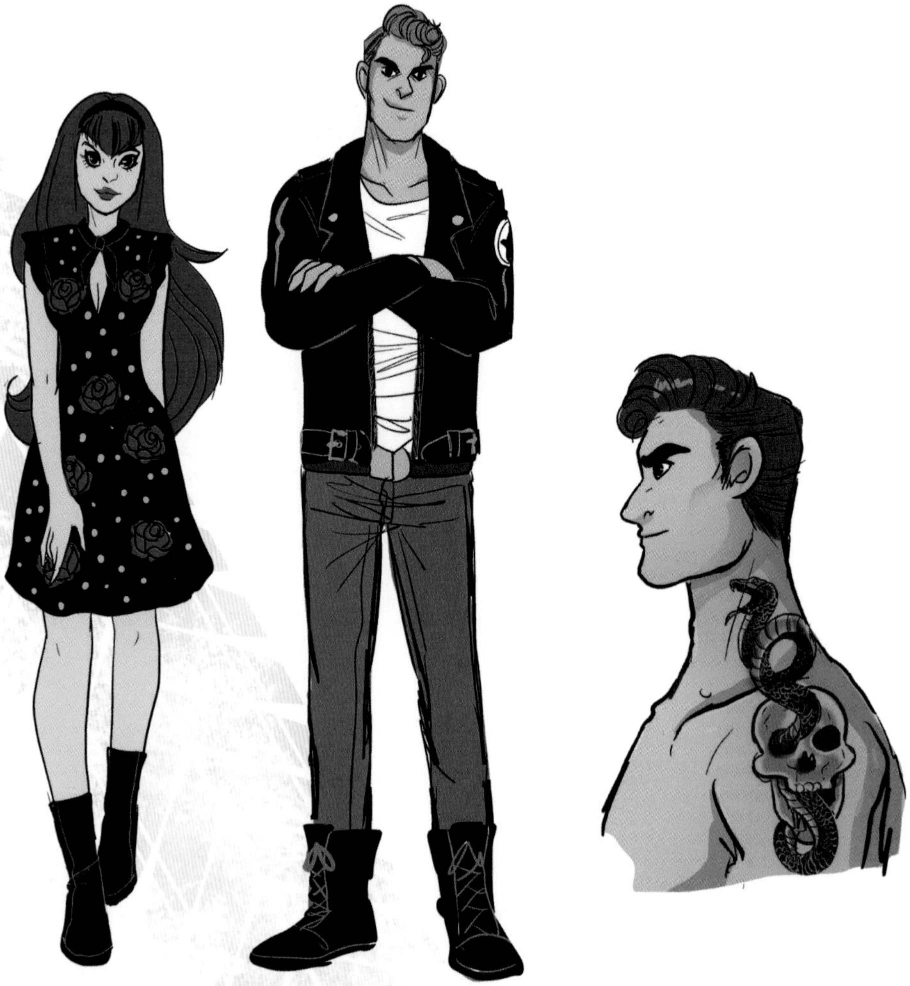

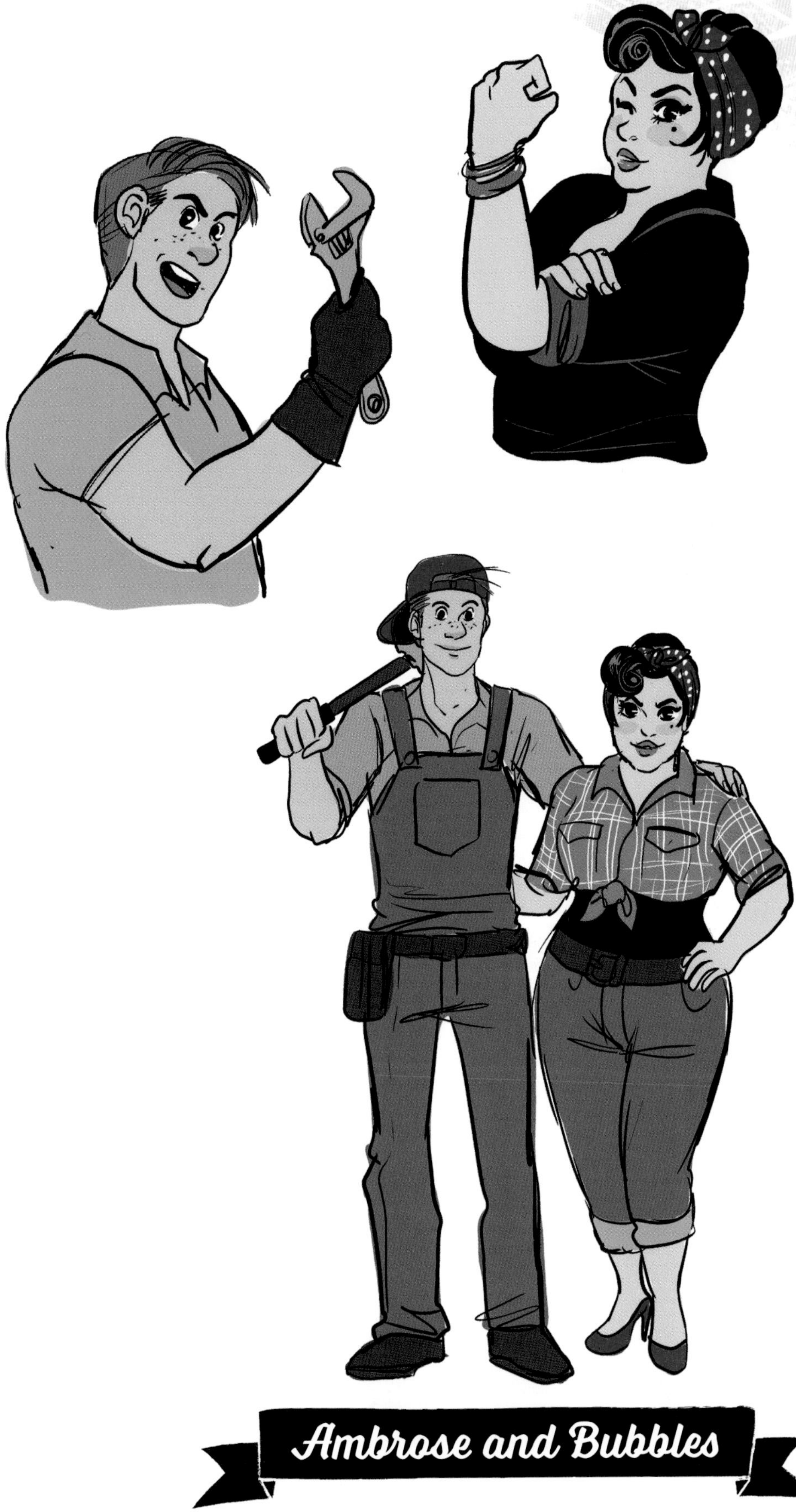

Ambrose and Bubbles

SPECIAL PREVIEW

RIVERDALE®

STORIES BY: ROBERTO AGUIRRE-SACASA

WRITER: GREG MURRAY
ARTIST: THOMAS PITILLI
COLORS: ANDRE SZYMANOWICZ
LETTERS: JANICE CHIANG

Here's a very special preview of the ongoing series RIVERDALE, based on the SMASH-HIT CW TV series. RIVERDALE offers a bold, subversive take on Archie, Betty, Veronica, Josie & the Pussycats and their friends, exploring small-town life and the darkness bubbling beneath the town's wholesome facade.

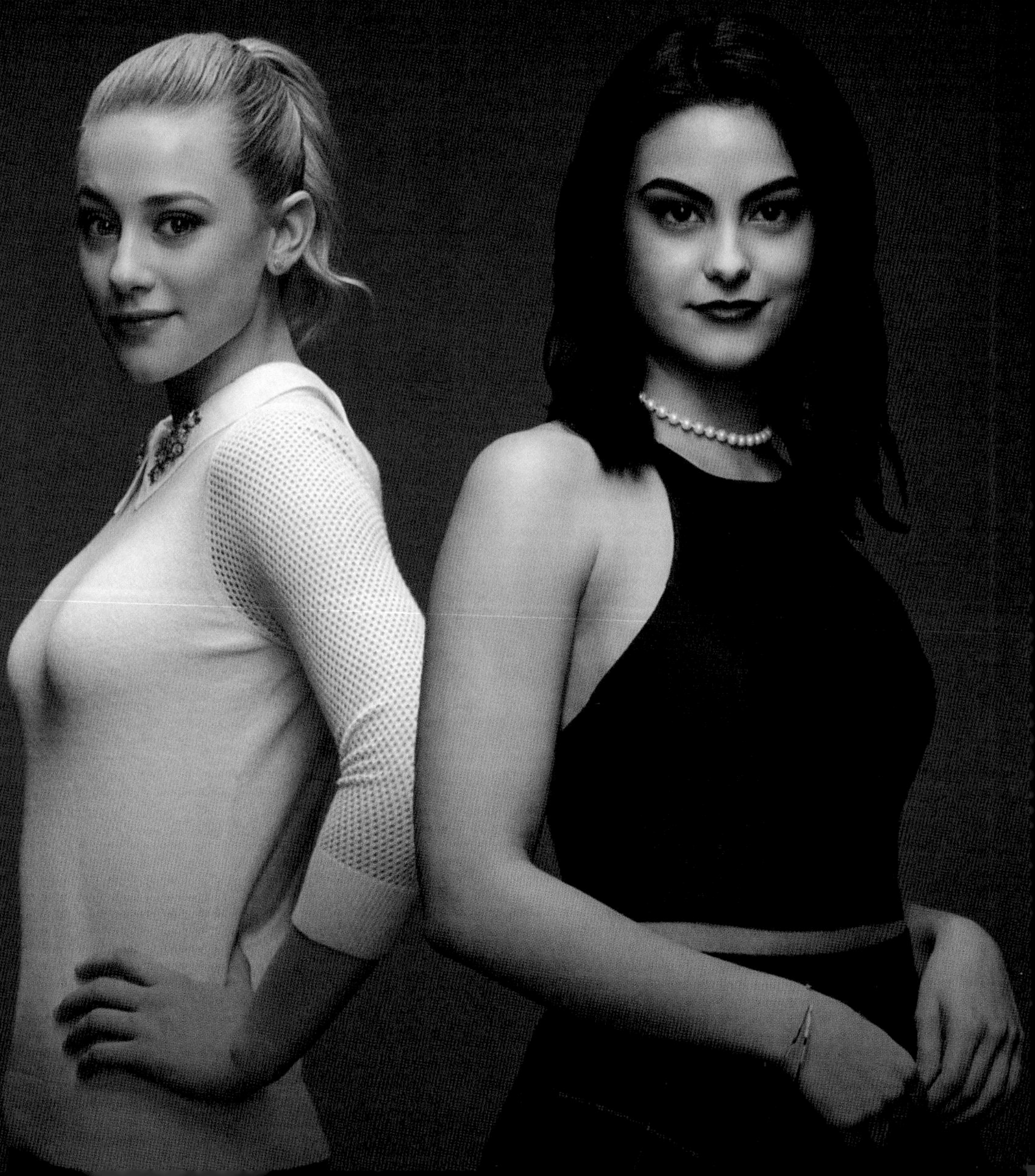

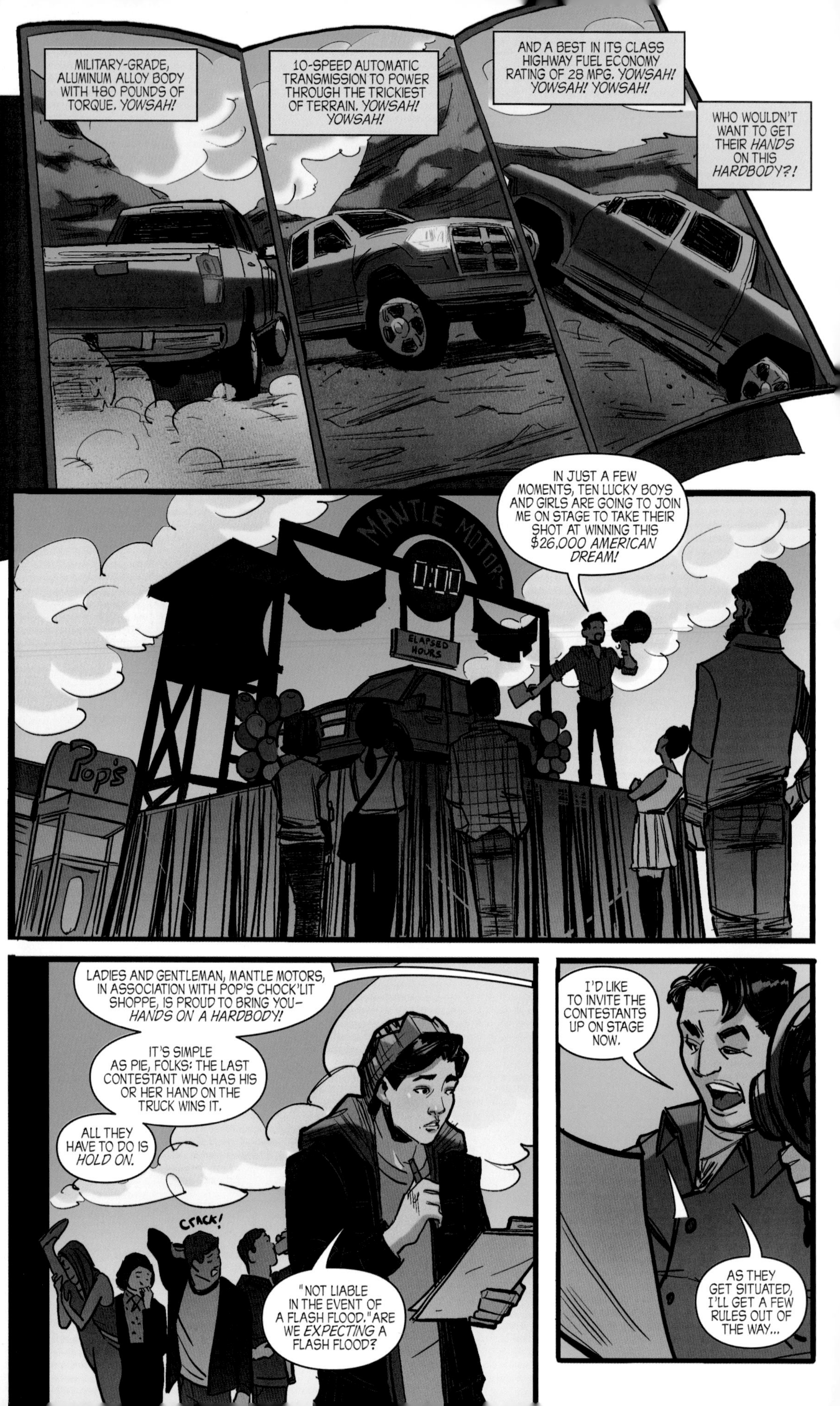
MILITARY-GRADE, ALUMINUM ALLOY BODY WITH 480 POUNDS OF TORQUE. YOWSAH!
10-SPEED AUTOMATIC TRANSMISSION TO POWER THROUGH THE TRICKIEST OF TERRAIN. YOWSAH! YOWSAH!
AND A BEST IN ITS CLASS HIGHWAY FUEL ECONOMY RATING OF 28 MPG. YOWSAH! YOWSAH! YOWSAH!
WHO WOULDN'T WANT TO GET THEIR HANDS ON THIS HARDBODY?!
IN JUST A FEW MOMENTS, TEN LUCKY BOYS AND GIRLS ARE GOING TO JOIN ME ON STAGE TO TAKE THEIR SHOT AT WINNING THIS $26,000 AMERICAN DREAM!
MANTLE MOTORS
0:00
ELAPSED HOURS
Pop's
LADIES AND GENTLEMAN, MANTLE MOTORS, IN ASSOCIATION WITH POP'S CHOCK'LIT SHOPPE, IS PROUD TO BRING YOU– HANDS ON A HARDBODY!
IT'S SIMPLE AS PIE, FOLKS: THE LAST CONTESTANT WHO HAS HIS OR HER HAND ON THE TRUCK WINS IT.
ALL THEY HAVE TO DO IS HOLD ON.
CRACK!
"NOT LIABLE IN THE EVENT OF A FLASH FLOOD." ARE WE EXPECTING A FLASH FLOOD?
I'D LIKE TO INVITE THE CONTESTANTS UP ON STAGE NOW.
AS THEY GET SITUATED, I'LL GET A FEW RULES OUT OF THE WAY...

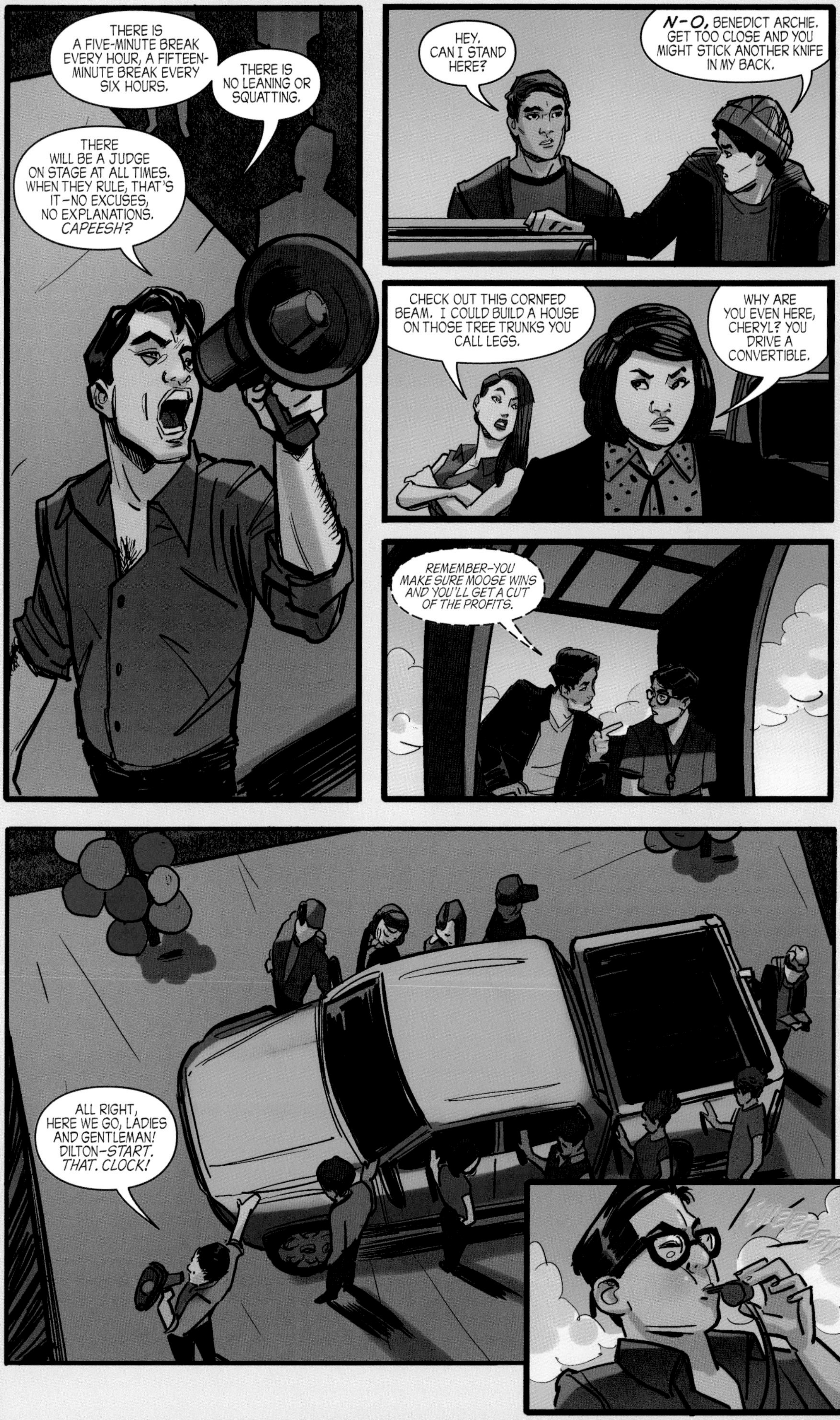
THERE IS A FIVE-MINUTE BREAK EVERY HOUR, A FIFTEEN-MINUTE BREAK EVERY SIX HOURS.
THERE IS NO LEANING OR SQUATTING.
THERE WILL BE A JUDGE ON STAGE AT ALL TIMES. WHEN THEY RULE, THAT'S IT—NO EXCUSES, NO EXPLANATIONS. CAPEESH?
HEY. CAN I STAND HERE?
N-O, BENEDICT ARCHIE. GET TOO CLOSE AND YOU MIGHT STICK ANOTHER KNIFE IN MY BACK.
CHECK OUT THIS CORNFED BEAM. I COULD BUILD A HOUSE ON THOSE TREE TRUNKS YOU CALL LEGS.
WHY ARE YOU EVEN HERE, CHERYL? YOU DRIVE A CONVERTIBLE.
REMEMBER—YOU MAKE SURE MOOSE WINS AND YOU'LL GET A CUT OF THE PROFITS.
ALL RIGHT, HERE WE GO, LADIES AND GENTLEMAN! DILTON—START. THAT. CLOCK!

I'VE GOT 5/2 ODDS ON ANDREWS, 15/1 ODDS ON ETHEL, ANY TAKERS? IT'S A *BEAUTIFUL* DAY! WHO'S FEELING *LUCKY*?

THIS IS ALICE COOPER LIVE STREAMING ON THE RIVERDALE REGISTER'S WEBSITE....

...TO BRING YOU COVERAGE LIVE AT THE CHOCK'LIT SHOPPE!

ETHEL, TELL US WHY YOU WANT TO WIN.

I HAD HOPES OF GOING TO SPACE CAMP THIS SUMMER, BUT MY PARENTS CAN'T AFFORD IT. IF I WIN, I'LL SELL THE TRUCK AND USE THE MONEY TO GO.

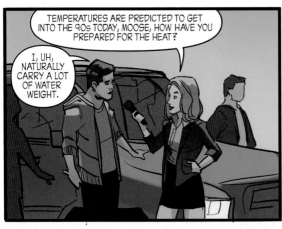

TEMPERATURES ARE PREDICTED TO GET INTO THE 90s TODAY, MOOSE, HOW HAVE YOU PREPARED FOR THE HEAT?

I, UH, NATURALLY CARRY A LOT OF WATER WEIGHT.

AND WHAT'S MOTIVATING *YOU* TO STAND HERE FOR HOURS ON END, ARCHIE?

OH, A FEW THINGS...

...THE OPEN ROAD, WINDOWS DOWN, VERONICA AT MY SIDE...

...DID I SAY THAT OUT LOUD?

Surfers Point 12 mi

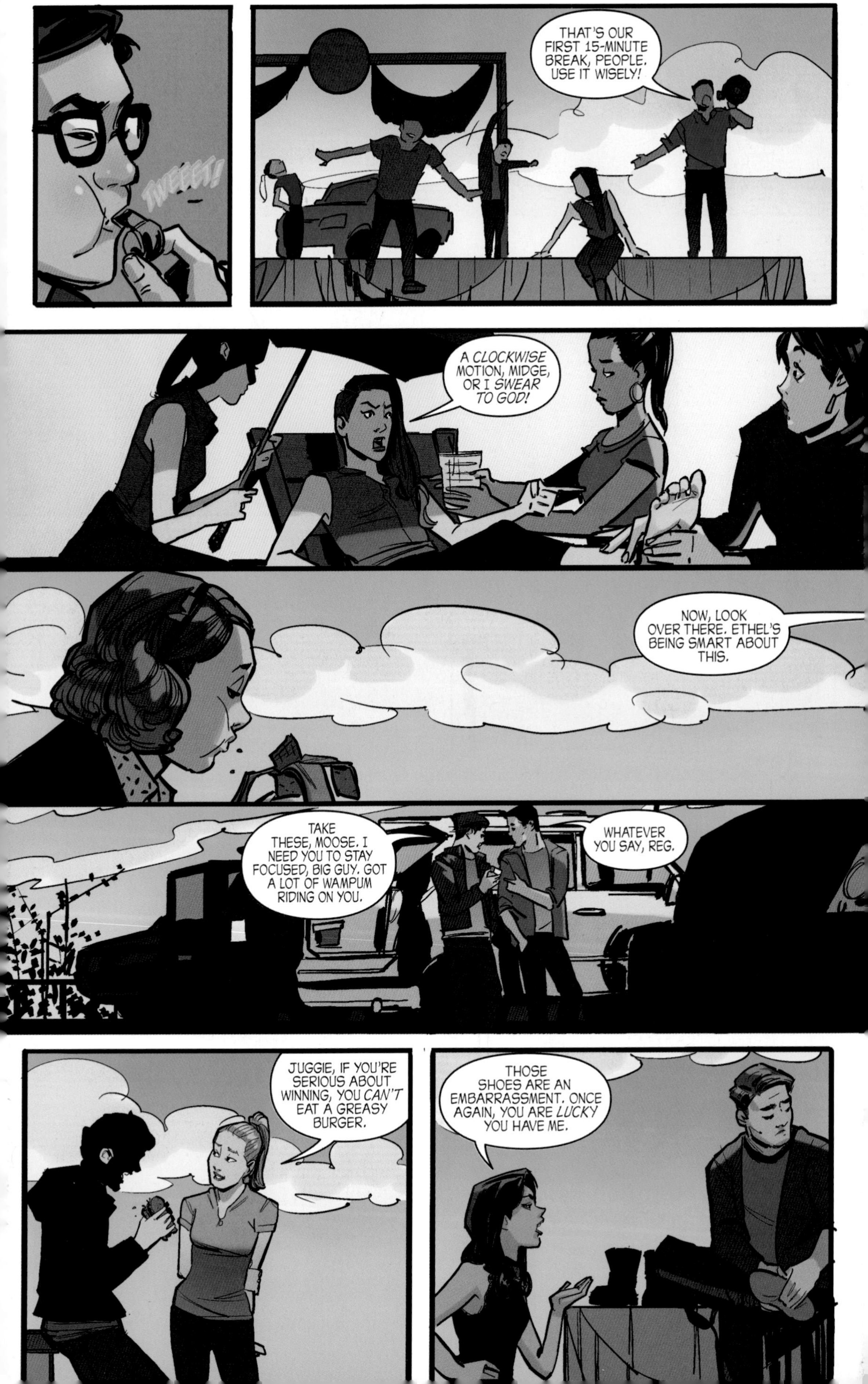
TWEEET!
THAT'S OUR FIRST 15-MINUTE BREAK, PEOPLE. USE IT WISELY!
A CLOCKWISE MOTION, MIDGE, OR I SWEAR TO GOD!
NOW, LOOK OVER THERE. ETHEL'S BEING SMART ABOUT THIS.
TAKE THESE, MOOSE. I NEED YOU TO STAY FOCUSED, BIG GUY. GOT A LOT OF WAMPUM RIDING ON YOU.
WHATEVER YOU SAY, REG.
JUGGIE, IF YOU'RE SERIOUS ABOUT WINNING, YOU CAN'T EAT A GREASY BURGER.
THOSE SHOES ARE AN EMBARRASSMENT. ONCE AGAIN, YOU ARE LUCKY YOU HAVE ME.

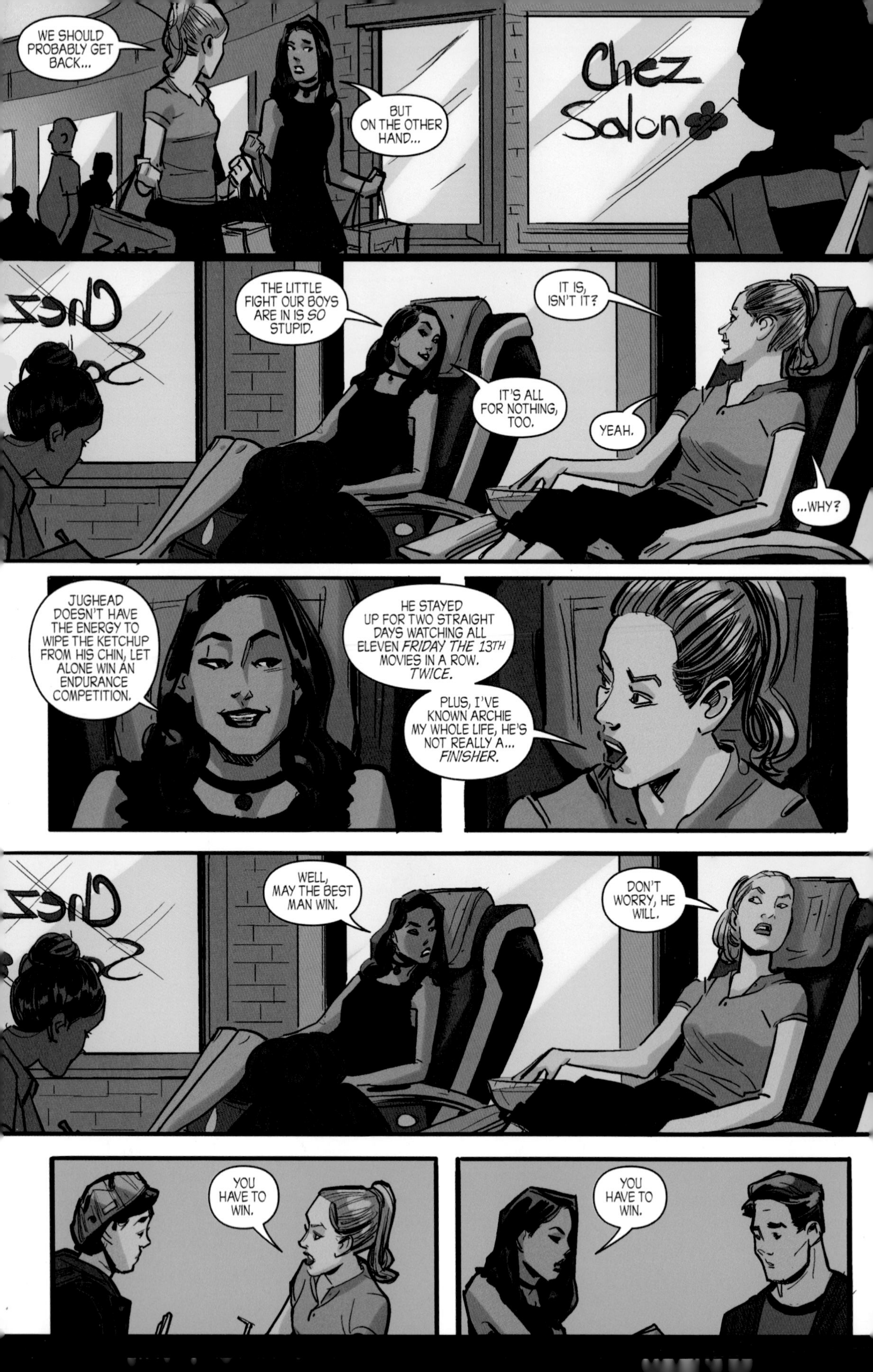

Chez Salon
WE SHOULD PROBABLY GET BACK...
BUT ON THE OTHER HAND...
THE LITTLE FIGHT OUR BOYS ARE IN IS *SO* STUPID.
IT'S ALL FOR NOTHING, TOO.
IT IS, ISN'T IT?
YEAH.
...WHY?
JUGHEAD DOESN'T HAVE THE ENERGY TO WIPE THE KETCHUP FROM HIS CHIN, LET ALONE WIN AN ENDURANCE COMPETITION.
HE STAYED UP FOR TWO STRAIGHT DAYS WATCHING ALL ELEVEN *FRIDAY THE 13TH* MOVIES IN A ROW. *TWICE.*
PLUS, I'VE KNOWN ARCHIE MY WHOLE LIFE, HE'S NOT REALLY A... *FINISHER.*
WELL, MAY THE BEST MAN WIN.
DON'T WORRY, HE WILL.
YOU HAVE TO WIN.
YOU HAVE TO WIN.